IMAGES
of America

GREEN RIVER AND THE GUNNISON VALLEY

ON THE COVER: On the porch from left to right are John Thomas "Tom" Farrer, John Thomas "J. T." Farrer Sr., Ernest E. Farrer (riding the bicycle), Matt Hartman (handling freight), and unidentified. (Courtesy of the Green River Archives.)

IMAGES
of America

Green River and the Gunnison Valley

Jo Anne Chandler, Annalee Thayn,
and the Green River Archives

ARCADIA
PUBLISHING

ISBN 978-0-7385-5877-6

Published by Arcadia Publishing
Charleston SC, Chicago IL, Portsmouth NH, San Francisco CA

Printed in the United States of America

Library of Congress Catalog Card Number: 2008925022

For all general information contact Arcadia Publishing at:
Telephone 843-853-2070
Fax 843-853-0044
E-mail sales@arcadiapublishing.com
For customer service and orders:
Toll-Free 1-888-313-2665

Visit us on the Internet at www.arcadiapublishing.com

To the residents of Green River, both past and present,
for your support and generosity to the Green River Archives
and for making this book possible.

Contents

ACKNOWLEDGMENTS

We would like to thank all those who have contributed to this work—Muriel Smith for her written histories of Blake, Greenriver, and Green River (*They Were Here*, vols. 1 and 2; and *The Green River Crossing*, vols. 1 and 2), and the Green River Library for its two-volume set of *Memories* with old photographs of the town and valley. Also, we appreciate all the great help the family historians have done to fill in some of the blank faces and for allowing us to use their photographs.

We realize that not all of the early families are represented. In the three and one half years that we have been collecting the history of this town and valley, the collection of family histories and photographs has grown. To ensure a complete collection for future generations, we will continue to collect and preserve the history of this town and valley, including the river. Remember to visit us for your research needs. We can only share with others what materials we have in our collection.

All images are courtesy of the Green River Archives.

INTRODUCTION

Green River and the Gunnison Valley cover a large area full of history. Green River is located in the eastern part of Utah surrounded by the Book Cliff Mountains. Green River has an altitude of just over 4,000 feet, with a population of fewer than 1,000 residents.

Green River is unique in Utah's history. It was one of the few towns not settled by Latter-day Saint (Mormon) pioneers. The Mormons did come here but decided the area could not be farmed. Lt. Joseph Christmas Ives came to the area in 1858. He also thought little of the area when he said, "The region . . . is, of course, altogether valueless. Ours has been the first and will undoubtedly be the last party of whites to visit the locality. It seems intended by nature that the Colorado River along the greater portion of its lonely and majestic way shall be forever unvisited and undisturbed."

John Wesley Powell came here on his first exploration in 1869. He came on a second exploration in 1871. Although Powell started in Green River, Wyoming, he did float by Green River, Utah. Green River the settlement was one of the few places where the river could still be crossed easily. Many of the geologic formations around Green River still carry the names Powell gave them.

The Farrer family, one of the first residents of Blake, as it was named at the time, did not have the same concerns, and they were able to earn a living here. They deliberately chose Green River because of its remote location; they wanted fewer neighbors. The Farrer family operated a store and ferry here.

Green River City started as Blake. It is rumored that a Mr. Blake worked for Tom Farrer and that the town was named after him. A more likely possibility is that the town was named after Blake to honor him and his service to the community. Blake carried the mail from Salina to La Sal. The town of Blake was a way station, a place to sell supplies to travelers, hold spare horses, and serve as a river crossing. On December 5, 1895, the town's name was changed to Greenriver. On March 1, 1951, the town's name was changed again, this time to Green River (two words). This made less confusion for postal workers, who would confuse Greenriver, Utah, with Gunnison, Utah, especially when it was handwritten.

Green River is a major crossroads in the West. The town was settled because it was one of the few places that the river could be crossed easily. The people of Green River's history include Native Americans, Spanish priests and explorers, outlaws, trappers and traders, and river runners. Each group left a mark on Green River.

Denis Julien was one of the first European trappers in the Canyonlands area. He was looking for beaver and otter pelts; the pelts were highly prized on the East Coast. Denis Julien carved his name many times around the Green River. In 1836, near one of his names, he also carved a boat.

William Ashley, another person who made his mark near Green River, did not intend to be a mountain man. He just wanted to be known as an "important man in society." His only interest in the fur trade was to gain enough money to be considered important. He partnered with Andrew Henry. They put an advertisement in the newspaper calling for any young man seeking adventure to come help them in the fur trade. Some of the men who responded to that advertisement are well known in their own right. Two of the men who responded were Jedediah Smith and Jim Bridger.

In 1825, Ashley and his men were in Green River. They divided into four groups and made plans to reunite at a later date downstream along the Green River. Ashley said he would "make such Marks as would designate it as a place of General Rendezvous for the men in my service." It appears that it was Ashley who made the words *mountain man* and *rendezvous* synonymous.

Nathaniel Galloway was innovative with boat design. He designed a boat that was lighter weight and easier to maneuver than previous boats. He was also one of the first river runners to face forward in a boat, rowing against the current.

The Kolb brothers Emery and Ellsworth were river runners and photographers. In 1911, they wanted to re- create John Wesley Powell's trip. They recorded their trip through words, photographs, and motion photography. Ellsworth wrote a book about the experience: *Through the Grand Canyon from Wyoming to Mexico.*

Haldane "Buzz" Holmstrom, after an unsuccessful attempt to join the geologic survey team from Cal-Tech when its members were planning to run the Colorado River, decided to run the river alone. He patterned his boat after the Galloway boat and started his adventure in Green River, Wyoming. He eventually passed the Cal-Tech team. Less than a year after this river run, he returned with Amos Burg to run the river again. Each of them in separate boats photographed the river. Holmstrom died in 1946 after serving in World War II.

In 1909, Bert Loper took a trip with two men down the river and began a lifelong love affair with the river lasting more than 40 years. He helped with several river expeditions, including the Hoover Dam survey and a government survey of the San Juan River. In July 1949, while running Marble Canyon in the Grand Canyon and marking his 80th birthday, he died of an apparent heart attack. He was lost until 1975, when a hiker found his body 47 miles downstream.

Green River is a town that has been influenced by many nationalities and cultures. Among these groups of people were the Chinese, who mostly built the railroad. There were Caucasian men also, who were much better paid, as well as Italian and Hispanic workers. The town of Green River today would not survive without the industry of the Hispanic workers.

In this book are the people and events that shaped the town Green River, affecting what Green River is today. Read about a fight over a horse that sent a man to the state penitentiary. Find out that the Hastings Water Wheel is not the only water wheel used in the valley. Discover why the water wheels were used.

Green River is a great place to create one's own adventure with all of the outdoor recreational activities available. For a more relaxed visit to Green River, there is plenty of history to read about or discover within an easy distance. This book will whet your appetite and give you a taste of what Green River is all about.

One

They Came from Everywhere

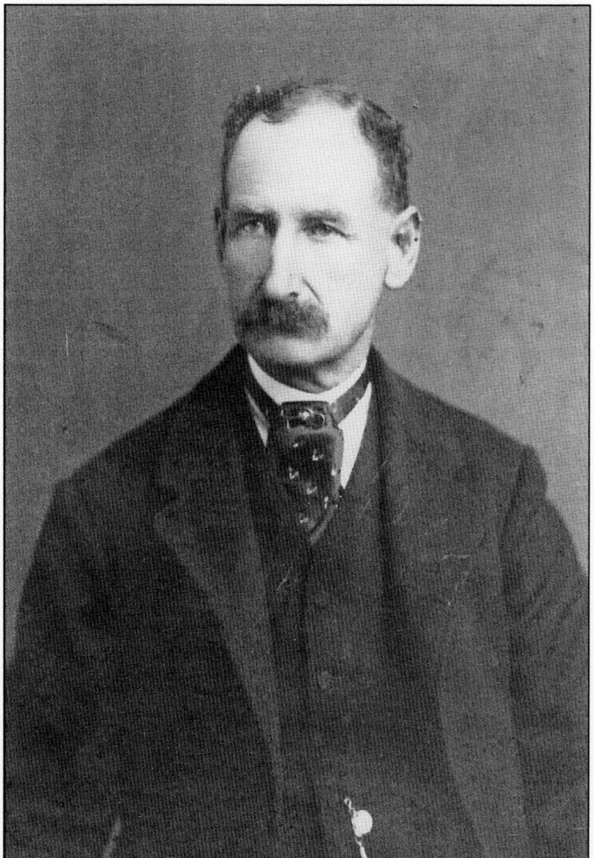

John Thomas "Tom" Farrer was born in England and came to the United States in about 1868. He and his family lived about 20 miles southwest of Salt Lake at St. Johns. They later moved to Sevier County for a number of years before coming to Green River in 1878–1879. He was married twice and had eight children. He served as the Emery County sheriff for 15 years and was known to say he "never came back without his man."

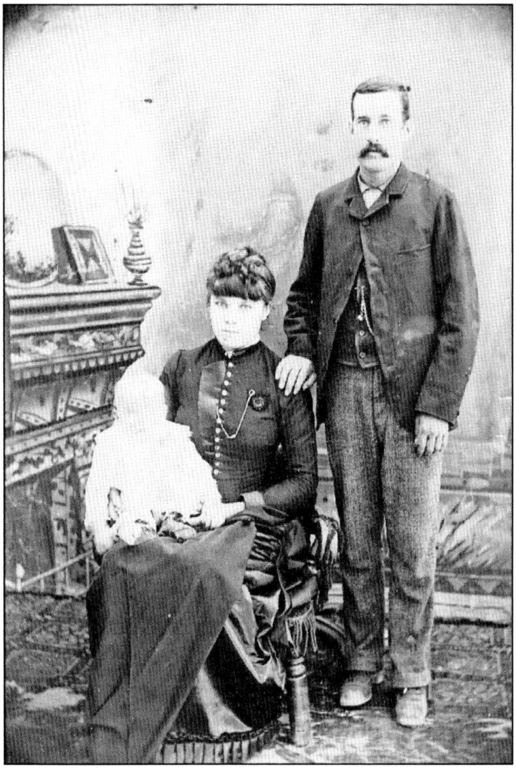

John Thomas "J. T." Farrer, Elizabeth "Libby" Sophia Larsen Farrer, and J. T. Farrer Jr. came to Green River in 1878–1879 with J. T. Sr.'s father, Tom. J. T. met and married Libby in Green River. He held the office of justice of the peace for 18 years, was the coroner and notary public in Green River, and was involved in many businesses—the ferry, store, post office, cattle, and sheep.

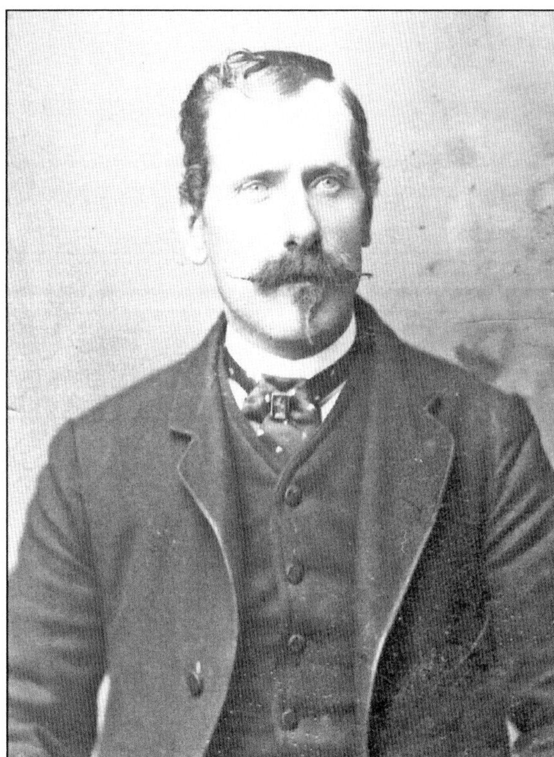

Matt Hartman, friend and business partner of J. T. Farrer, came from Switzerland and met J. T. in Utah. It is not known if he ever married or had children. Matt, it has been written, was a "character." He remained in Green River for several years after J. T. moved to California. They were close friends throughout their lives.

Herman Dahling was born in Sweden and came to Utah about 1863. He married Beatrice Farrer, daughter of Tom and Hannah Farrer (Tom's first wife) in Castle Dale, Utah, in 1881. They had 11 children; 10 lived to have families of their own. Dahling was a cowboy, teamster, cattleman, and railroader, and he died in 1954 at the age of 98 in Fruita, Colorado, where he had lived for many years.

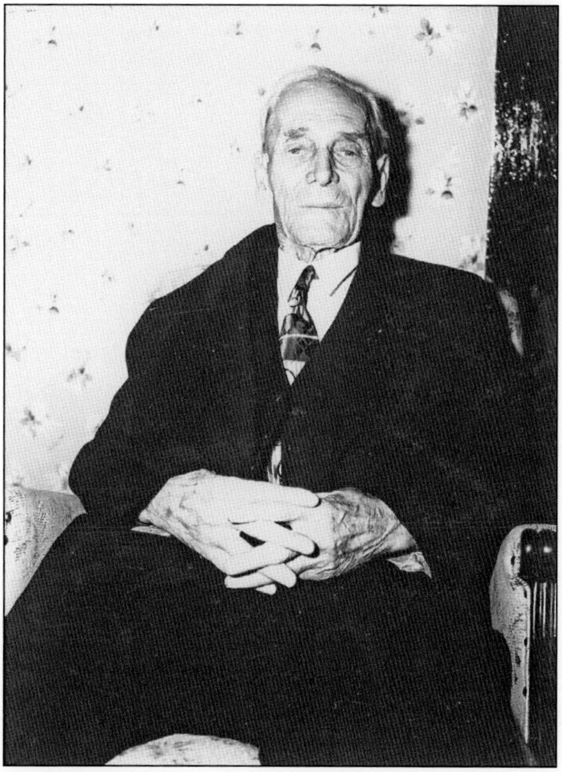

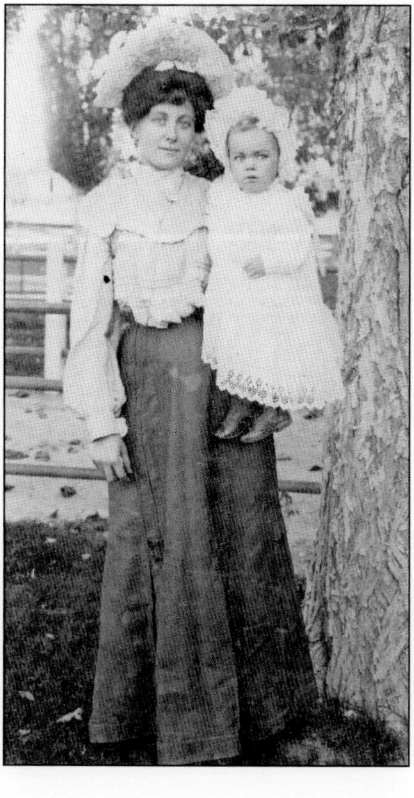

Lillie Maglene Dahling married Aultmer Leslie "Mirt" Tomlinson in 1903 in Green River. Lillie and Mirt had nine children. Lillie was the daughter of Herman and Beatrice Elizabeth Farrer Dahling, one of the first families in Green River. They moved to Fruita, Colorado, in 1922. Shown here are Lillie Maglene Dahling Tomlinson and her son Leslie Aultmer Tomlinson.

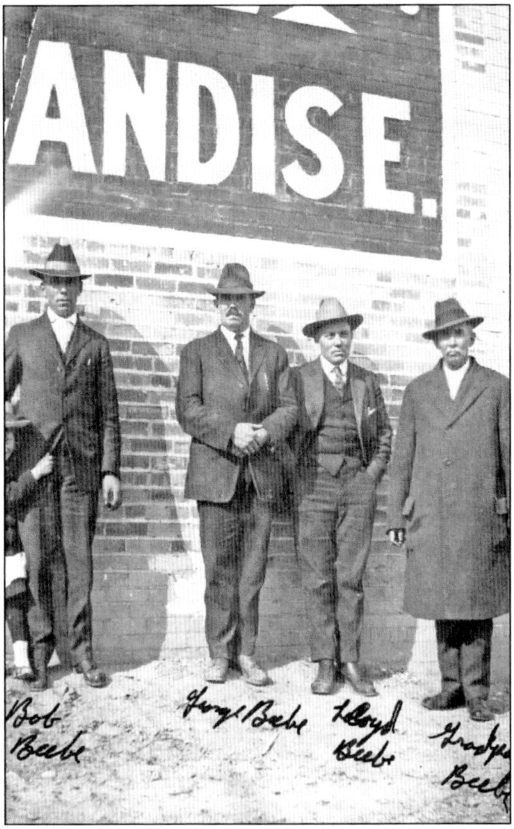

In this photograph are, from left to right, brothers Bob, George, and Lloyd Beebe, along with their father, Alvaro D. Beebe. The Beebe men are next to the store they ran for many years, which was started by Alvaro in 1910. The building had many owners but was demolished in 2006. The Beebe men were known in both Emery and Grand Counties, having many business interests.

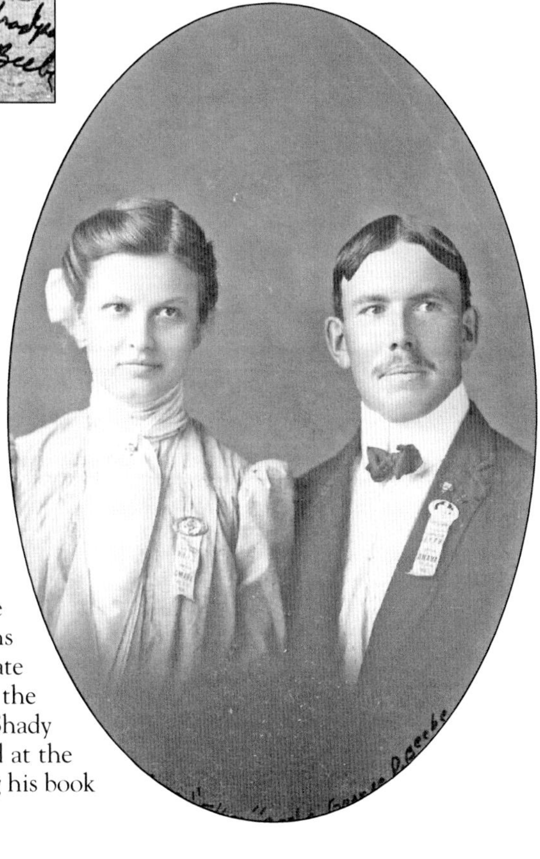

George Beebe, son of Alvaro D. and Sarah Beebe, married Mary Estelle Eller in 1911. They moved to Green River in 1919, where he was part owner of the Beebe and Sons store until 1932. He worked for the State Highway Department until 1942. He built the first campground in Green River, the Shady Rest Auto Camp. Author Zane Grey stayed at the Shady Rest about 1932 when he was writing his book *Robbers' Roost*.

William Fritz "W. F." Asimus is shown standing inside the W. F. Asimus Grocery and Hardware Store. He owned the store from 1909 until his death in 1947. He was born in Stuttgart, Germany. At 18, he came to the United States, where he married Jenny Haley and had two children. After Jenny's death, he left his children in Washington and came to Utah. He married Callie Otte on October 10, 1900. They arrived in Green River in 1909.

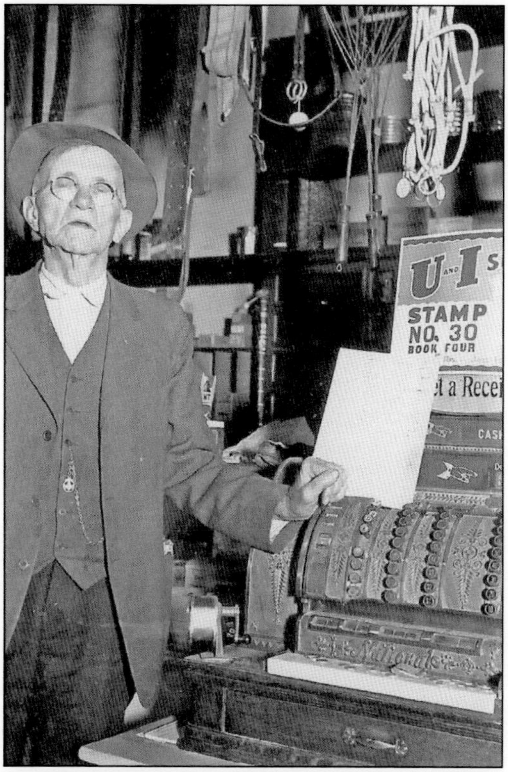

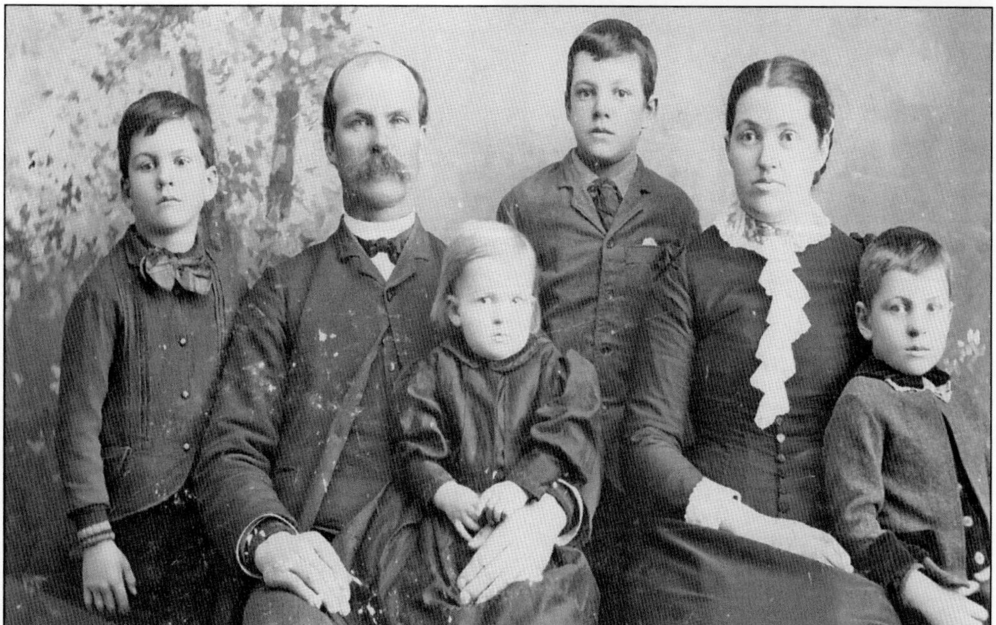

Photographed here is the Hastings family: (from left to right) Howard Johnston Hasting, Thomas Jefferson Hastings holding Cloyd Oscar Hastings, Berkley Monroe Hastings, Ida Ellen Pixley Hastings, and George D. Hastings. This photograph was taken in Nebraska. Berkley died at the age 16 of dropsy. Howard Hastings's son Tom still lives in Green River on Hastings Road.

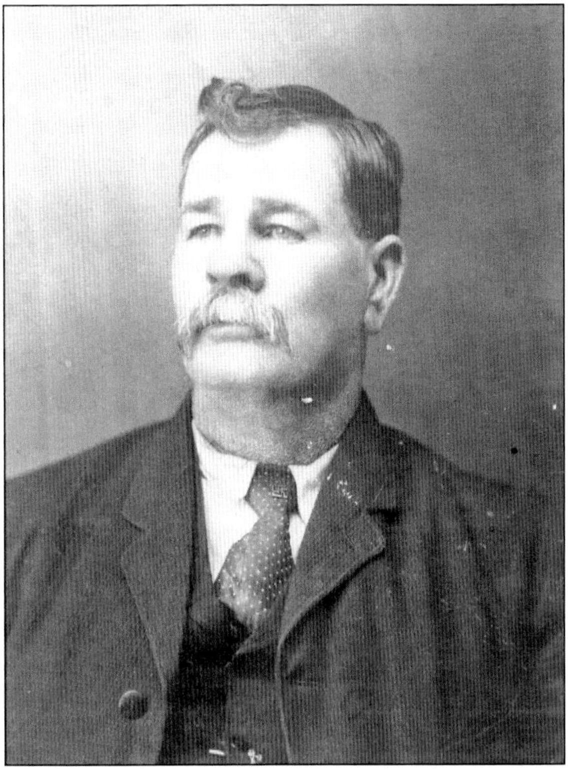

Daniel Gillies—born on May 3, 1849, in Newcastle, England—came to the United States with his parents in 1856. They settled in the Beaver County, Utah, area. It was about 1900 that Daniel brought his wife, Susannah, and 12 children to Green River. They ranched on the San Rafael River south of Green River. It is still known as the Gillies' Ranch. Later they moved into town.

Susannah Gillies married Daniel Gilles in 1877. She met him in Beaver, where they had their first home. They later moved to Circleville, Utah. In June 1900, Susannah and her family moved again, this time to Green River. Susannah always said that when civilization caught up with Dan, he moved. During World War I, she sent three of her sons off to war on the same day, and when it was over, they all came home.

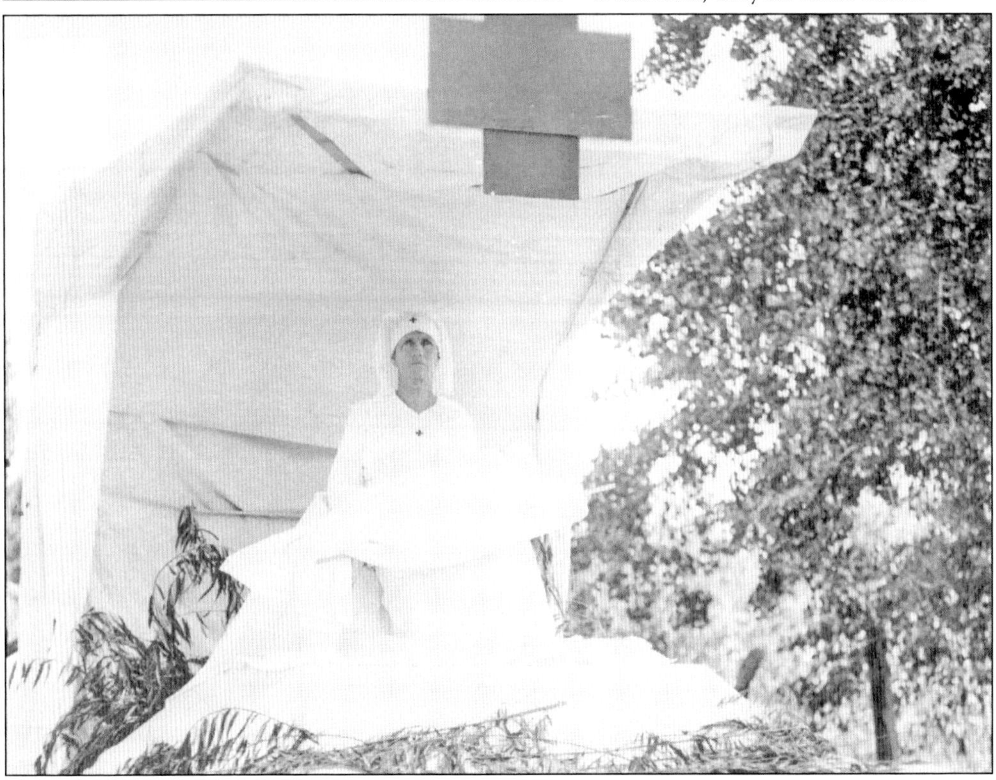

Pete and Rose Politano came from Italy to Green River in 1893 by way of Canada. Pete was a farmer, and Rose raised three sons: Frank, Joseph, and Malcolm. Two of their sons, Frank and Malcolm, went into the mercantile business. Joseph went on to work for the railroad. Rose lived to be over 100 years old; she always held on to her religious beliefs.

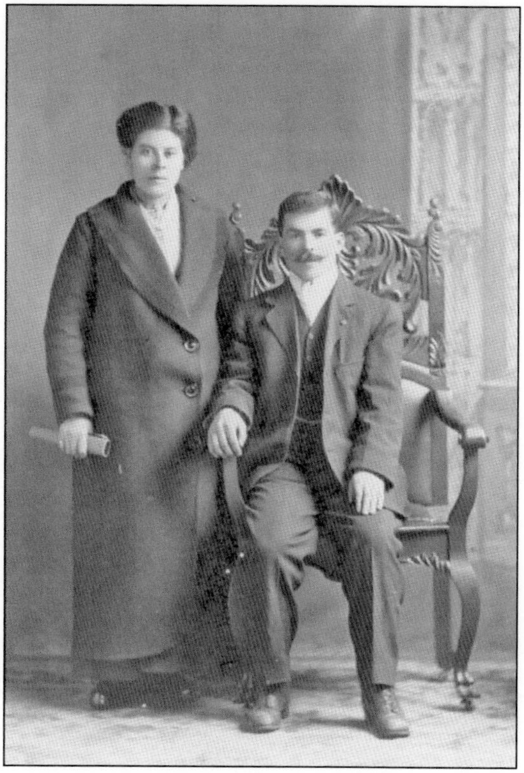

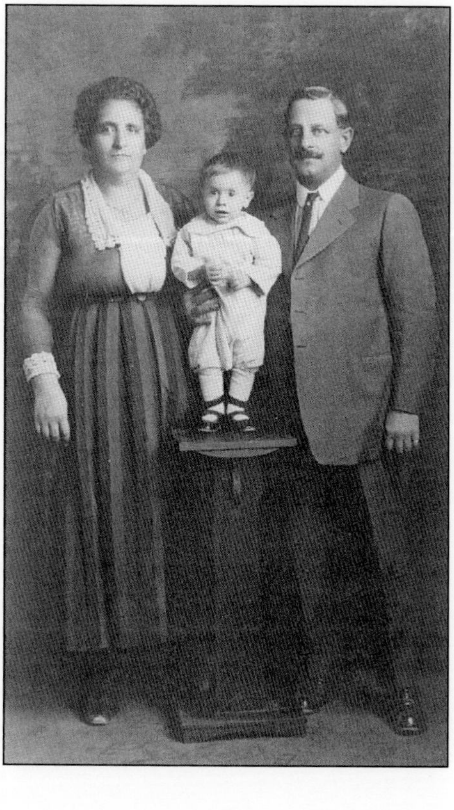

Many of Carmine "Charlie" and Teresa Spadafora's descendants still live in the Green River area. Both were born in Italy. Charlie came to Green River in 1903 and the following year returned to Italy for Teresa. They had seven children; one died in infancy. Charlie built the Metropole Hotel and Bar with his cousin Joe Politano. Later they purchased another building and established an amusement hall.

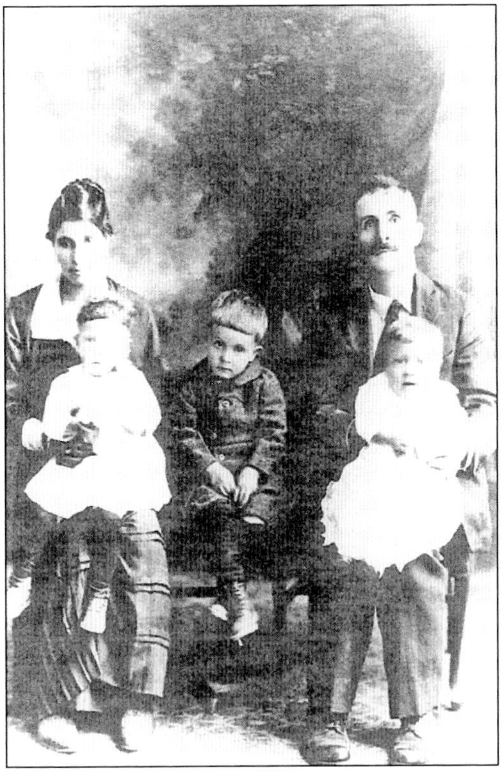

Giovanni "John" and Maria Vetere were early arrivals in Green River and residents of the town for over 50 years. John came to the United States, as many others from Italy did, for a better life. He came to the coalfields of Scofield, Utah, first and then to Green River. John was a hard worker and raised his family to be that way as well. He farmed north of town before moving into town on Clark Street in the 1950s.

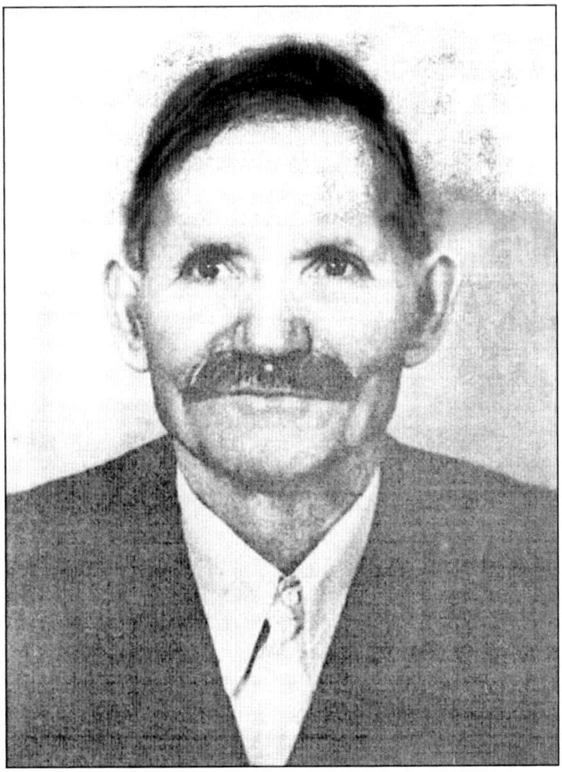

Joe Chiodo was born in 1873 in Italy. He married Santa Angotti in Italy in 1893. They came to the United States in 1896, first to New York and then in 1901 to Green River. There he worked for the Denver and Rio Grande Railroad and was a farmer. Joe and Santa had six children. Santa passed away in 1919. Joe later married Rose Cundarie in 1920 and had two daughters by her. Joe passed away in 1944, and Rose then moved to California to be near her daughters.

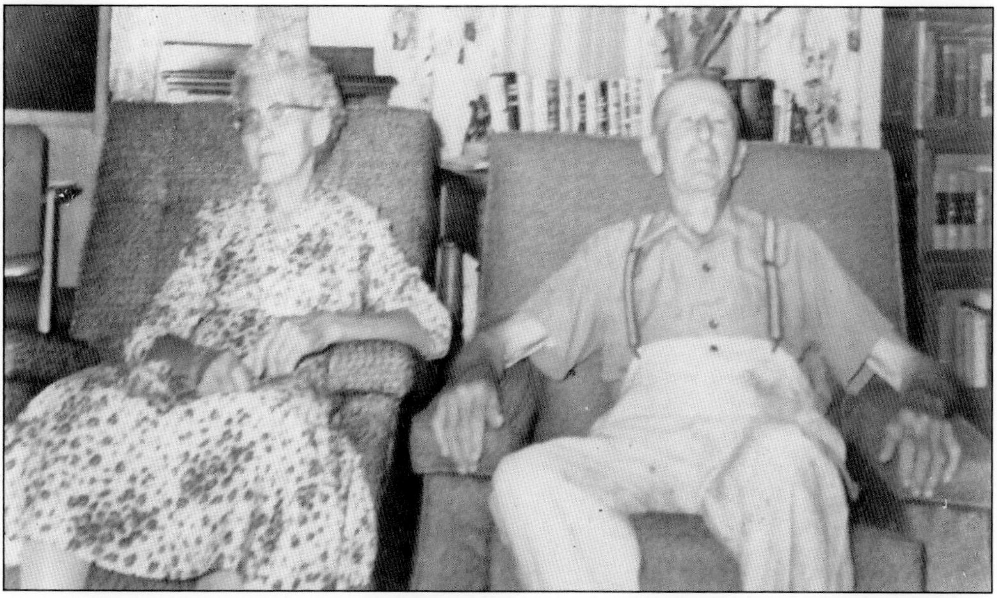

Bertram Joseph "B. J." Silliman, born 1875 in Illinois as an only son, married Mina Lois Adams, who was born in 1878 in Indiana, on June 20, 1907. B. J. had a son, Joseph B. Silliman, from his first marriage and one daughter and three sons with Mina. B. J. and his family moved to the Green River area in 1915, where he was in charge of the local bank and a farmer. B. J. was also involved with research on the Old Spanish Trail.

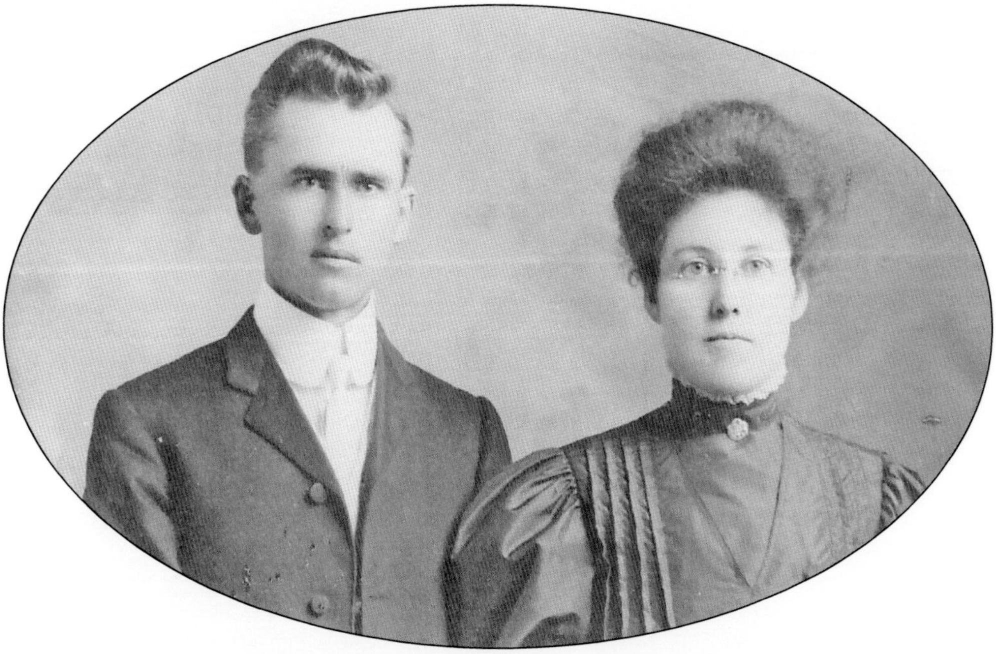

The Wilson family arrived in 1909 from Kansas. They brought with them their six children. Samuel Moore Wilson worked as a foreman for the Hiram Silliman holdings on the east side of the river. Later, in 1922, they moved to the west side of the river, where he began farming 35 acres. In 1929, they purchased the 42 Ranch, consisting of more than 2,000 acres. By 1960, the family had raised cattle and farmed melons. The ranch was later purchased by the Thayn family.

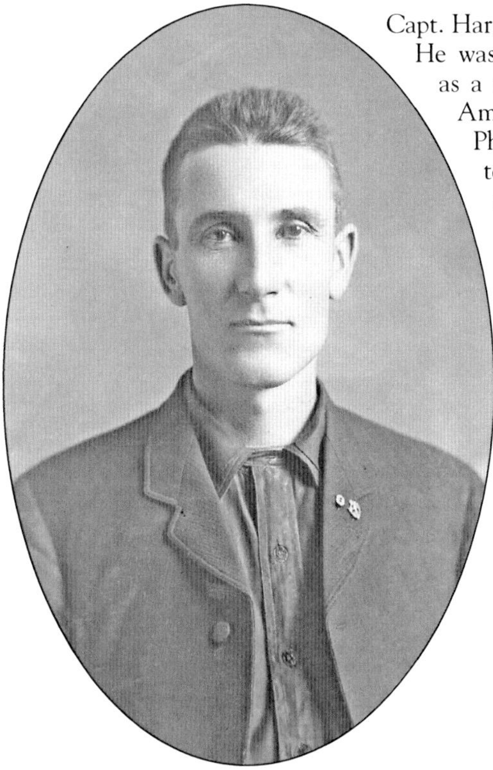

Capt. Harry T. Yokey was originally from Ottumwa, Iowa. He was a military man, first with the army in 1892 as a cavalryman. At the outbreak of the Spanish-American War, he reenlisted and saw action in the Philippines until the war ended in 1898. He came to Green River with the railroad as an operator of the pumping plant. His home south of the railroad tracks on the river still exists. He never married. Found in some papers was poetry he had written.

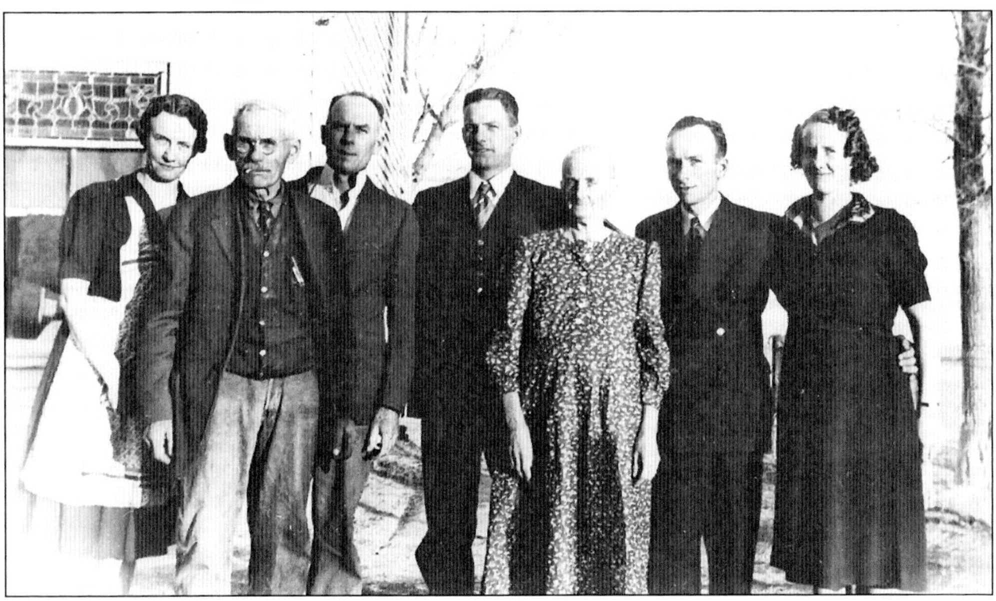

Standing from left to right are Ruth Thurman, George Thurman, Carl Thurman, Raymond Thurman, Anna Thurman, George J. Thurman, and Mamie Thurman. George Thurman helped construct many buildings in Green River. One building still standing is the Bible Church. It is listed on the National Register of Historic Places. Thurman paid for the stained-glass windows in the church. Thurman also had stained-glass windows at his house on North Long Street. The house burned down, but the windows were saved.

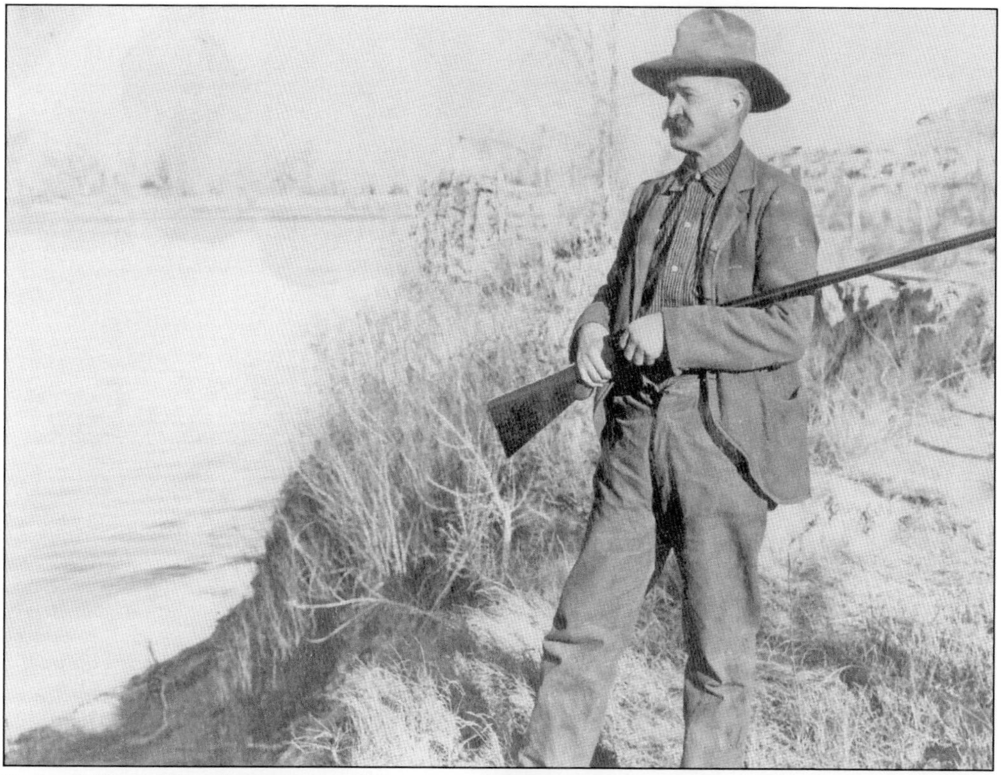

Roswell "Ros" Wheeler and two of his brothers, Arthur and Wallace, came from the state of New York and settled about 15 miles south of Elgin in 1884. They installed three waterwheels for irrigation and farmed Little Valley. Arthur and Wallace left for Yukon River country in 1898 in search of gold. Ros stayed in the valley and worked for the Utah Power and Light Company. He never married and died at the age of 70 in 1920.

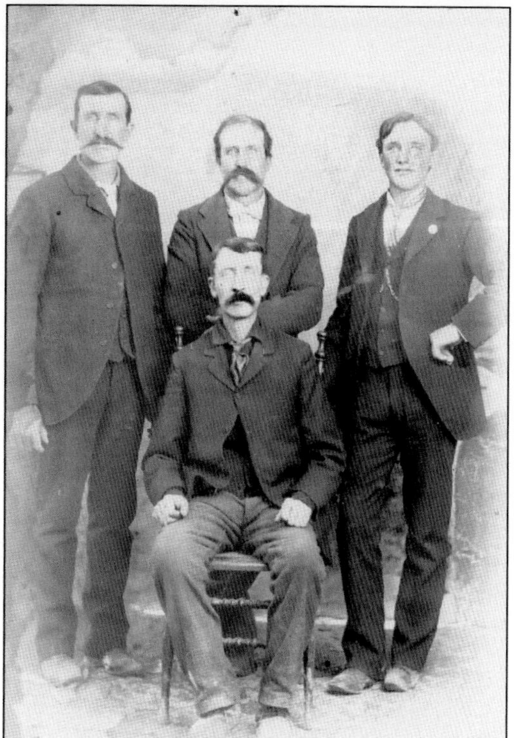

Standing from left to right are Ben, Charles, and Frank Gibbons; seated is Fred Gibbons. These four brothers were from Wayne County. In 1909, Charles A. Gibbons bought into the business of McCarty and Pace, a mercantile store. He came from Hanksville, where he was interested in quartz and placer mines in the Henry Mountains. His store was one of the neatest in the state, being equipped with a general stock of merchandise and all the modern appliances.

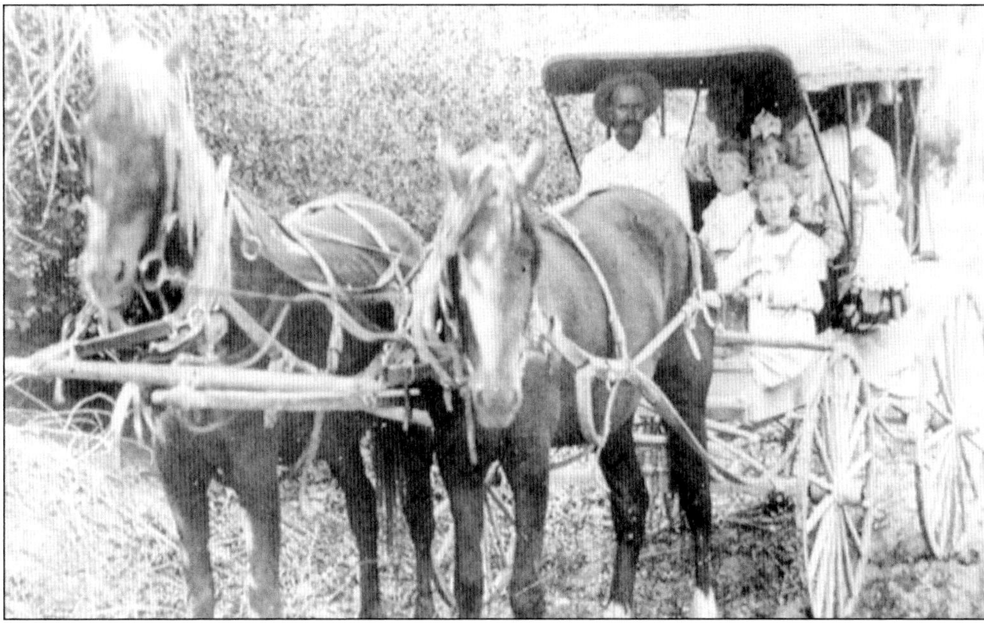

Chris Halverson came to America from Norway in 1882. His first trip to Green River was to work on the new railroad abutments for the Denver and Rio Grande. Chris married Anna Eliza Zabriskie of Mount Pleasant, Utah, in 1892 in a ceremony at the Palmer House. Chris and Anna had seven children. Two children died in infancy, and one died at the age of 20 when shot by a friend playing with a loaded gun.

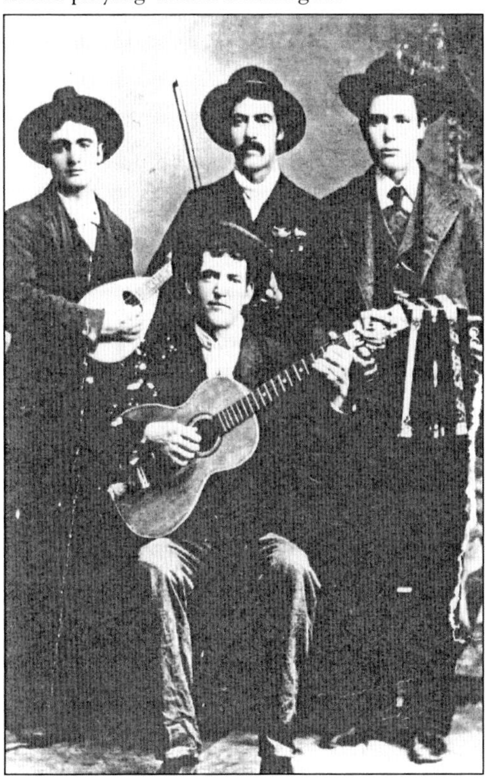

The Hunt Family Orchestra featured Elias Hunt (seated in front with the guitar). Hunt married Eva Johnson on October 23, 1907. Their first four children were born in Aldridge, Utah. When Erma, their oldest daughter, became seriously ill with a heart condition, the family moved to Aurora, Utah, where Hunt farmed for a few years. While in Aurora, Erma died and was buried there. The Hunts then moved to Green River and had six more children.

When electricity was installed in 1915, in Green River, it was Orin K. "O. K." Anderson's job to turn the streetlights on at night and off in the morning. Anderson was a member of the Green River Service Club, organized in 1944. One of the goals accomplished was the building of a city park. The park was named for Anderson because no one had worked harder for the town of Green River or its people.

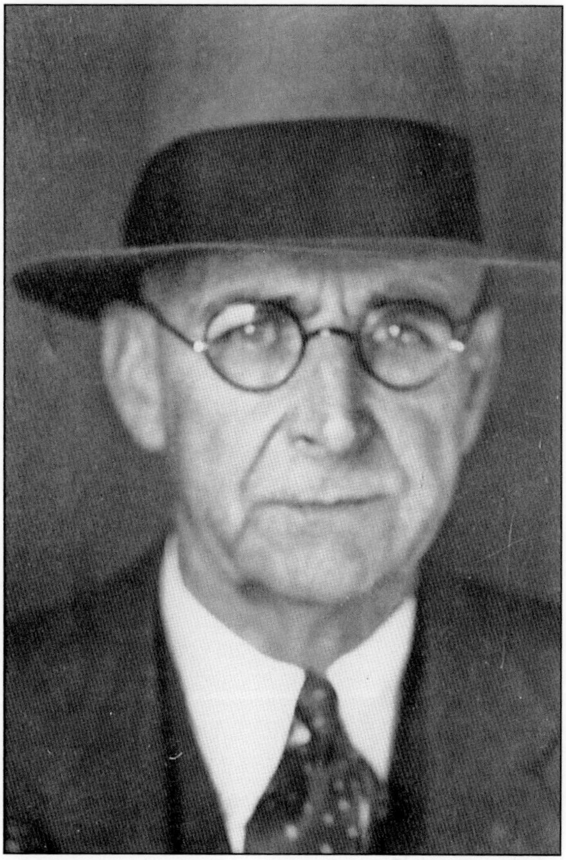

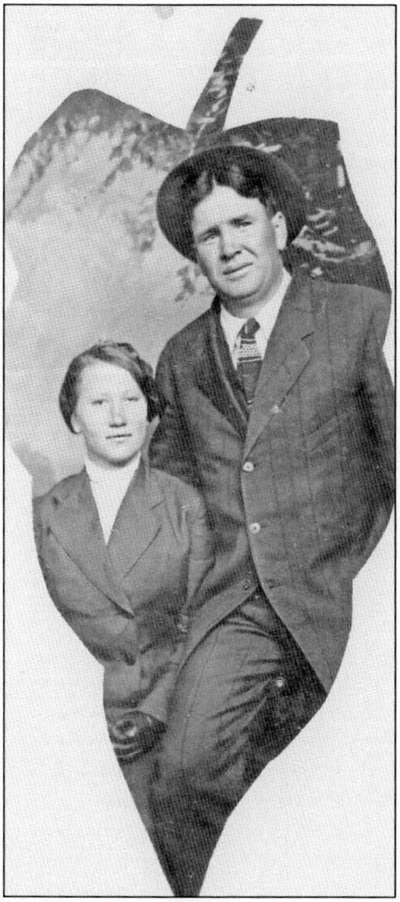

George and Pursy Seely moved to Green River prior to World War II. They had been married on February 19, 1913, in the Salt Lake Temple. They raised a family of six daughters and one son. Their first home was a tent in Price, Utah. George had many skills during his life: logger, farmer, butcher, cattle and sheep man, deputy sheriff, blacksmith, and railroad man. Pursy liked to do her housework at night in order to have more time for her family. Many of their descendants still live in Green River.

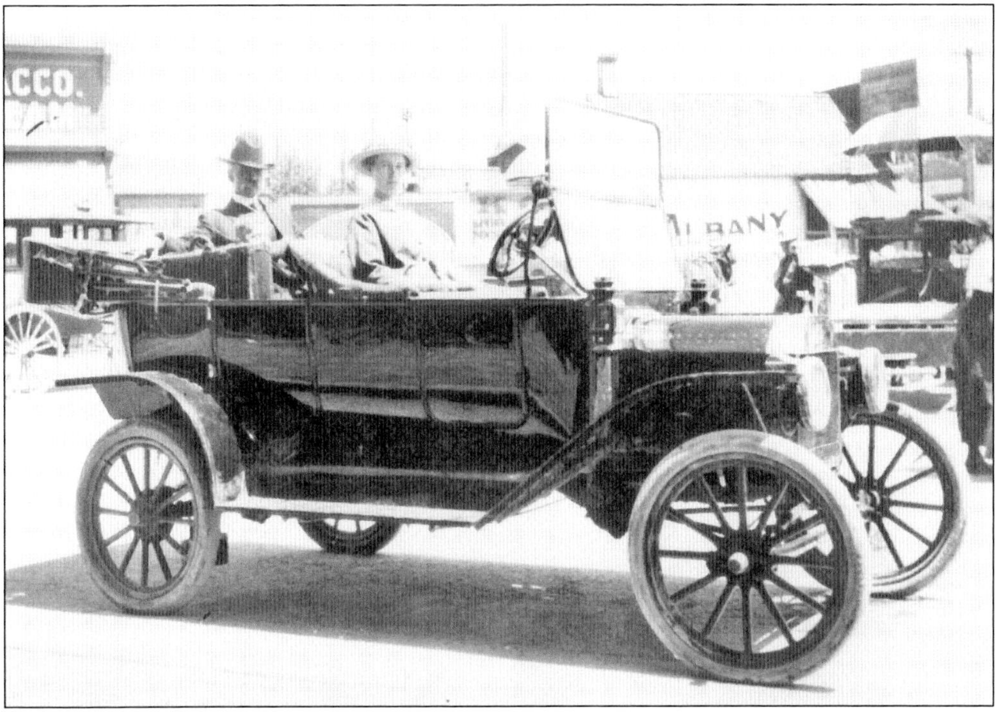

Lafayette Henry "Bud" Milton was born in Georgia and spent time in Colorado and Texas before coming to Green River. Early in his life, he became a cattleman. He was about the age of 21 when he drifted into Utah. Bud married Verna McCrillis in 1914 in Grand Junction, Colorado. In 1919, they bought a farm in Green River. They raised three daughters and one son. This is their wedding photograph.

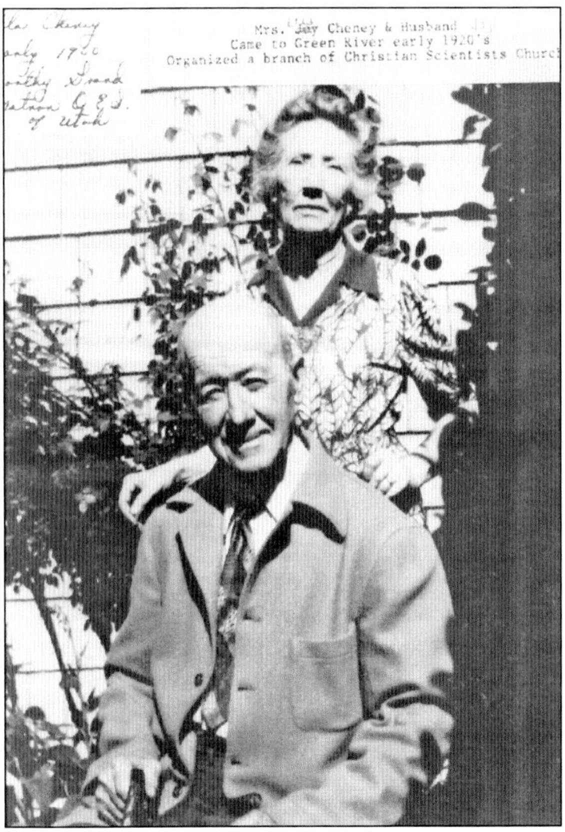

Lila Cheney (standing behind her husband, Joy Cheney) came to Green River in 1906 when the largest group of people moved in. Lila taught piano for a large group of students. Both Cheneys were born in Iowa and married there on November 17, 1892. They had three children: Harold C., Lauris R., and Florence C. The Cheney house still stands and today is owned by Duane and Penney Riches.

A familiar face to most of Green River's students for more than 50 years, Albert Weber was more than just the school custodian. He also drove the school bus and was a justice of the peace from 1955 to 1970. Albert married Vera Hanks in 1921, and they had seven children.

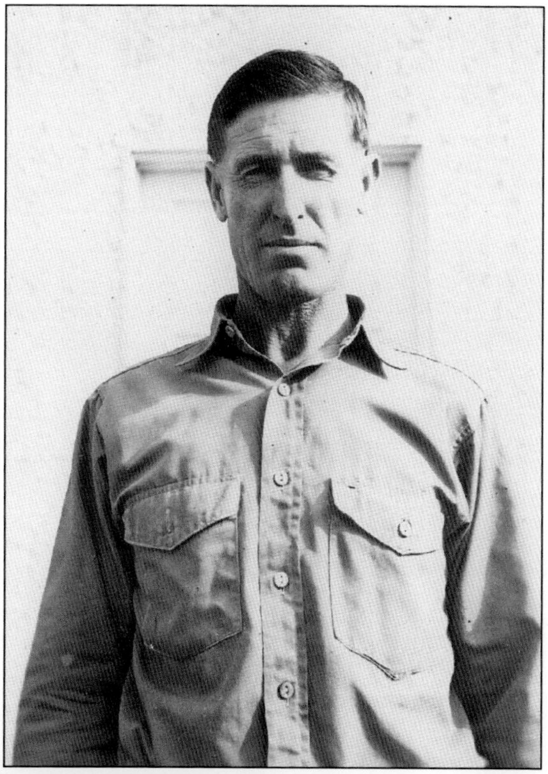

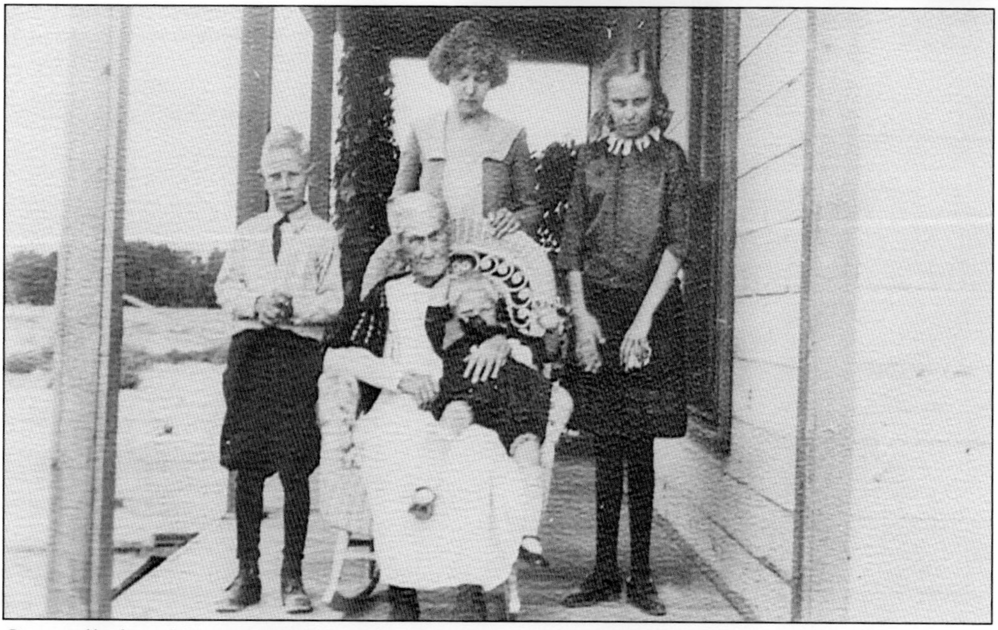

Originally from Virginia, Nancy and LeRoy Harris moved their cattle from Colorado to Utah in 1888. They later established a stage station at Old Woman Wash, which was named after Nancy. In the photograph, Nancy is photographed with four of her grandchildren—(from left to right) Larry, Goldie, Sylvia, and Ballard Harris—belonging to Gilmore A. "Ink" and Laura Clarinda "Clara" Larsen Harris.

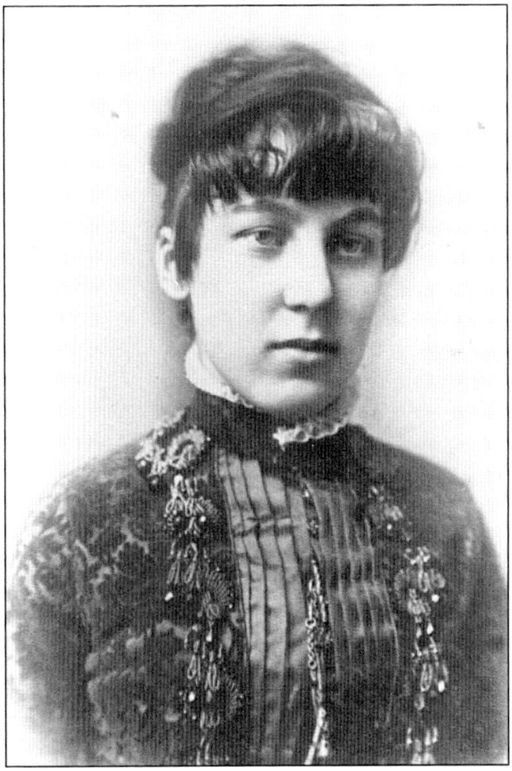

Florence "Bote" Harris Fuller is known as the cattle queen of the Colorado Plateau. She left her family in Telluride at the age of 15 and headed to Texas. While in Texas, she entertained in saloons and dealt cards. When she came back to Utah, she was said to have many beautiful dresses and could play any instrument with strings.

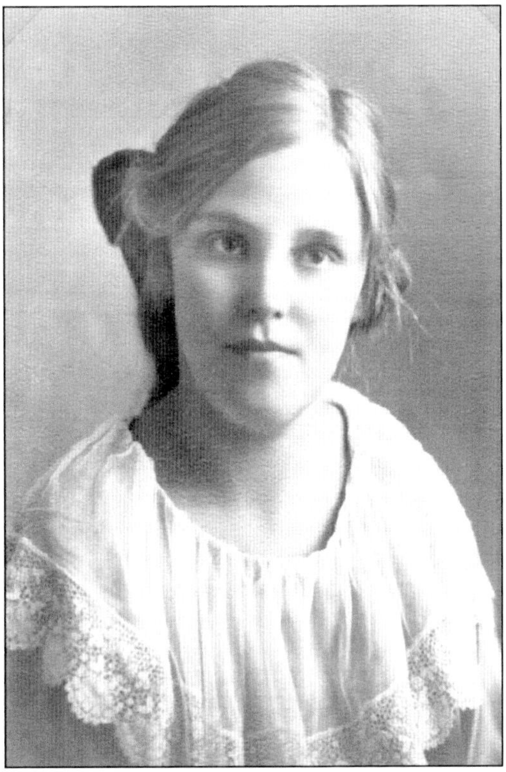

Sylvia Harris Ekker, daughter of Gilmore A. "Ink" and Laura Clarinda "Clara" Harris, was born in Elgin, Utah, in 1908. The family home is still standing. Her grandchildren remember playing at her home. Sylvia spent five years teaching in a one-room school in Valley City, Grand County, Utah, which is now a ghost town. She married Horace Ekker in October 1935 and moved to Trackyte Ranch in the Henry Mountains.

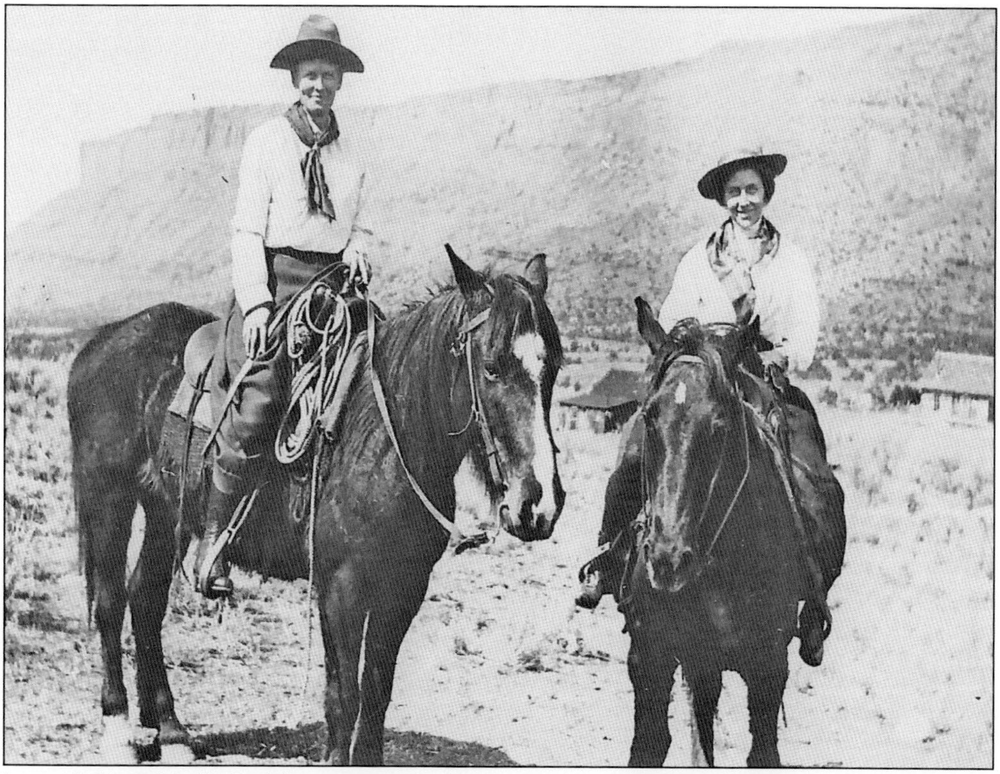

Lizzie (left) and Lillie Dahling are pictured here. These are the twin daughters of Herman and Libby Dahling. They were born in 1886. They are riding their horses in Castleton, a small town east of Moab, Utah. Lillie married a local boy, Aultimer Tomlinson.

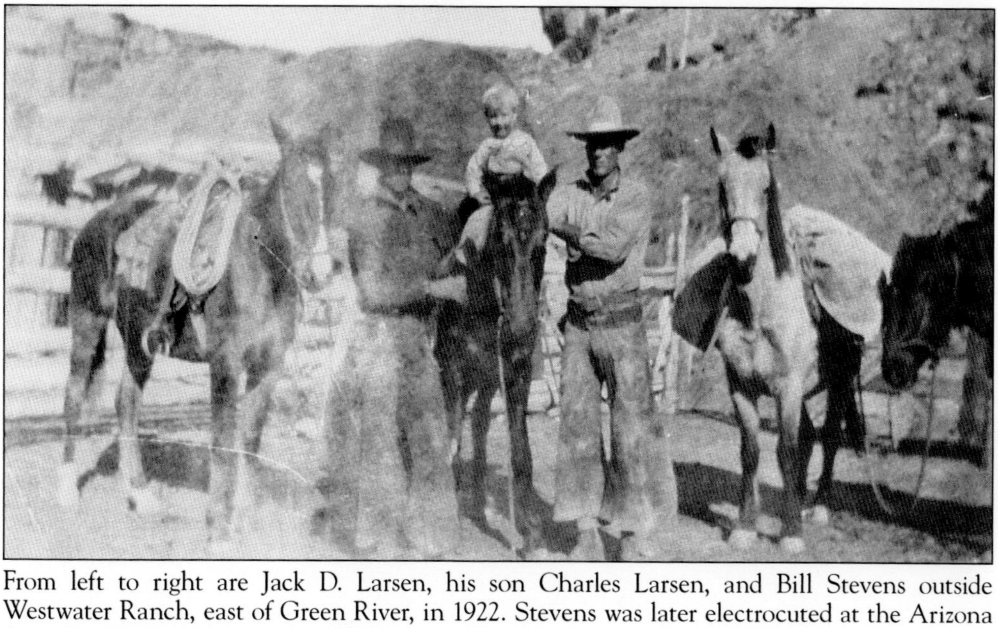

From left to right are Jack D. Larsen, his son Charles Larsen, and Bill Stevens outside Westwater Ranch, east of Green River, in 1922. Stevens was later electrocuted at the Arizona State Penitentiary for murder. The cause of the murder was the black horse in the center of the photograph.

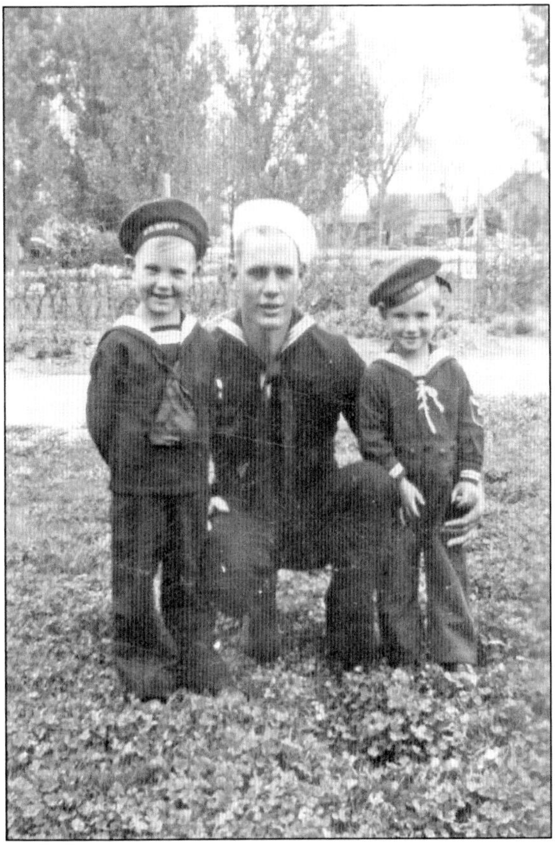

Nolan Richard Curtis was born the ninth of 10 children in Wayne County, Utah, to Wallace and Amanda Watson Curtis. They moved to Green River in 1919. He is photographed with his two oldest sons, Kenneth (left) and Ward, during World War II. Nolan and his wife, Mazel, had seven children. They ran the Frosty Circle and made the best onion rings. They also taught square dancing and formed a dance club for adults, the Melon Busters Square Dancers.

Below, from left to right, are James T. McPherson, Tora (Seamount) McPherson, Ione McPherson, Fern McPherson, and James McPherson on their ranch at Florence Creek. Florence Creek is part of the Bookcliff Mountains. The Florence Creek Ranch is 30 miles north of Elgin, Utah. On the ranch, the McPhersons raised an orchard, vegetables, and alfalfa. The McPhersons always gave river travelers a warm welcome.

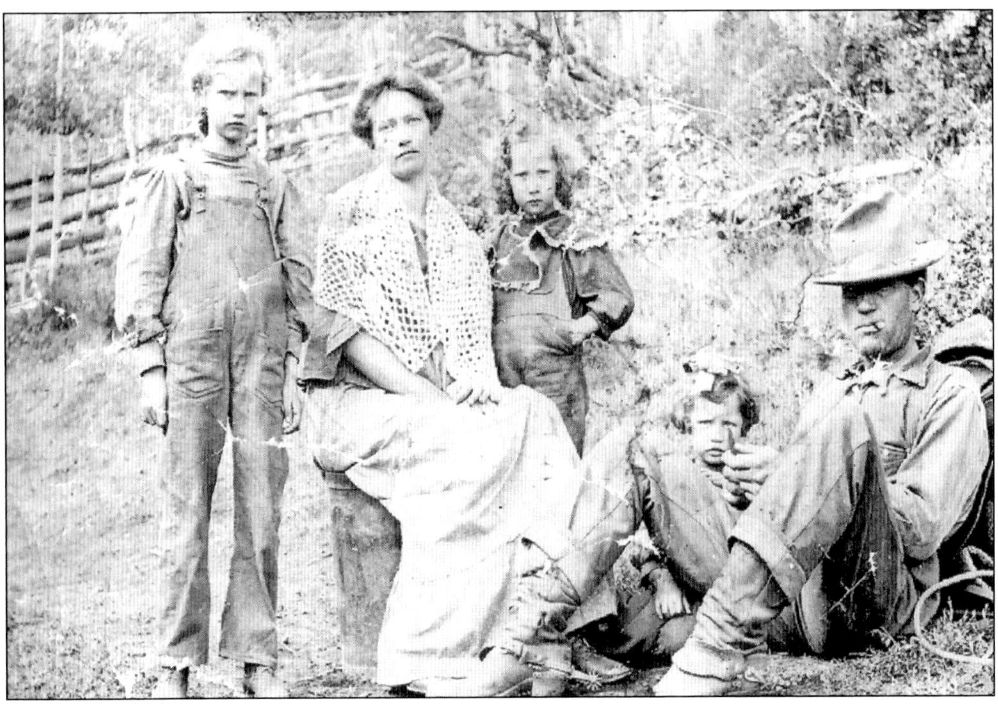

Leona May Bigelow married Alma Scovill on June 22, 1932, in Green River. They are the parents of six children. Alma and Leona moved to Green River in 1934. Each year, to mark their wedding anniversary, the Scovills would take a trip. Alma was the official storyteller on the Utah Centennial Train in 1996. Alma was born in 1909 and is the oldest male resident of Green River in 2008.

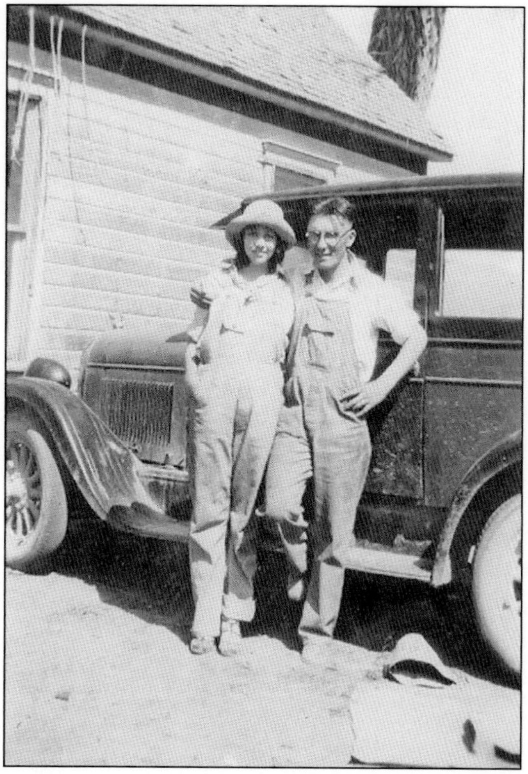

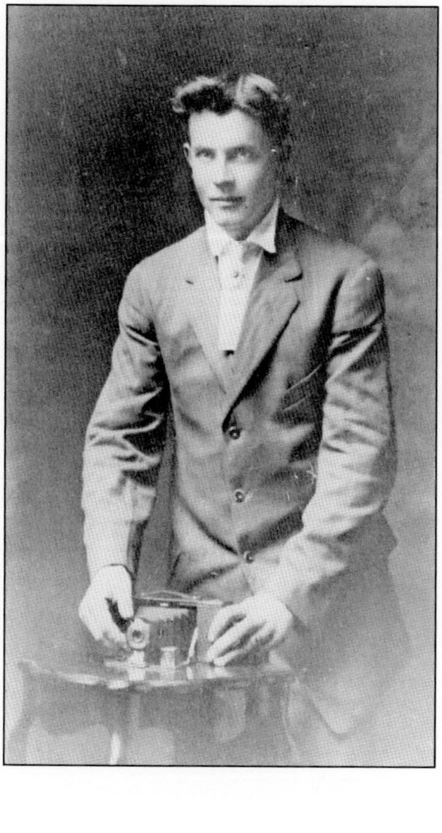

In October 1925, Isaac Stott and his wife, Elvira (Lance) Stott, with their children Lance, Errol J., Don L., and Max L. moved to Green River. There Stott opened a service station, which later burned down. In 1946, he began building the Stott Motel. He did most of the plumbing and carpentry work himself. He also had a great interest in photography and passed that down to his children.

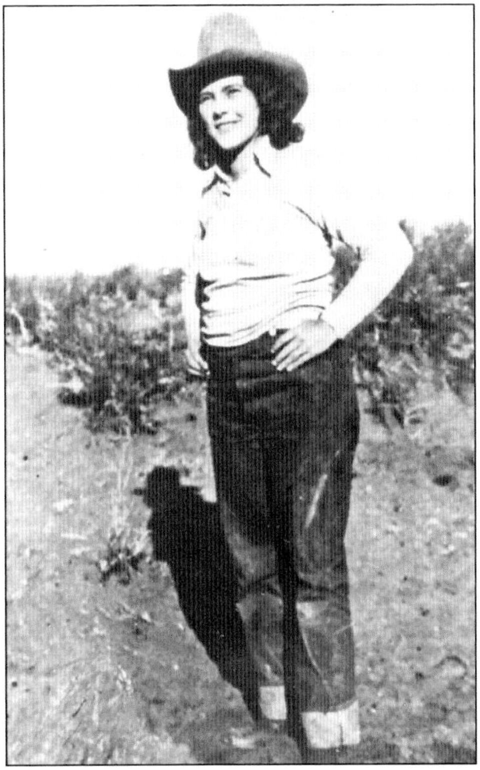

Pearl Baker was the daughter of Joe and Amelia Mae "Millie" (Scharf) Biddlecome. Baker's family owned and farmed Robbers Roost. The Roost is famous for its visitors, among them Butch Cassidy and the Sundance Kid. Baker was the first City Library Committee chairman to raise money for a new library in Green River. Baker is a well-known author of several books. This is Baker's favorite photograph of herself.

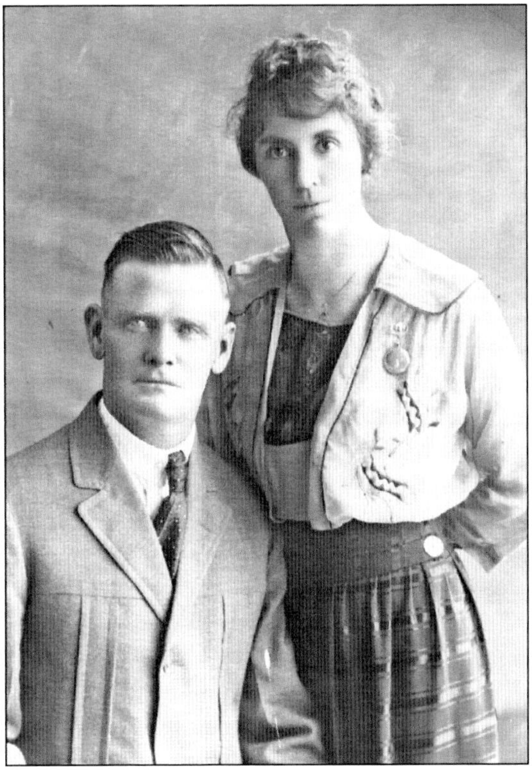

Thomas W. "T. W." Smith was involved in cattle his entire life. Sarah Ann (Gledhill) Smith kept a neat and tidy house in Green River but loved to be out on the desert. They moved to Green River in 1922 in a covered wagon. Their son Lee, who was six at the time of the move, remembers arriving in Green River in the late summer, where they ate cold watermelon. Many descendants of this union still live in Green River.

Two

SCENIC AND FUN

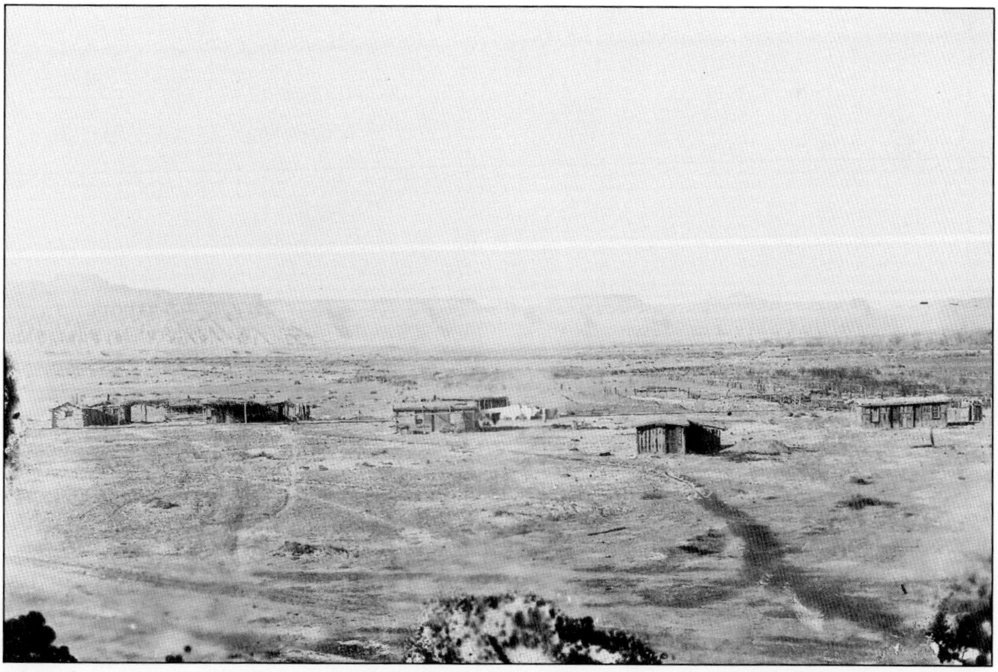

This photograph was taken around 1900 before the Green River Land and Townsite Company plotted the city. The view is from Reservoir Hill looking north on what would later become Broadway Street. Green River was not a well-populated town at the time, and it is still small today, with a population of less than 1,000 residents.

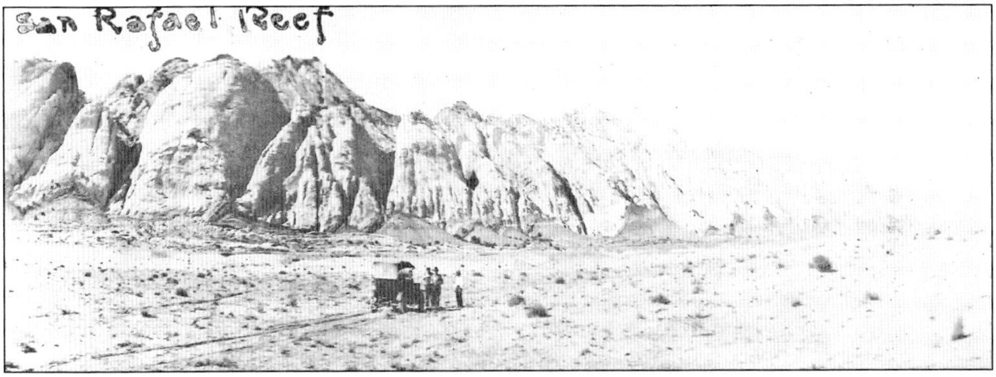

The San Rafael Swell is about 30 miles wide and 50 miles long in size and is located between Green River and Castle Valley. The area received its name from the river, located to the north. The San Rafael Swell is a massive swell in the earth resembling an inverted bowl. Erosion from wind and rain has caused crags, canyons, towers, buttes, and rock lands.

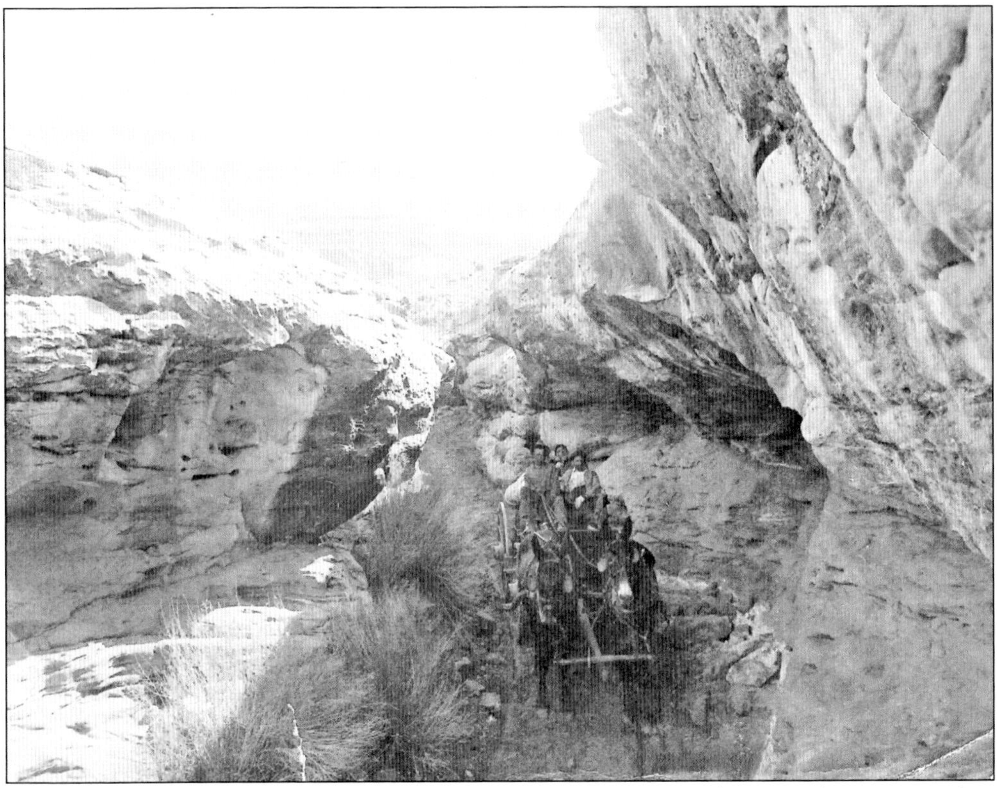

Sam Wilson and Henry Baines (in front, from left to right) came down Coal Canyon with a load of coal. Today, 75 years later, the road down the canyon has washed out. Now a steep grade, using four-wheel drive is the only way to the top. At the top, the road into Coal Canyon exists for approximately one mile; to reach the mine site is a 45-minute hike.

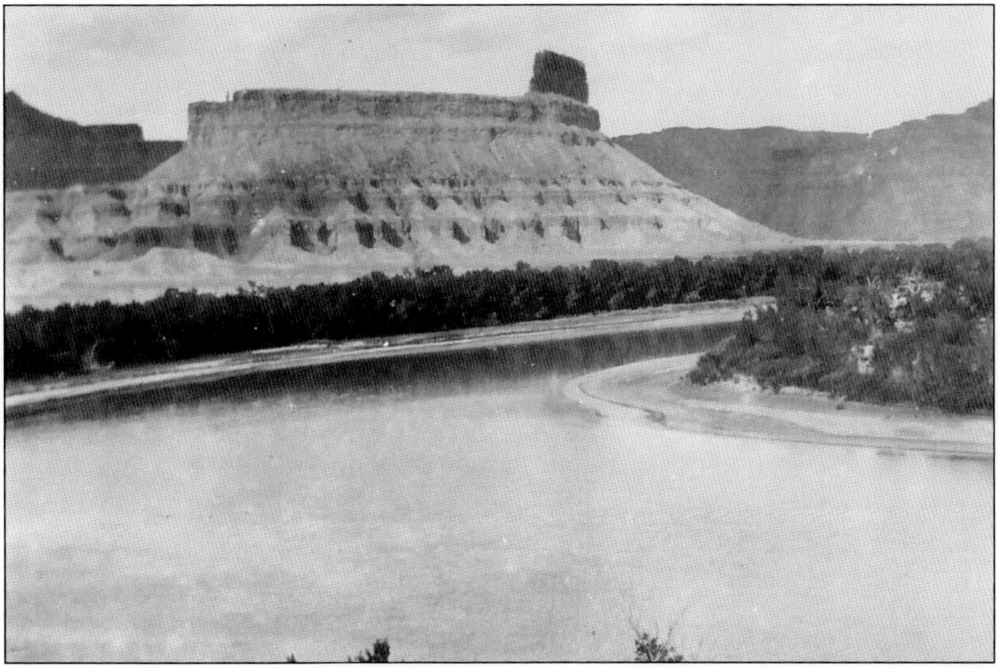

Gunnison Butte is part of the Bookcliff Mountains. It was originally named Cathedral Butte, but John Wesley Powell changed the name to honor Capt. John W. Gunnison, a member of the U.S. railroad team working in the area. In August 1853, Pavant Indians murdered Gunnison and several members of his group in western Utah.

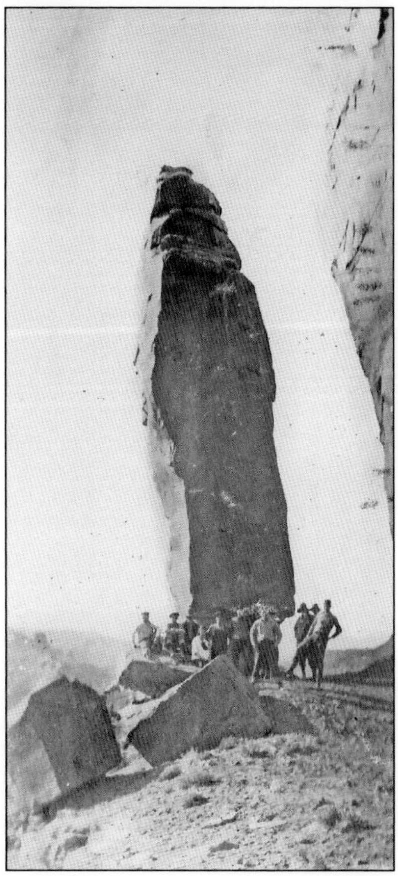

Old Brigham was a pinnacle on Gunnison Butte. It was rumored in Green River that as long as Old Brigham was still standing, Green River would never prosper. It is not known whether Old Brigham fell as a result of dynamite and alcohol or wind and rain erosion, but Green River has continued to have its economic booms and busts.

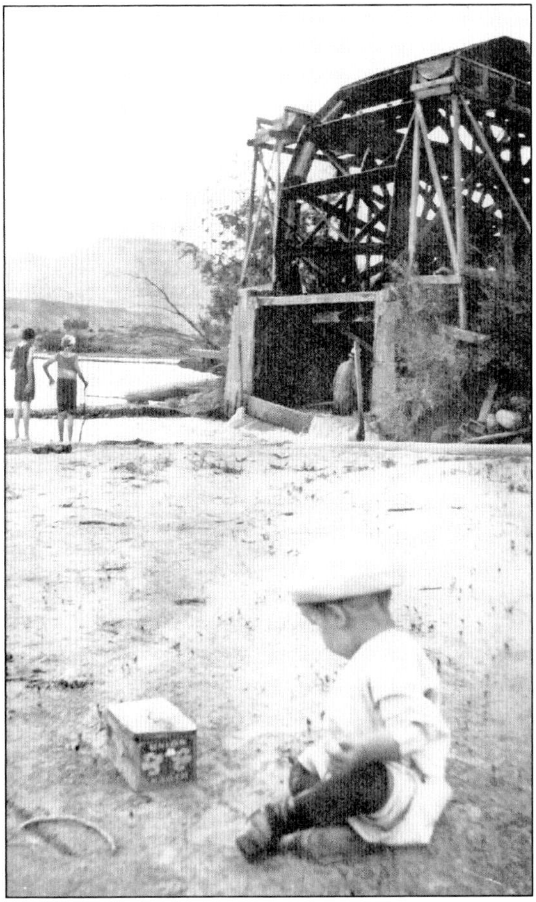

Visible in the background is the Hastings water wheel. The young people look like they are having a great time. The Beebes originally built the waterwheel, and later the Hastings purchased the ranch. Many changes were made to it over the years, and today it no longer runs.

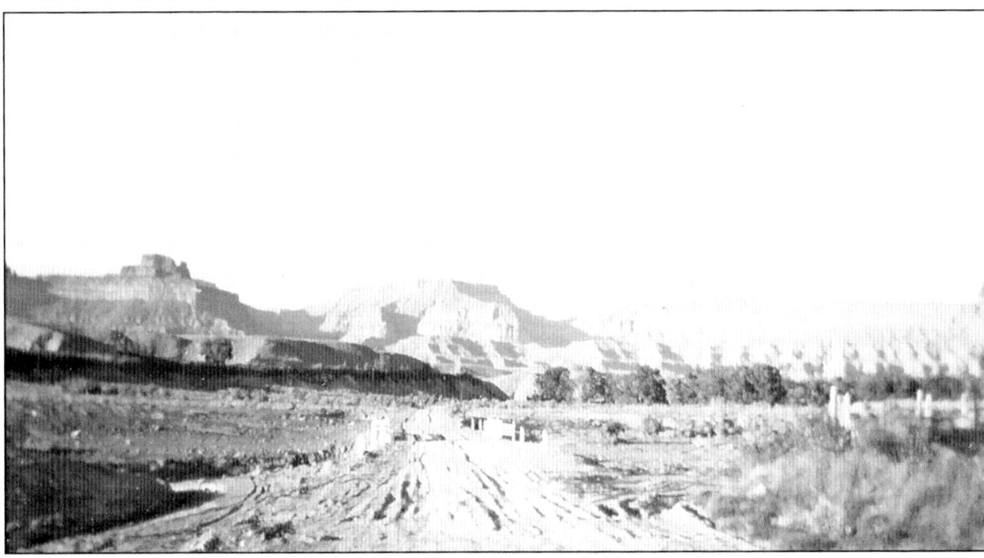

This road follows the west side of the Green River. Along the way is the pump house. Today the Thayn family owns the pump house, using it to generate electricity and to water their corn, hay, watermelons, and cantaloupes.

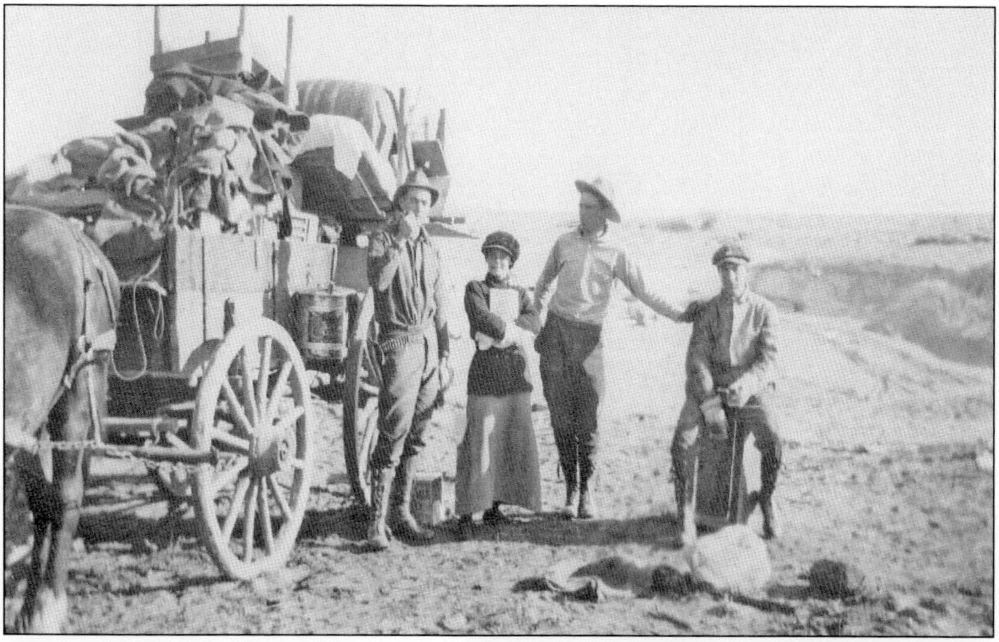

This is a photograph of the Gillies family, early residents of Green River. It is unknown whether they were moving to or from their ranch near the San Rafael River. The family members are unidentified, but it is believed that the young woman in the photograph is Una Gillies.

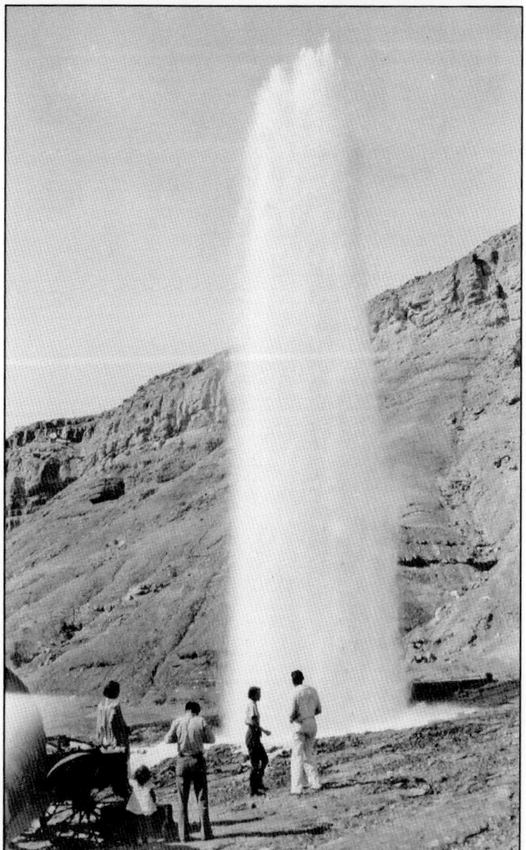

Crystal Geyser was drilled in 1934, when oil companies were looking for oil. What was found instead was a pocket of carbon dioxide. The geyser does erupt, but 12 to 17 hours pass between each eruption. At one time, it did erupt at a scheduled time, but trying to regulate it and vandalism have changed its schedule and made it more irregular.

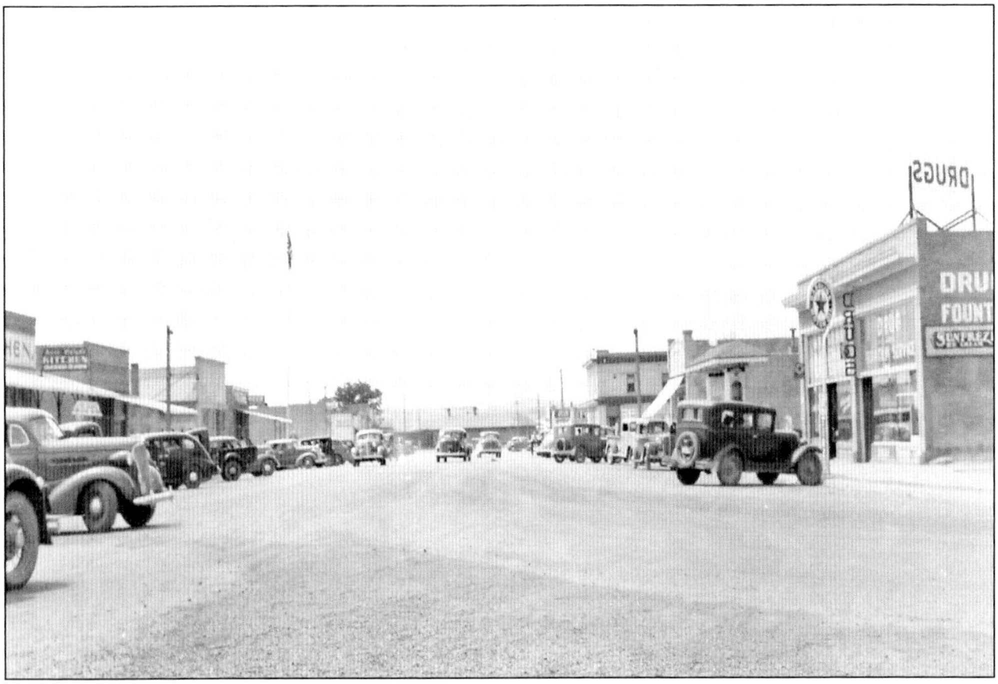

This photograph is looking south on Broadway Street. Ray's Tavern would in the future be located on the left-hand side of the street and was well known by anybody who runs the Green River. It was also across the street from the future Melon Vine Grocery Store and up the street from the future Green River Community Center.

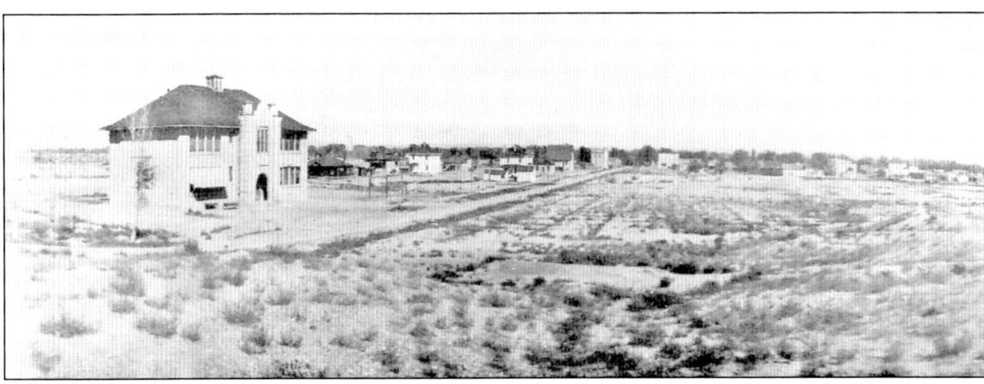

Floyd Kelly took this photograph in the early 1920s. The Green River School is on the left and the dirt road in front later became Highway 6 and 50. The weed patch on the right is the Young Men's Christian Association. The YMCA plot is from the 1906 layout of Greenriver during the land boom.

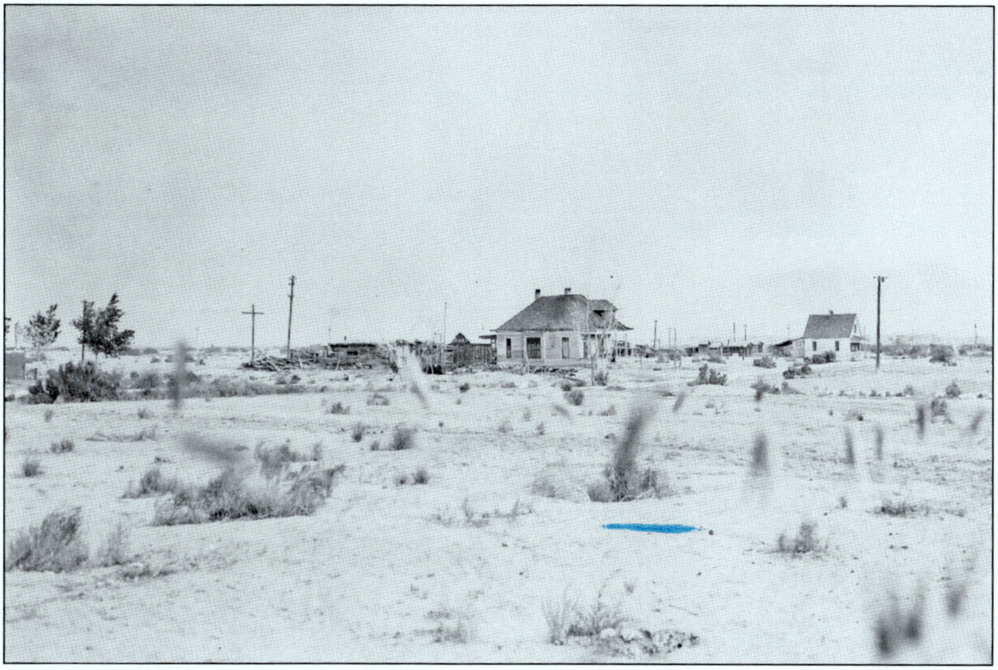

Pat Brown's house was in Elgin, which is a town on the east side of the Green River. Elgin was the first settled area of the valley. With the coming of the railroad, Elgin became east and Greenriver became west, with the river dividing the two towns.

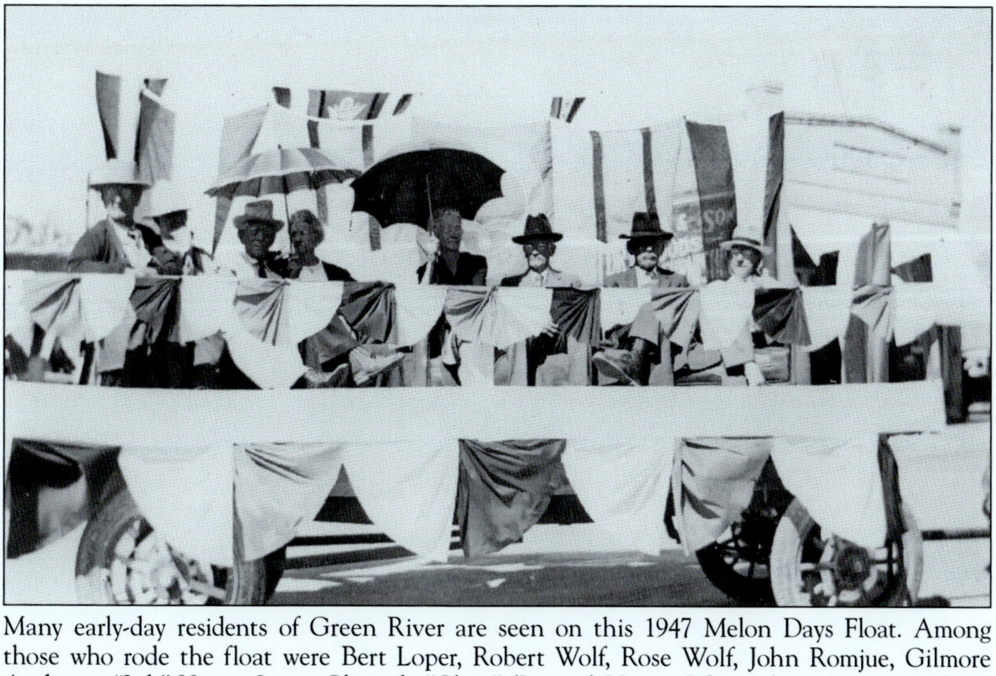

Many early-day residents of Green River are seen on this 1947 Melon Days Float. Among those who rode the float were Bert Loper, Robert Wolf, Rose Wolf, John Romjue, Gilmore Anderson "Ink" Harris, Laura Clarinda "Clara" (Larson) Harris, John Adams, Lorena Wilcox, Chris Halverson, George and Anna (Horton) Thurman, Frank Politano, Bud and Verna Milton, Capt. Harry T. Yokey, John Byers, Rose Politano, Bob Gillies, Una Gillies, and Lou M. Chaffin. Several residents who were on the float had gotten off before the photograph was taken.

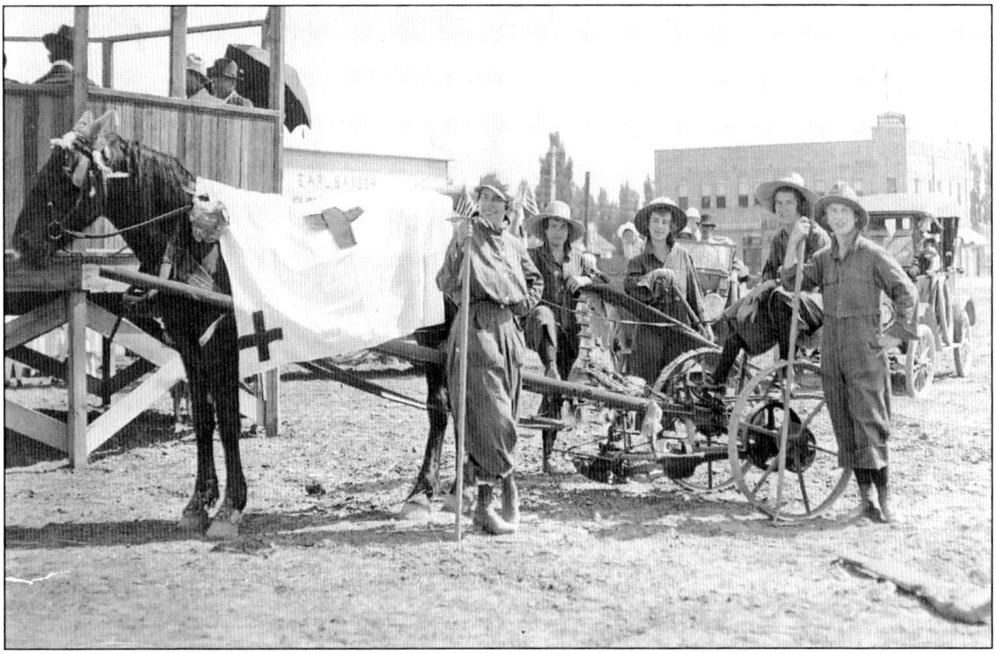

This Red Cross Parade was held in 1918. From left to right are Thurza (Adams) McDougall, Florence (Beebe) Riley Howland, Celestine Moon, Bernice Steel, and LaRata Waddell. In the background is the Metropole Hotel. Many of these women were descendants of early Green River residents. This was the second Red Cross Parade held in Green River.

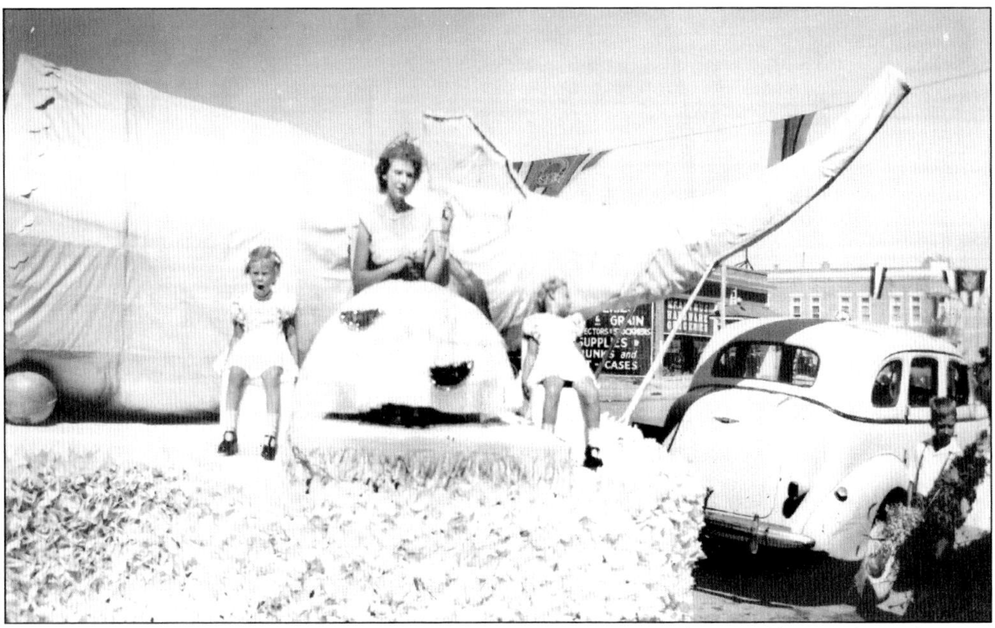

Ina Hunt (Spadafora) was the first Melon Days Queen in 1947. She is still a resident of Green River, a mother to seven children, and a grandmother to numerous grandchildren. Adolph Spadafora, her boyfriend at the time, now her husband, helped her sew the melons visible on the dress and also helped with the earrings. The two attendants are Deanna Curtis (Mecham) and Carolee Allen (right).

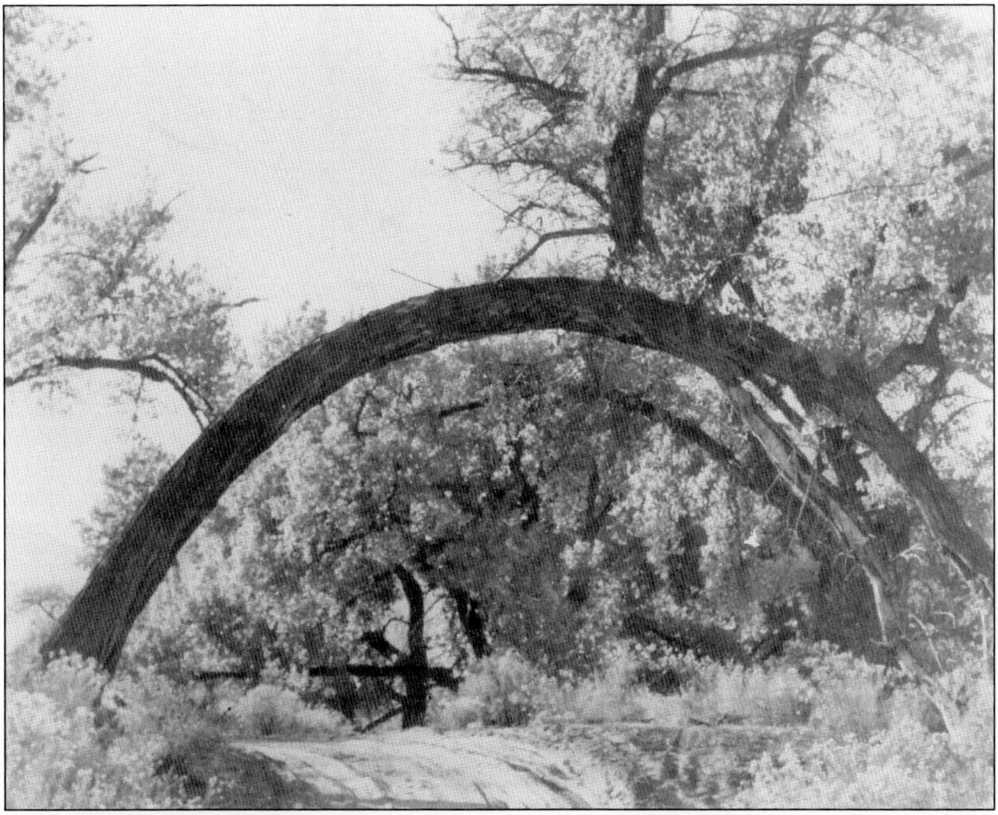

This is Willow Bend, located on the end of North Long Street at the mouth of Gray Canyon and at the beginning of the Bookcliff Mountains. It is obvious how the name for the area came about. Willow Bend as a location still exists today, but the Willow Bend tree is no longer there.

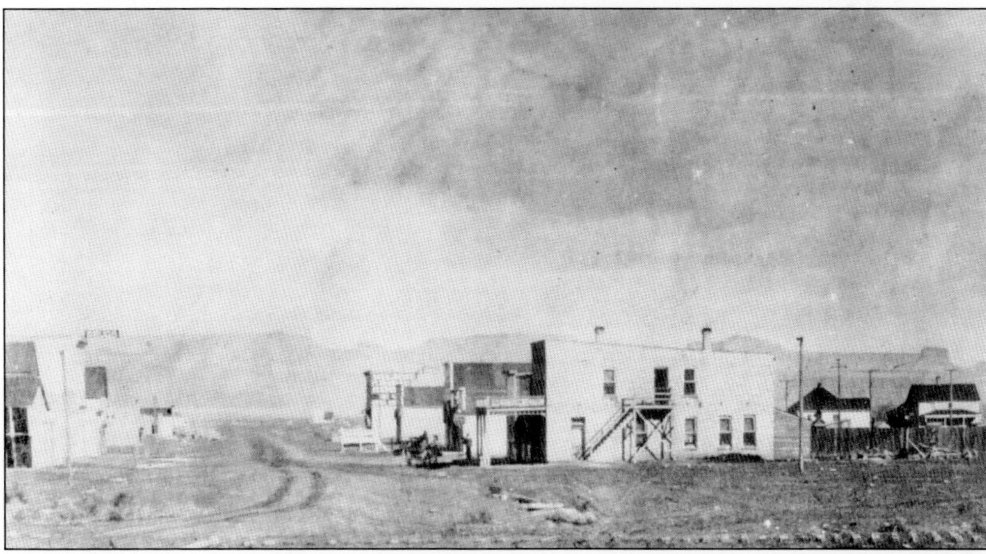

On Broadway Street in 1911, the large building in the foreground was a bakery. It no longer stands. The old Moab Garage was built in that location in the 1920s. Later it was the Midland Garage, and in the late 1980s, it was the location of Adventure River Expeditions.

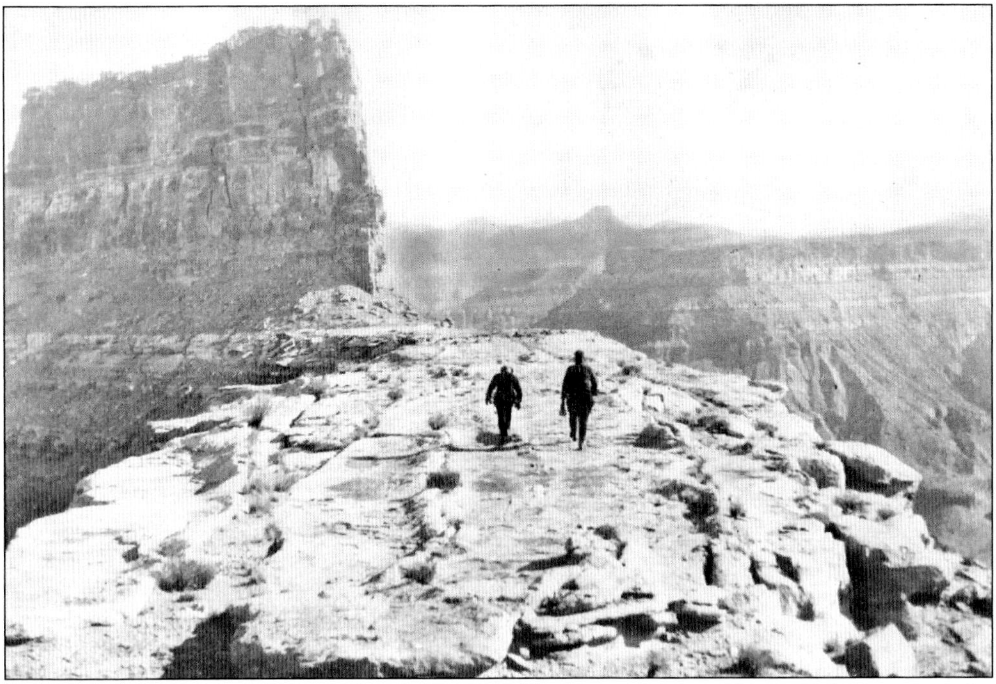

Floyd Kelly, a geology teacher in the early 1920s, liked to take his students on field trips to the Gunnison Butte and the surrounding area. Here are two of Kelly's students on top of Gunnison Butte. At one time, there was a trail on the back of the butte; now it is quite a climb.

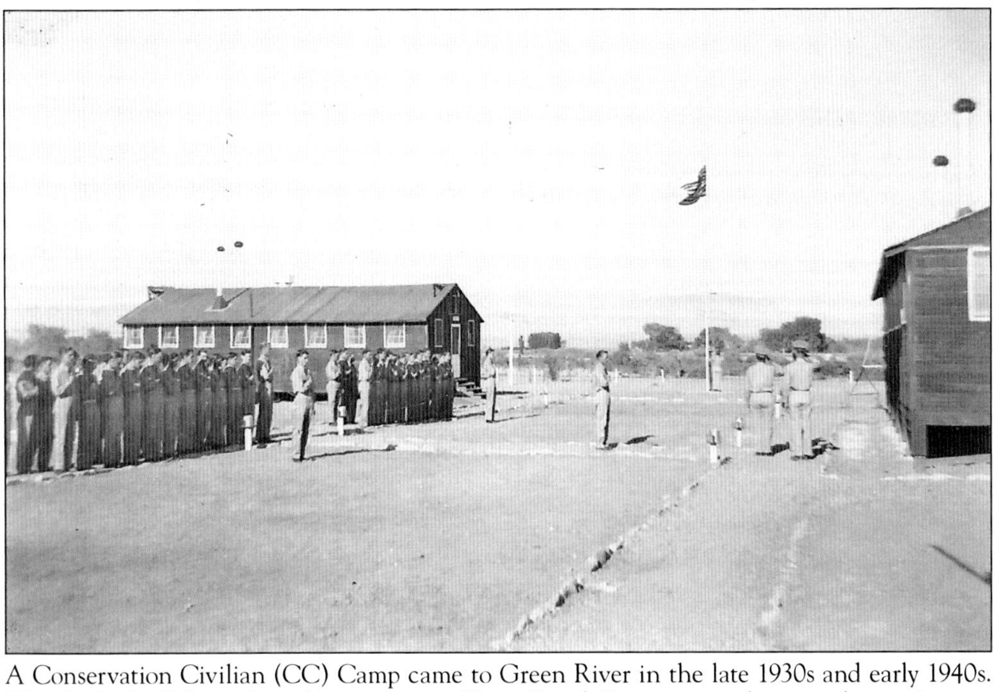

A Conservation Civilian (CC) Camp came to Green River in the late 1930s and early 1940s. They built the CC pond northwest of town, Horse Bench Reservoir, and many other projects in the area. Their base was located on North Long Street where the ball fields and Emery County Road Shed are today.

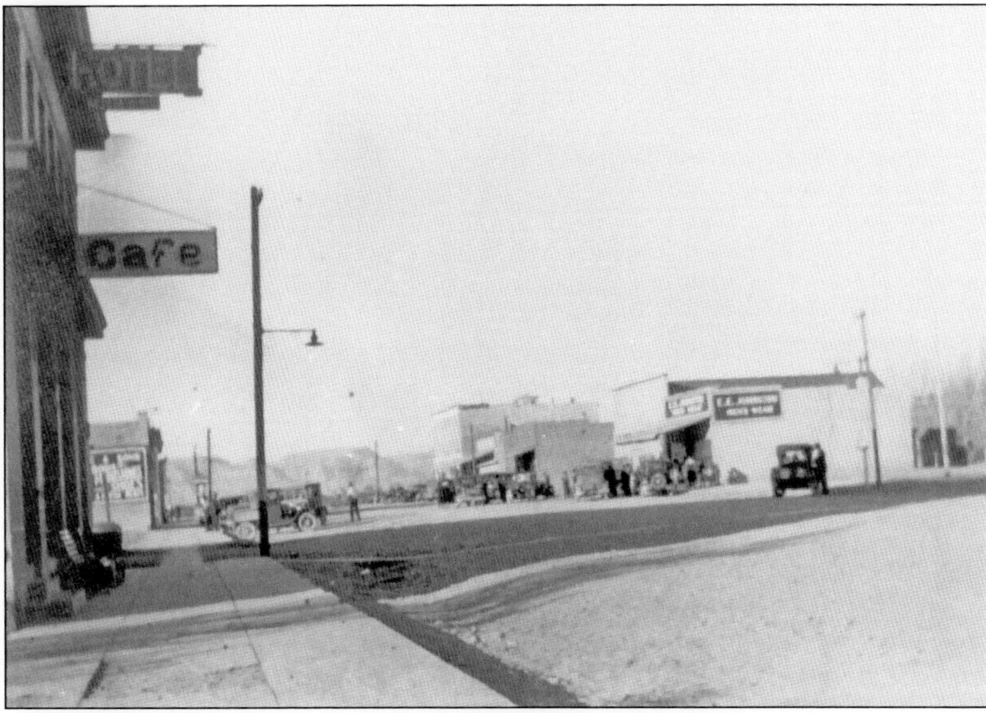

Broadway Street in 1915 is seen from the former location of the opera house next to the Midland Hotel; several of the buildings still stand today, though many are gone. Broadway was the original location for Melon Days celebrations, and the parade still goes up Broadway to Highway 6 and 50.

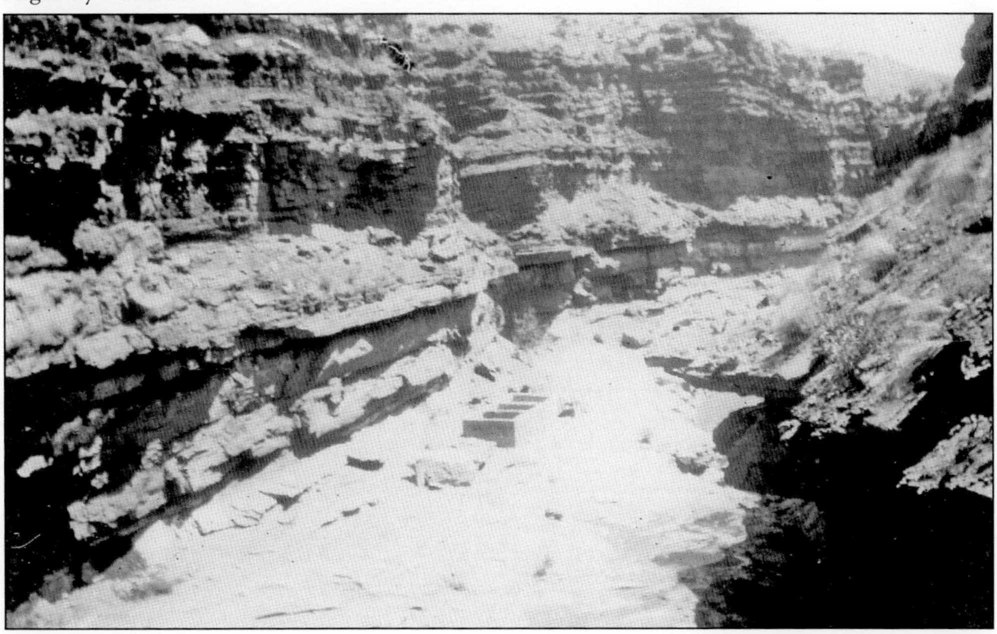

These abandoned tanks were used for making moonshine by Bill Tomlinson. He lived and ranched at the present Chaffin Ranch before the Lou Chaffin family arrived. It is a favorite hike for many today. Moonshine Canyon is located south of Green River below the San Rafael River.

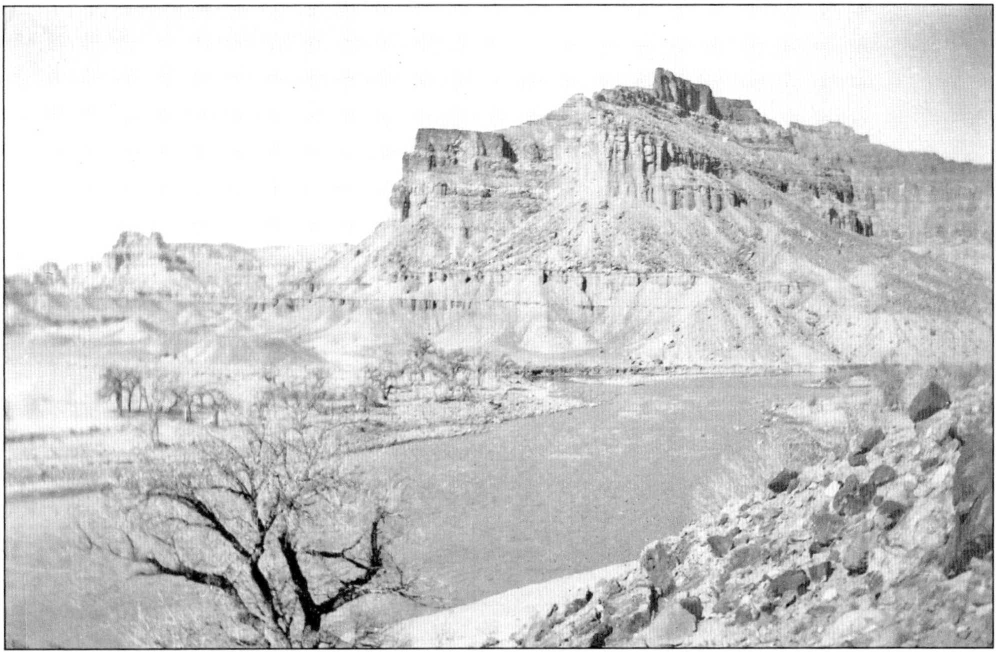

The mouth of Gray Canyon is located on the Green River north of town. It shows the "Beach," as the locals refer to the Swasey's Rapids area, with white sand as good as that on the ocean shores. The Beach is a favorite spot for camping, fishing, and just riding the rapids on an old inner tube. It is also the take-out place for the Desolation River trips.

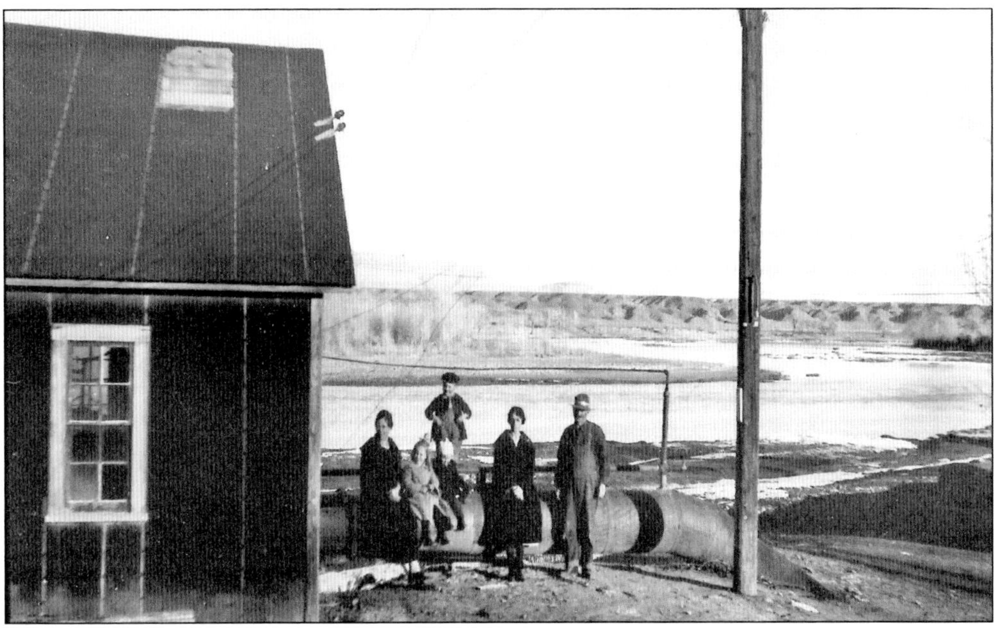

The pump house on North Long Street is pictured about 1924. From left to right are Mabel Smith and three of her children, Estelle (Cameron) Brown, and Thomas S. Brown. The pump house has since had many major repairs done to it, but it is still being used today to produce electricity and also to water farm crops.

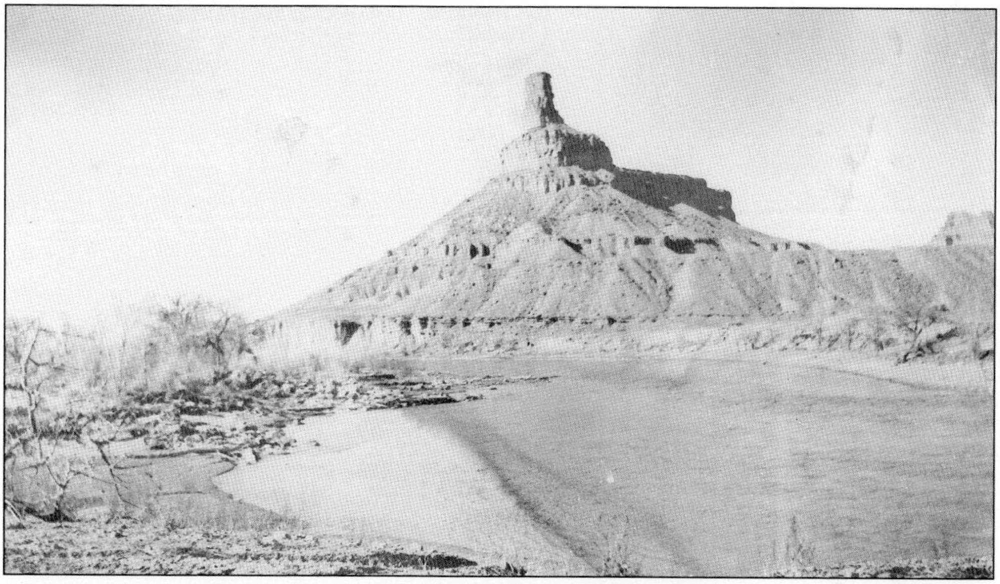

Gunnison Butte was originally named Cathedral Butte, but John Wesley Powell changed its name to honor Capt. John W. Gunnison, who was killed by Pavant Indians in western Utah. For those taking the float trips down the Green River, it is a beautiful sight, especially for photographers.

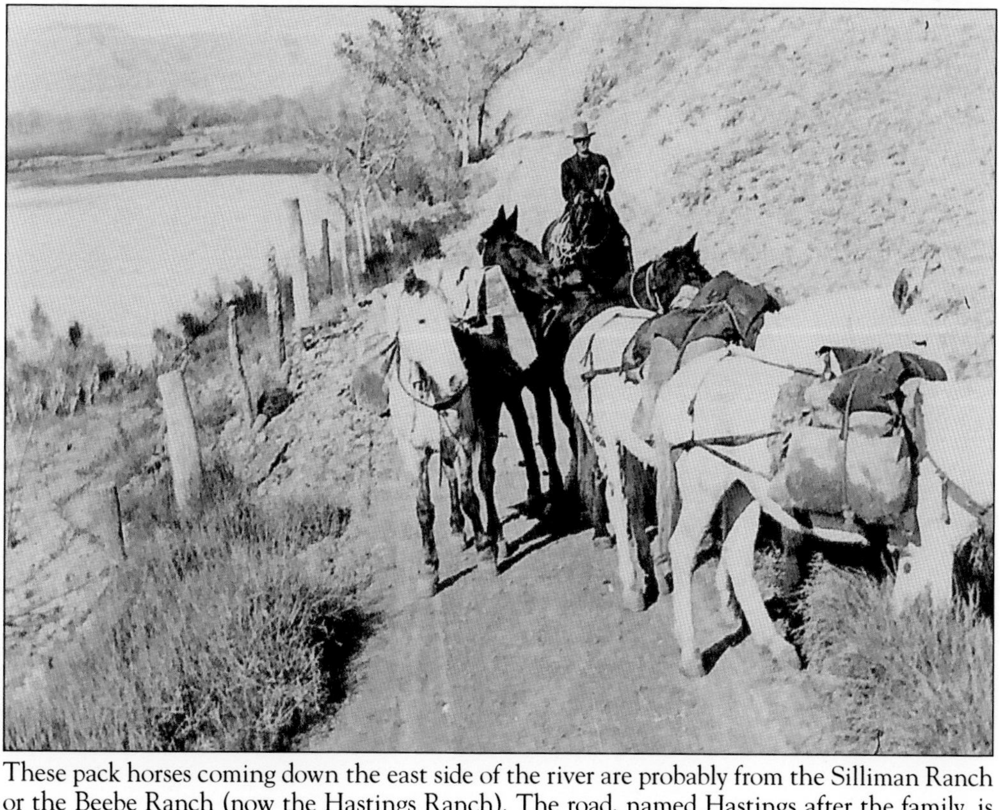

These pack horses coming down the east side of the river are probably from the Silliman Ranch or the Beebe Ranch (now the Hastings Ranch). The road, named Hastings after the family, is now much wider and paved. Just before the river swings back out is the location of one of the Old Spanish Trail crossings.

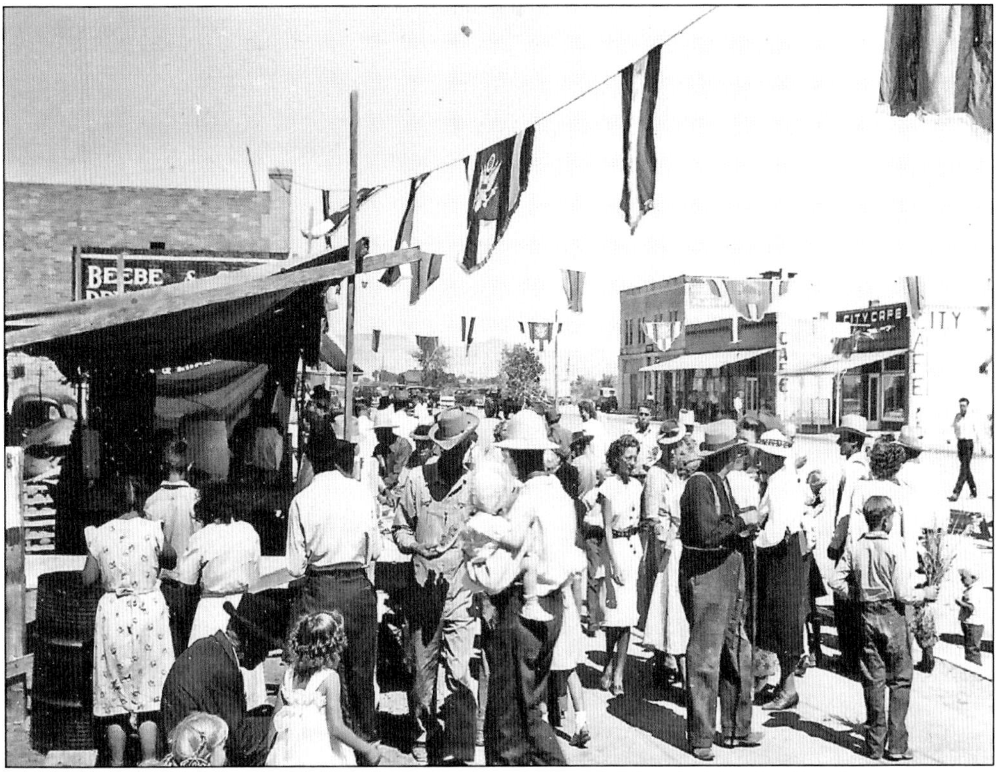

The Melon Days festival was held on Broadway Street in the mid-1940s. Booths were set up in what is now the Melon Vine Grocery parking lot. Research has not shown any information on there ever being a building previously on this spot. It was a good place to use for community activities.

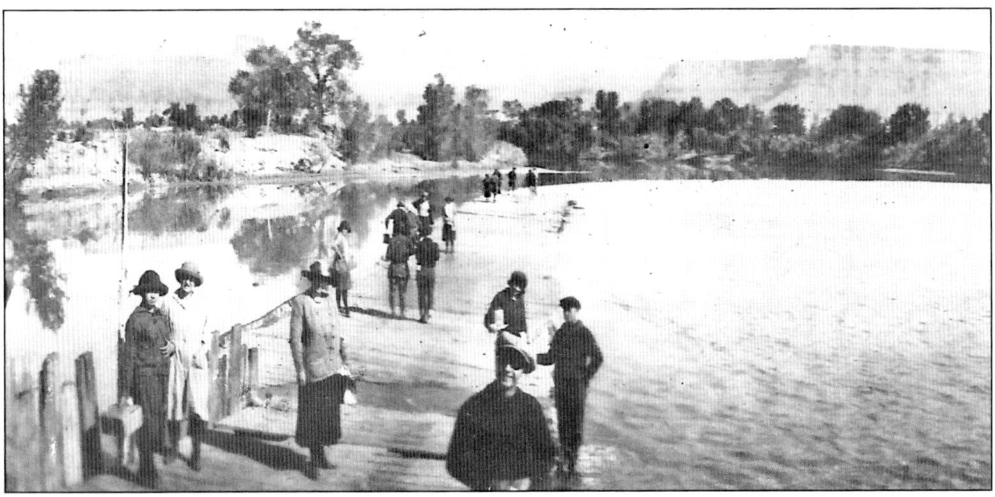

A geology field trip was taken by Floyd Kelly's class; this time, the class went to the diversion dam above town. Kelly was an avid believer in field trips. He liked to take his students to many different locations in the valley, and his numerous photographs recorded their adventures.

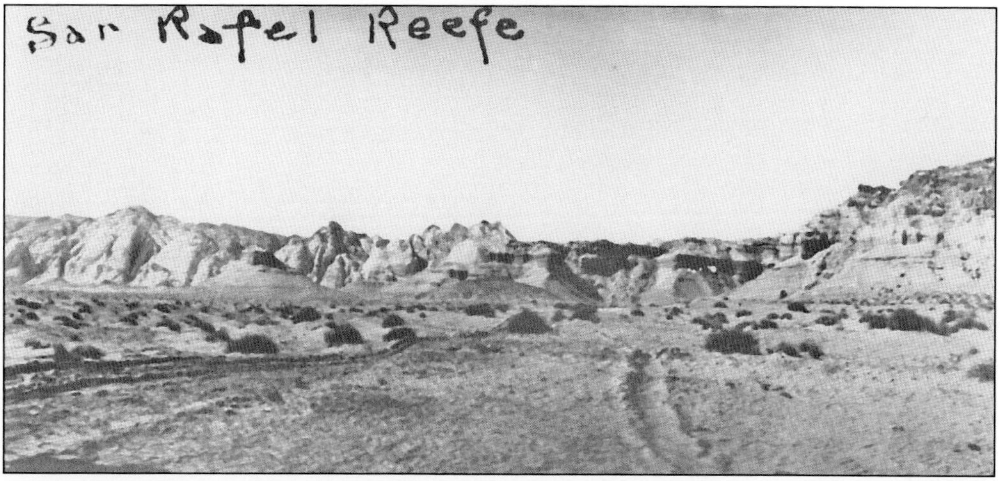

The San Rafael Reef and Swell are well known for their beauty. Some people are also aware of the ranchers, prospectors, and outlaws who have lived and worked in the reef. It is good cow country, has vanadium and uranium in quantities, and has great places for outlaws to hide. The swell is still used for ranching and mining, but a new twist has been added—hiking and bicycling.

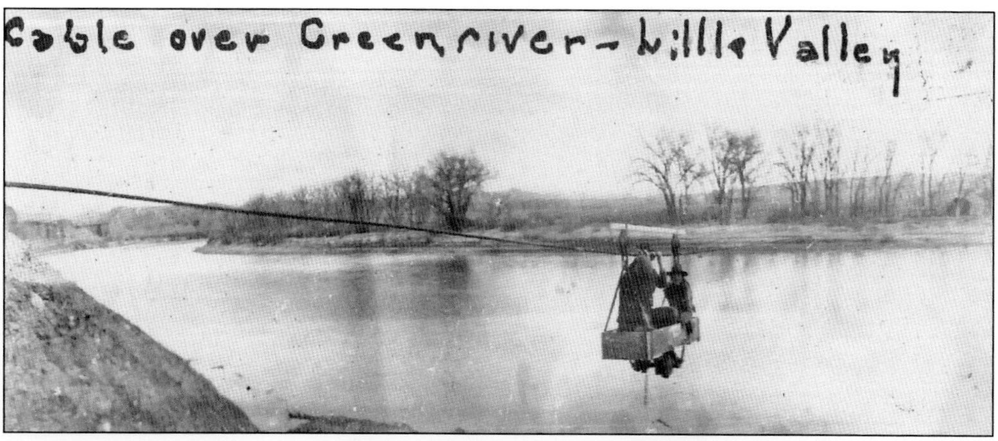

For ease and speed, many who ranched or farmed along the river built cable cars to cross it. One side might have a shorter way to town with a road or easier terrain to cross. This one was on the lower end of Little Valley about seven miles south of town. The east side was a long way to reach town, whereas the west side had a better and shorter road.

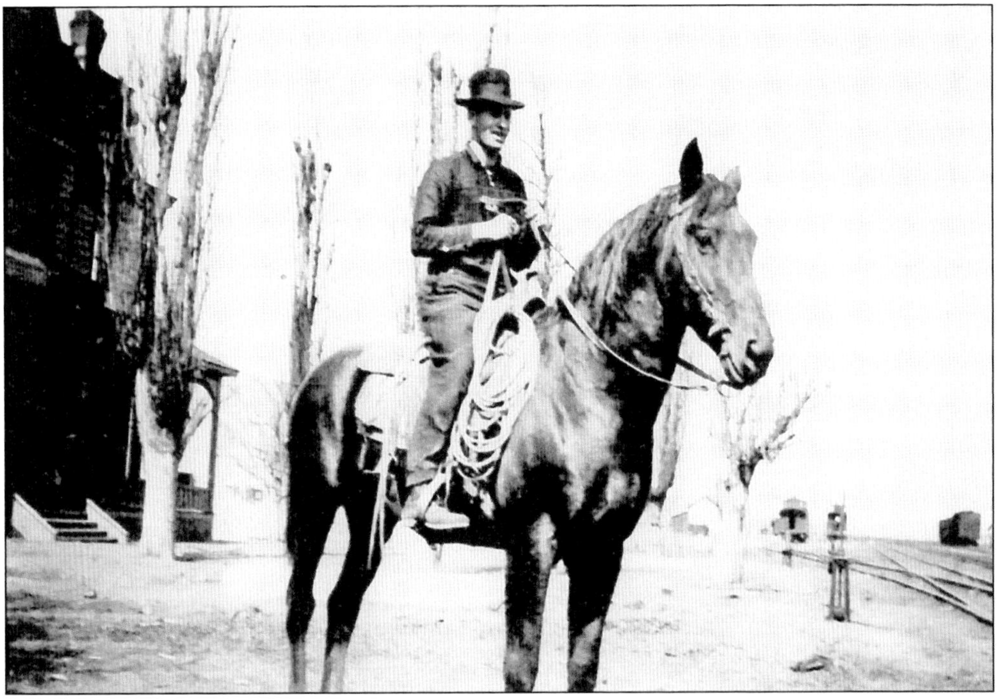

Bill Dahling rides his horse Prince in front of the Palmer House. This is the only known photograph from the 1920s of this angle for the Palmer House and the railroad tracks. Bill was the son of Herman and Beatrice Dahling. The house he grew up in still stands.

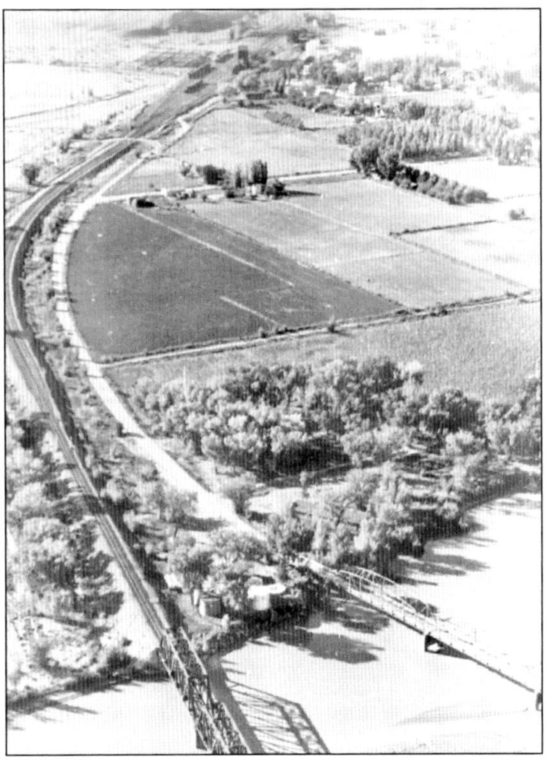

This is an aerial photograph of the town of Green River taken in the early 1940s. The railroad bridge can be seen in the foreground and the car or wagon bridge just slightly above it and to the right. In the central part of the photograph are several trees densely planted; today that is where the Green River State Park and Golf Course is located.

This photograph, taken from the air in the early 1940s of Green River, shows the road to the left, Broadway Street. At the bottom of the photograph is the Saleratus Wash, which changed its course many times. Visible are the stockyards just above the wash. The building in the center of the photograph is the Metropole Hotel. The long narrow building to the lower left is the roundhouse used to crate and ship melons.

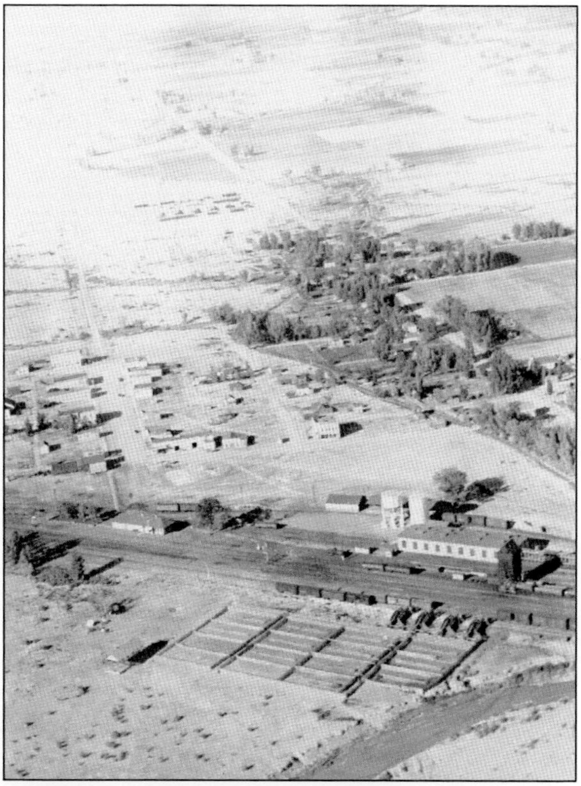

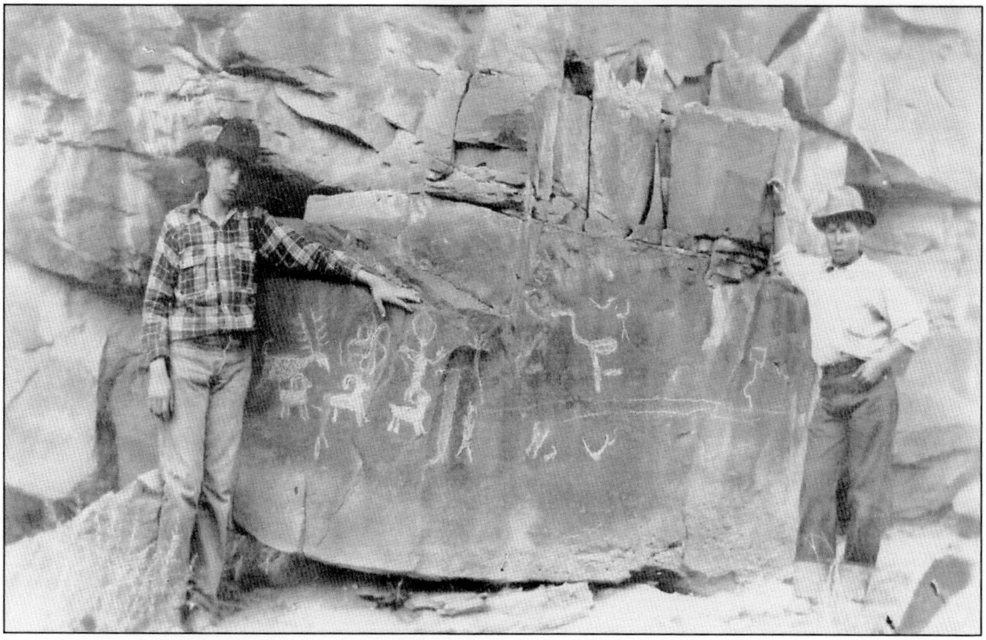

Standing from left to right are Chad Moore and Jay Marsing. The original caption for this photograph calls the Native American writings "hieroglyphics." Today they are called petroglyphs. It is unknown exactly where these are located. Both young men grew to adulthood but have since passed away. This is from an early-1940s Boy Scout trip.

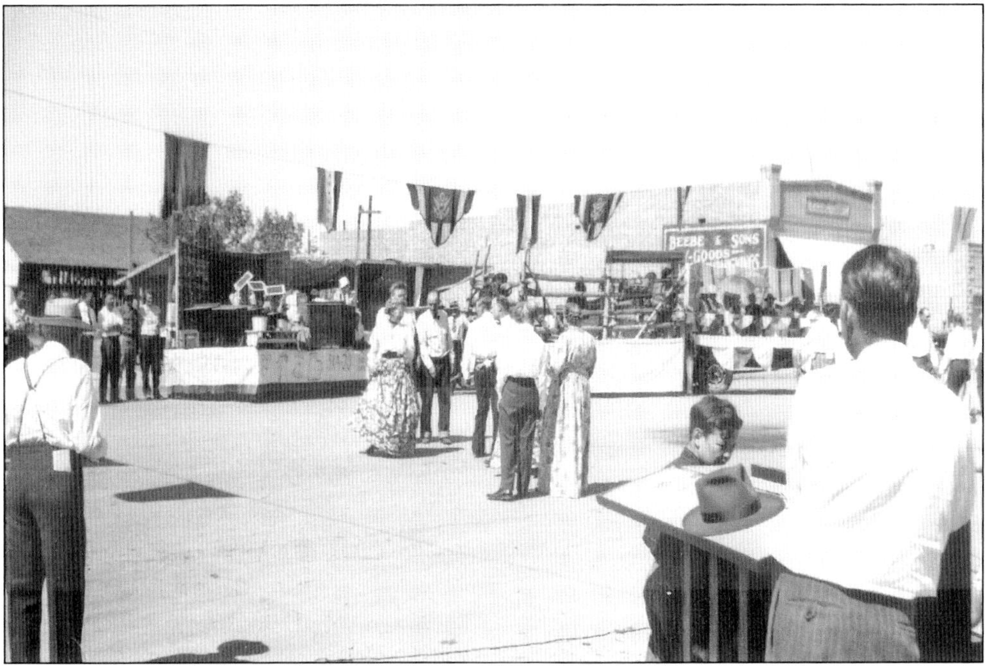

Nolan Curtis married Mazel Duncan on July 3, 1939; they are the parents of seven children. Curtis and his partner Wilford Durrant ran the Curtis and Durrant Service, a fuel business. Curtis eventually sold his half of the business. The Curtises ran the Frosty Circle from 1966 to 1976. Nolan and Mazel formed the Melon Busters Square Dancers. In 1998, Nolan received the Cole Award for his 50 years of promoting square dancing.

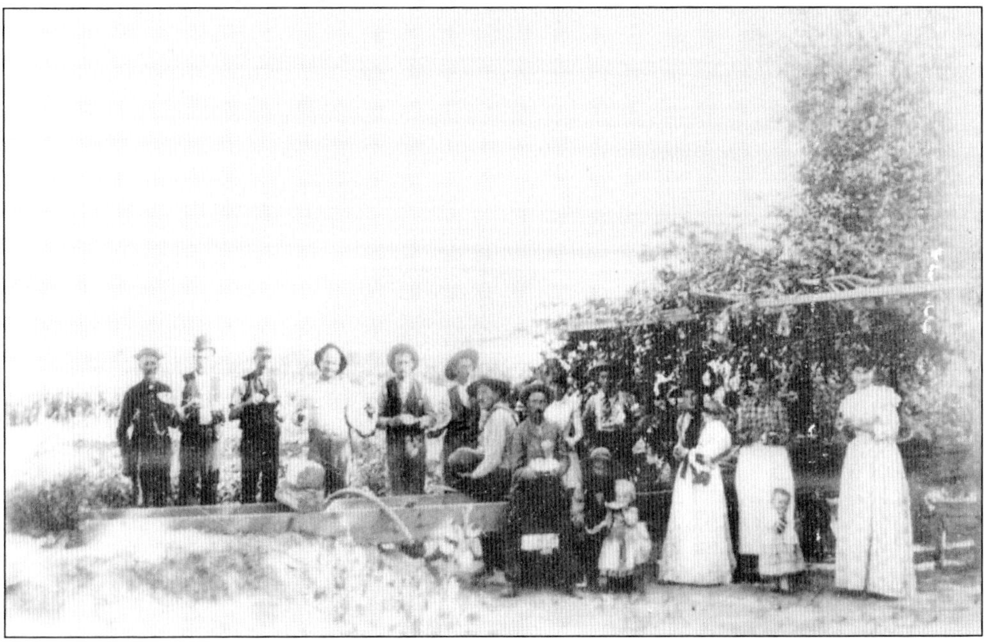

One of the first Melon Days celebrations held in Green River was in approximately 1907. The bower was built to shade the melons as well as the people. Green River has celebrated more than 100 years of Melon Days.

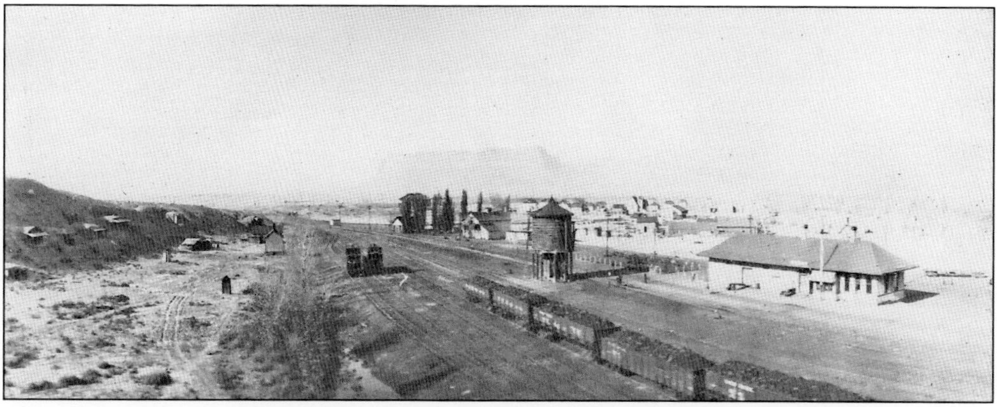

This photograph was taken in approximately 1924 by Green River's first geology teacher, Floyd Kelly. This view of the railroad tracks was taken from the Palmer House before the Palmer House was demolished in 1927. Floyd Kelly and his wife, Elizabeth (Coath-Miner), left soon after. To the northwest some of the homes of Green River can be seen.

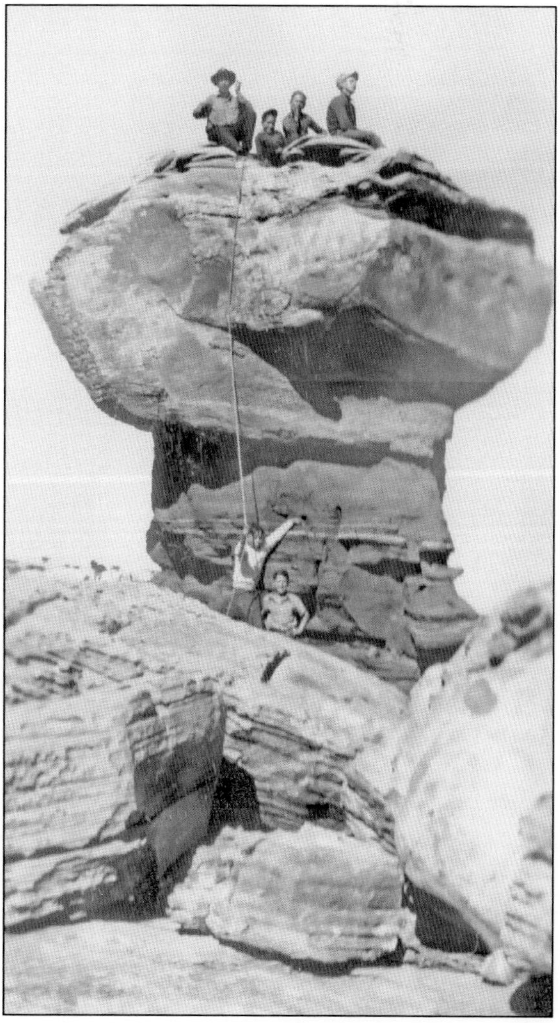

Boy Scouts climb on the rocks at Crystal Geyser. The photograph was taken in the early 1940s. The geyser is located just nine miles south of Green River. It still erupts to this day, just not as frequently as it did when this photograph was taken. It is now owned by the City of Green River.

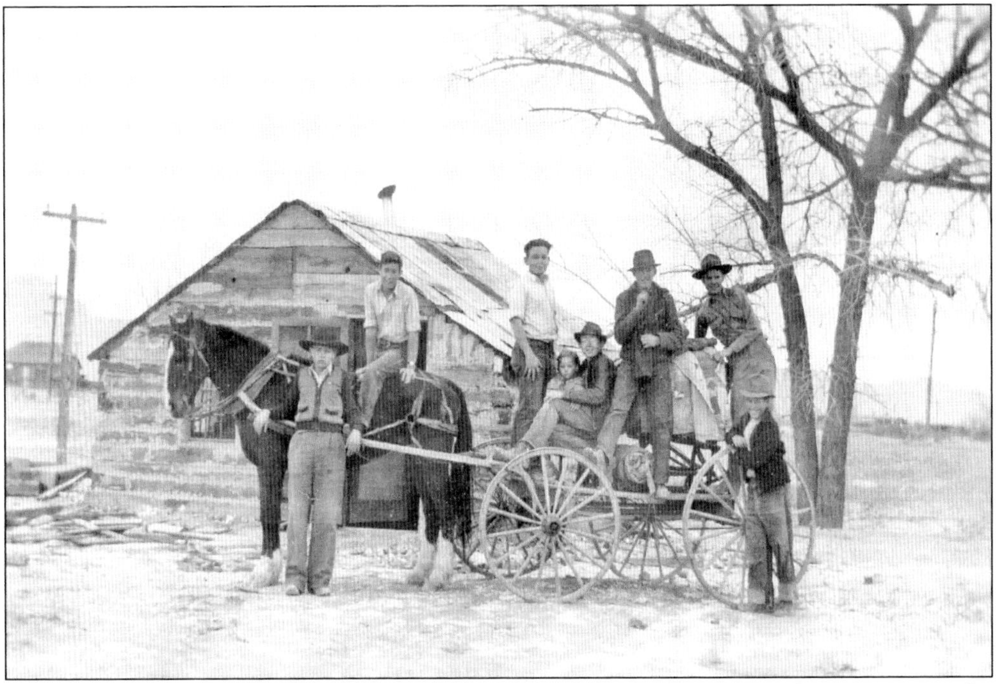

A Boy Scout troop prepares for an adventure and was sure to have one. They were using the wagon where the Boy Scouts of today would use an all-terrain vehicle (ATV). The identities of these early-1940s Boy Scouts are unknown.

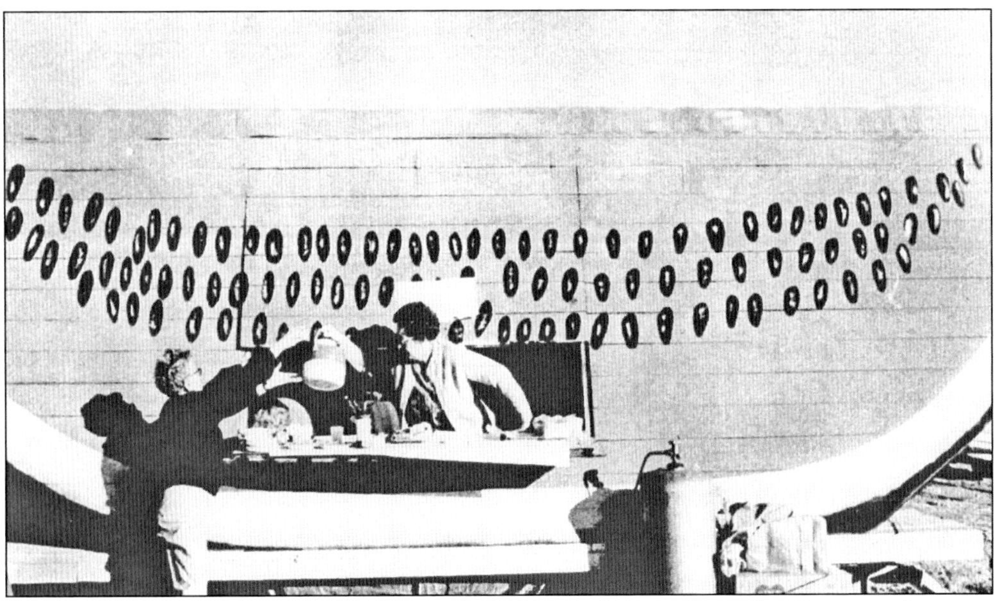

The famous watermelon slice was originally built to be a float in the Melon Days parade; it was also built as a concession stand. Helen Tidwell is passing the water jug to Mamie Weihing. The chamber of commerce built the float in 1960 as an advertisement for Green River. It is still used as a float for the Melon Days parade, but it is no longer used as a concession stand.

Three

Cowboys and Farmers

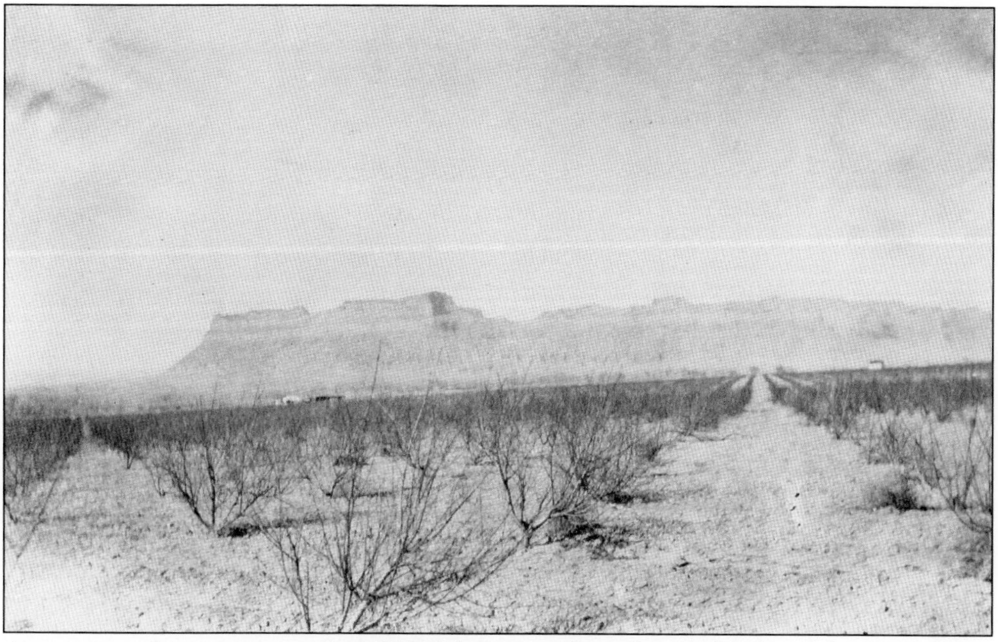

At one time, there were more than 50,000 fruit trees planted on both sides of the Green River. Several early warm springs and later extreme hard frosts caused devastating damage to the trees. It is said that one could hear the trees exploding from the freeze. Devastated, many left everything in Green River to start a new life somewhere else. For many years afterwards, the locals used the trees as firewood.

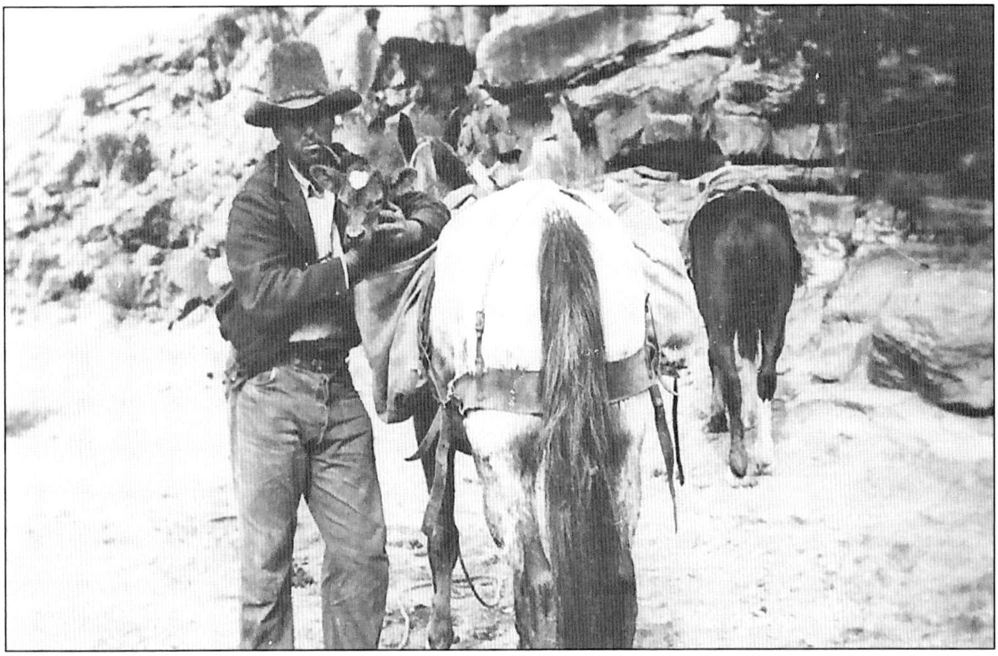

Lorin Wilson rescues a newborn calf. Apparently its mother died at its birth. It was common to save the new calf and try to get another cow to take it as its own. Notice the packs on the horse; they were used to carry the little ones back to the ranch because they were too small to make it on their own.

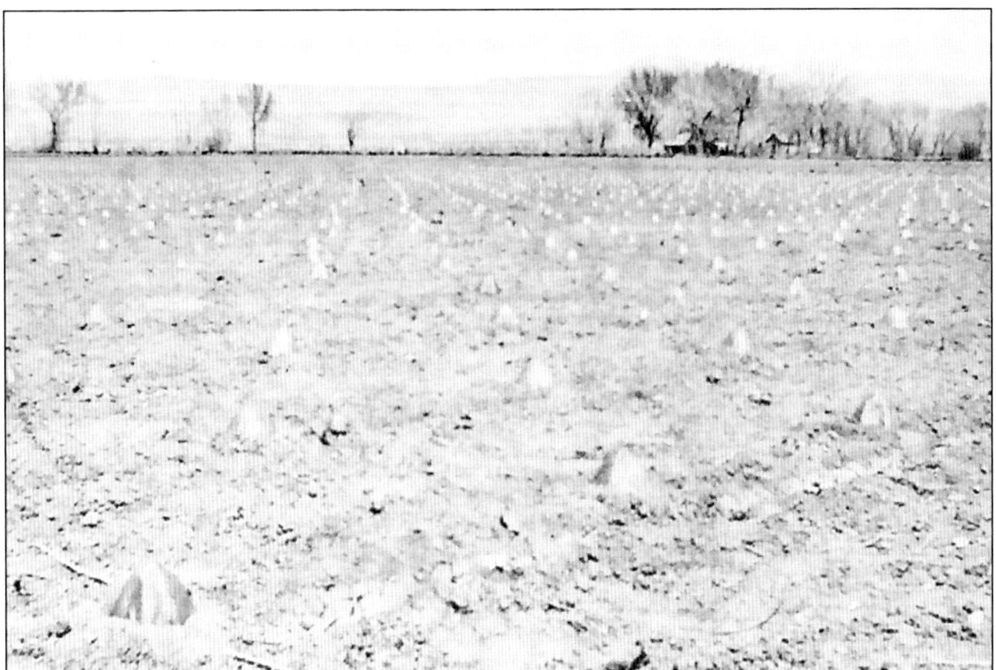

The Wilson family not only raised cattle, but also farmed. This photograph is of a newly planted melon field. This dates from about the 1930s, with the plants under hot caps. Hot caps are a smaller version of a greenhouse used to speed up the growth process of the fruit.

Andy Moore was a cattleman his entire life. He started working with his father and brothers as a child. When he married and had two sons of his own, he was still in the cattle business. This is a photograph of his cabin in the San Rafael Swell. It was not the first cabin he shared with his wife and children, but he moved his family here when he had a large herd.

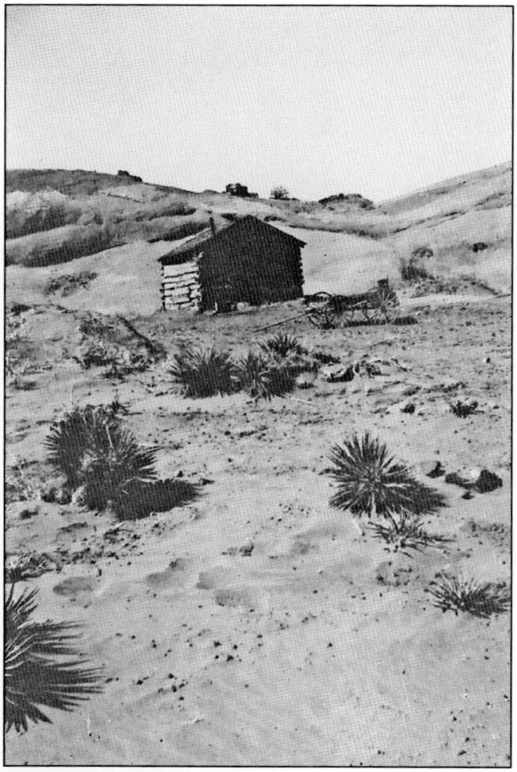

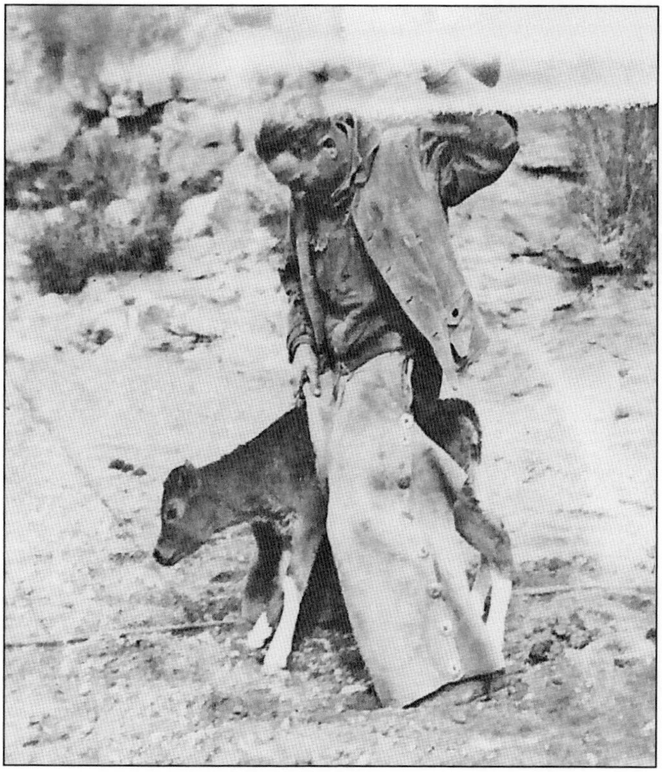

Lorin Wilson pretends to ride a new calf for the camera. Wilson was a busy man. He was co-owner of the Wilson Produce Company and was involved in the farming and livestock businesses. Wilson moved to Green River when he was three years old. He graduated from Green River High School and married Mildred Searson Ainsworth, another Green River resident. Lorin had a son with Mildred and also helped raise her three children.

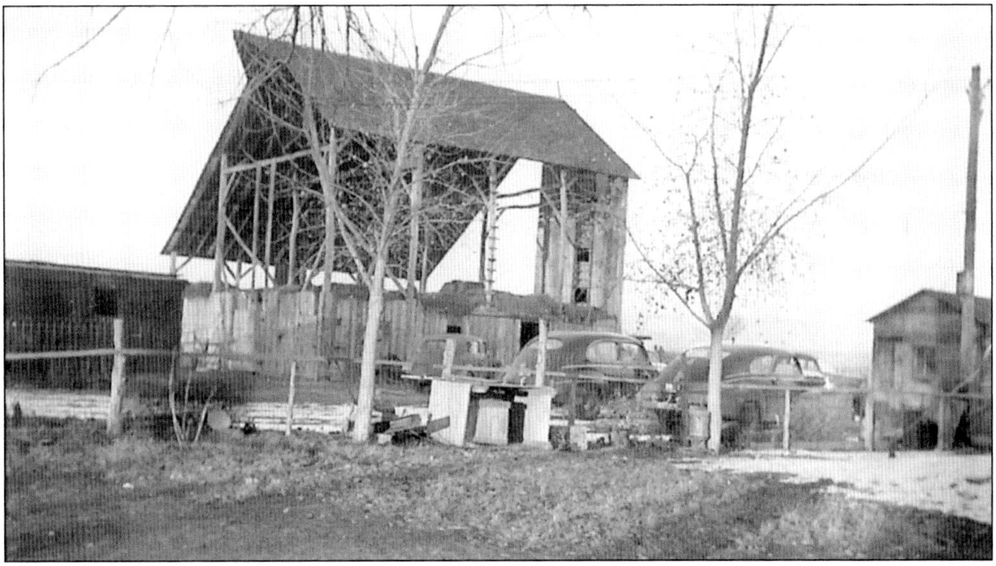

The Thurman ranch and farm on North Long Street boasted the only cement silo in the valley. According to the *Emery County Progress* in 1917, there were to be five cement silos built in Emery County. Thurman's was the only one on this side of the county. The silo still stands today. The barn is gone.

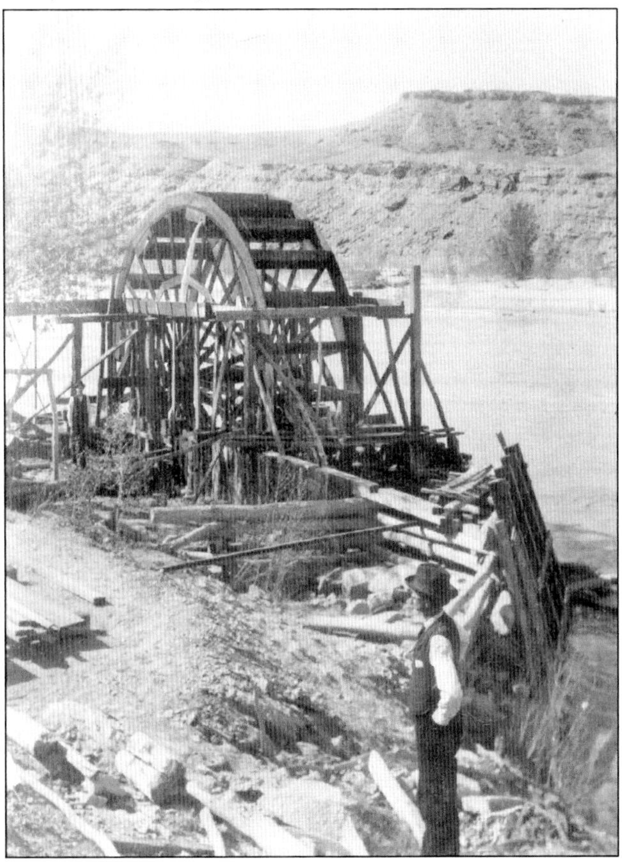

One of the first waterwheels built in the valley was located south of the railroad bridge on the east side of the river. The waterwheels were used where there were no canals. There were several waterwheels along the Green River, but none are in use today.

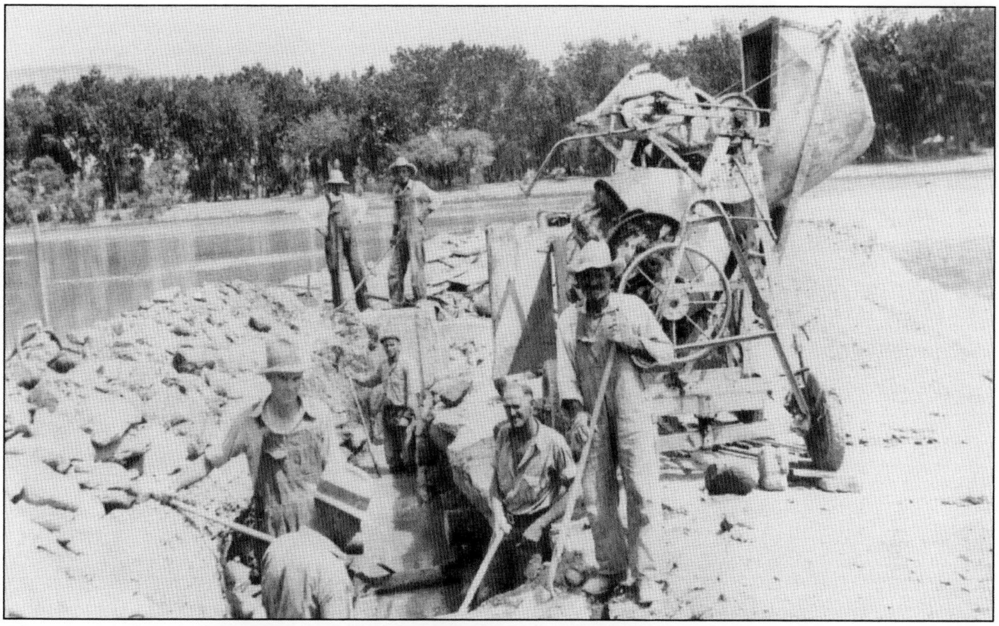

The Green River diversion dam has seen many changes. The first dam was reinforced with brush, rocks, and trees, but when high water hit in the spring, the dam was washed out. By 1932, the dam was reinforced with concrete. The photograph shows John Vetere Sr. (working down in the hole) and others working on the dam.

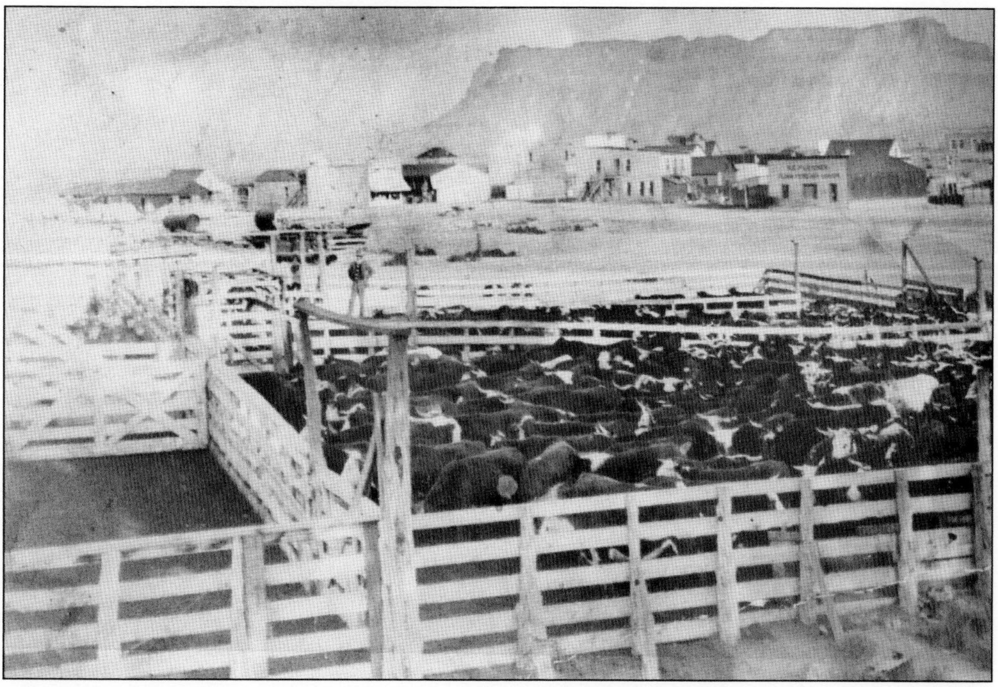

The stockyards are full of cattle ready and waiting for the trains to take them to market. Notice the horns on the cattle; now they are removed when they are still calves. In the background is the town of Green River. The Saleratus Wash removed the area where the stockyards were located years ago.

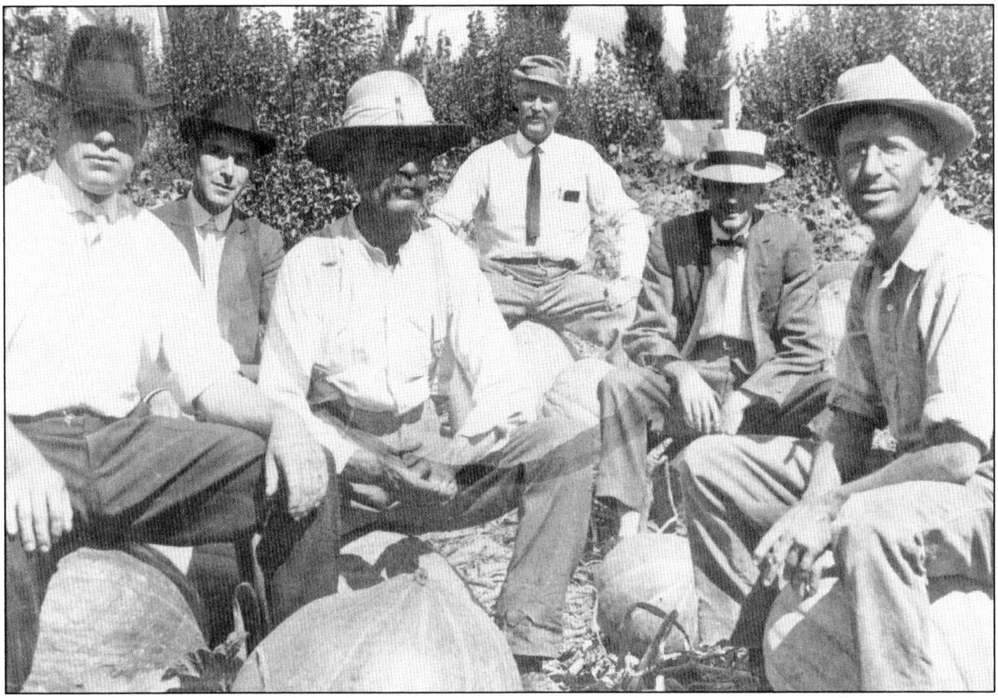

Many different crops have been grown in the valley over time. Here are some of the pumpkins grown in 1914. The Green River area has also grown beets, onions, peaches, and pears. Today Green River is famous for its melons. Seated at far left is Charles McPherson, the mayor of Green River from 1914 and 1915. Third from left is A. D. Lewis; the rest of the men are unidentified.

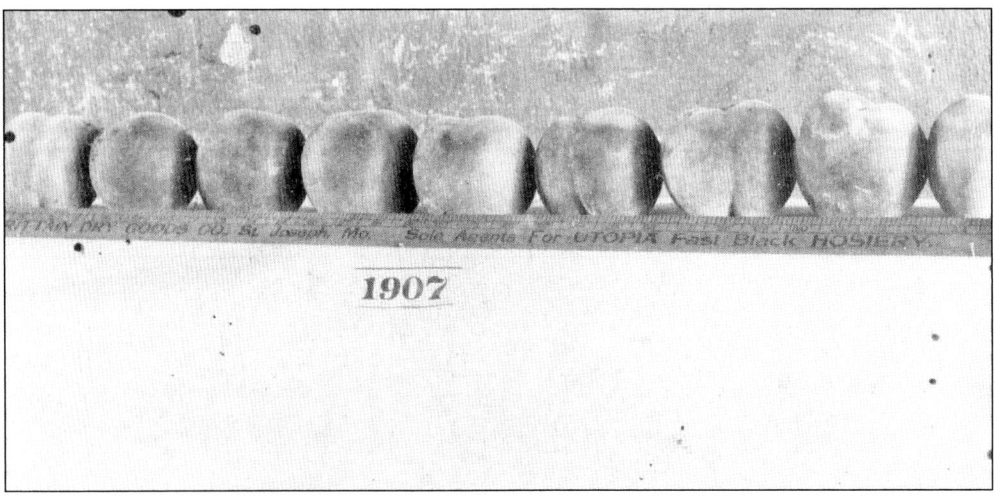

Peaches were some of the biggest crops grown in Green River before the weather destroyed the trees. These are from 1907 and are quite large. Notice the ruler placed in front of them to show the size comparison. In one newspaper article, they are compared more than favorably with the peaches grown in Colorado.

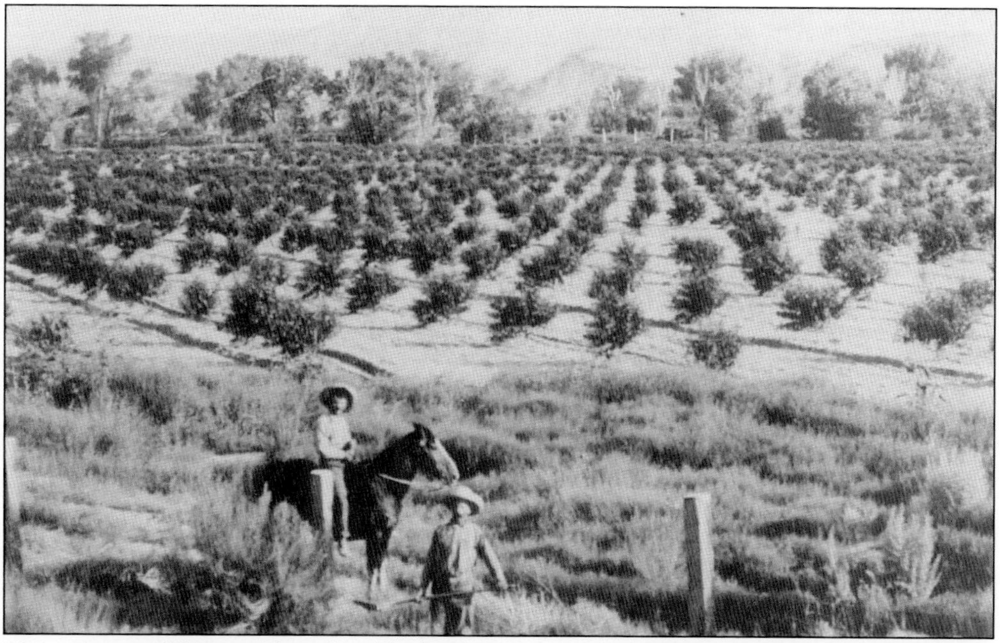

This is how an Elgin peach orchard looked before the freeze. Elgin is a small town on the east side of the Green River, almost a ghost town. That year the climate was particularly hard on the peaches, and many thousands were lost. The identities of the people in the photograph are unknown.

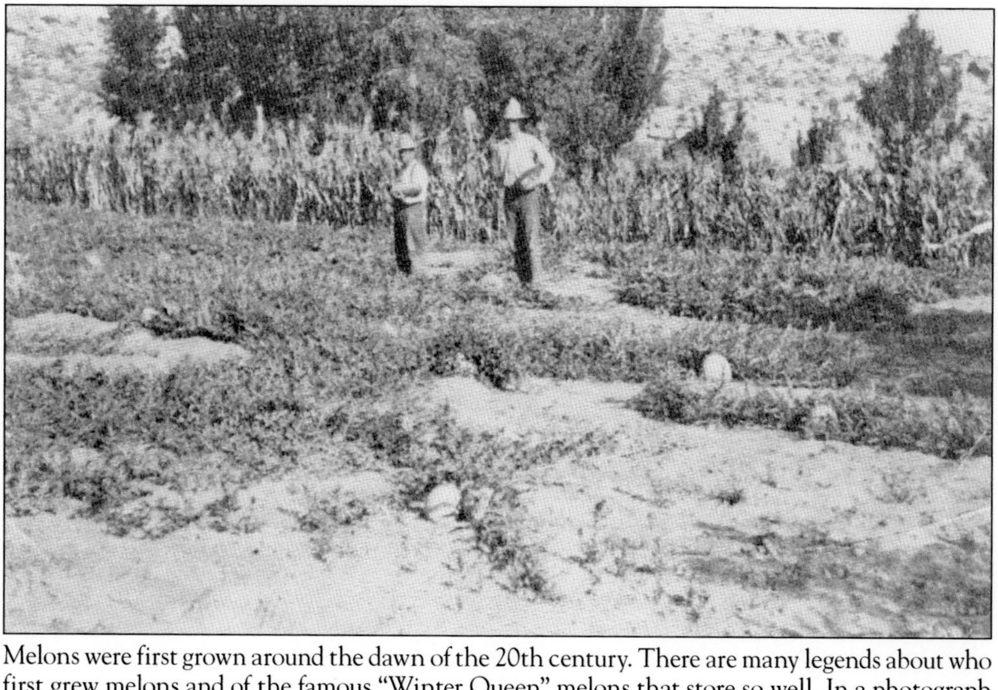

Melons were first grown around the dawn of the 20th century. There are many legends about who first grew melons and of the famous "Winter Queen" melons that store so well. In a photograph of the 1910 dedication of the Green River Bridge, the people are shown eating melons. The photograph was taken in December, which is out of season for melons.

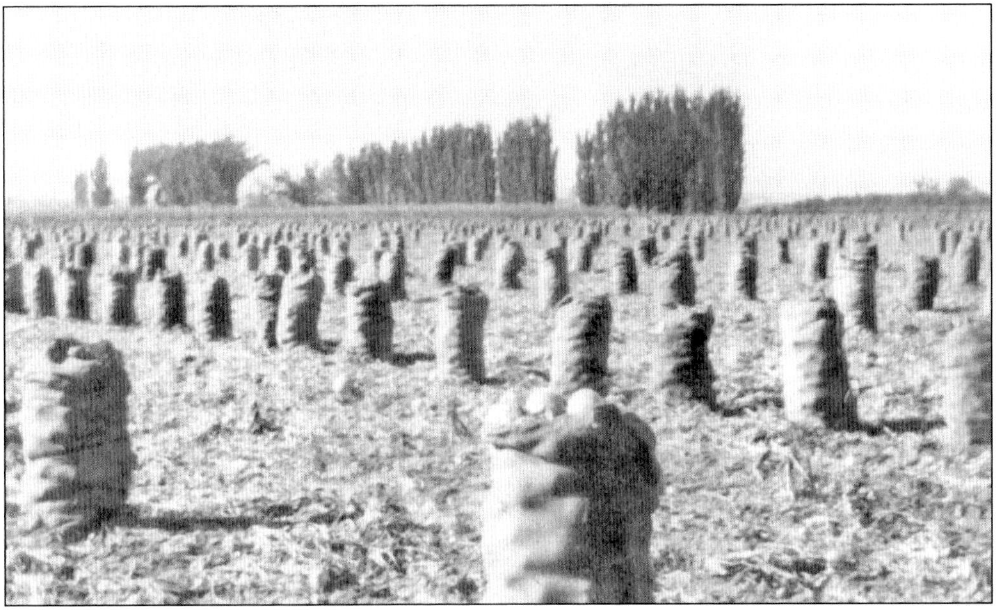

Onions were one of the crops grown in the valley. This 1927 photograph was taken of Peter H. Riley's crop of onions. The onions were harvested and placed in the bags seen here; eventually, the onions would be placed in a root cellar until they were needed.

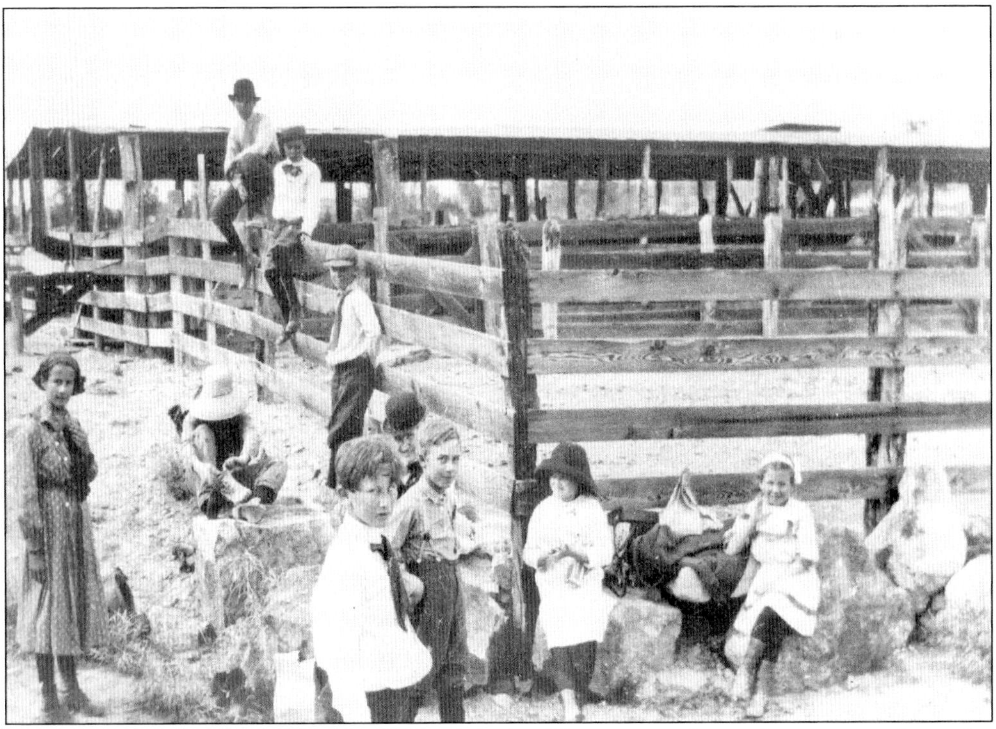

The stockyards were a fun place for children to play. This one was located approximately on the railroad duplex on Cherry Street, south of town in Green River. People who had sold their cattle and were waiting to have them shipped out of town would leave their cattle here until they went out on the railcars.

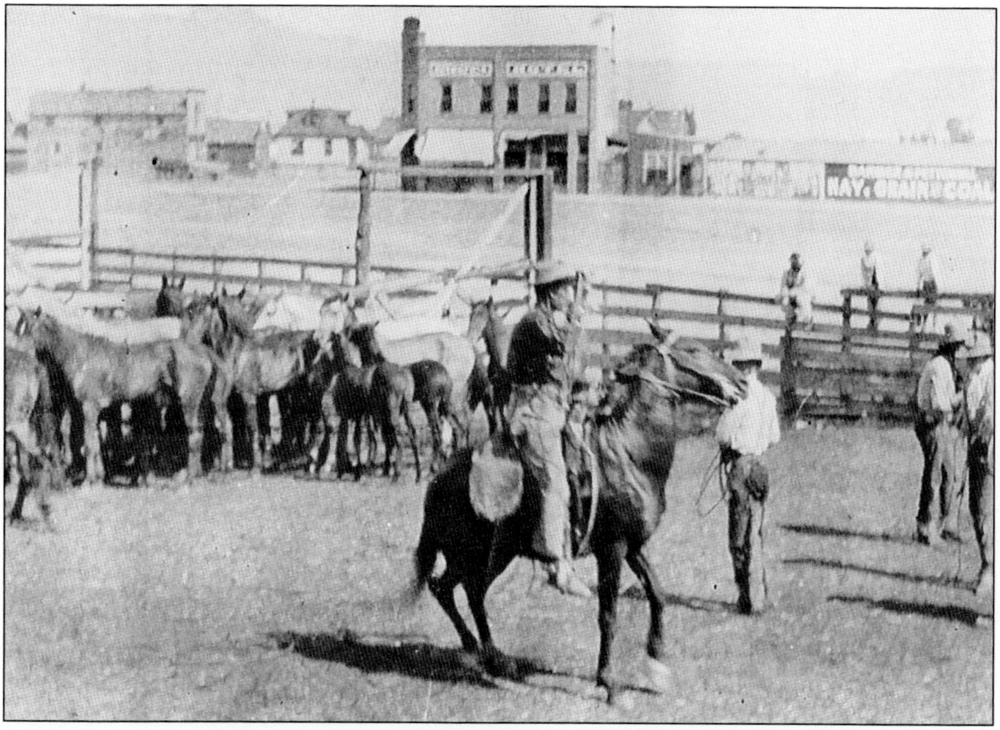

Before the automobile, horses were a necessity for everyone. The building featured in the center of the photograph is the Metropole Hotel. Allene Spadafora lives on the property today where the Metropole was located. The horses in the corral look like they are being herded to one area to make room for more.

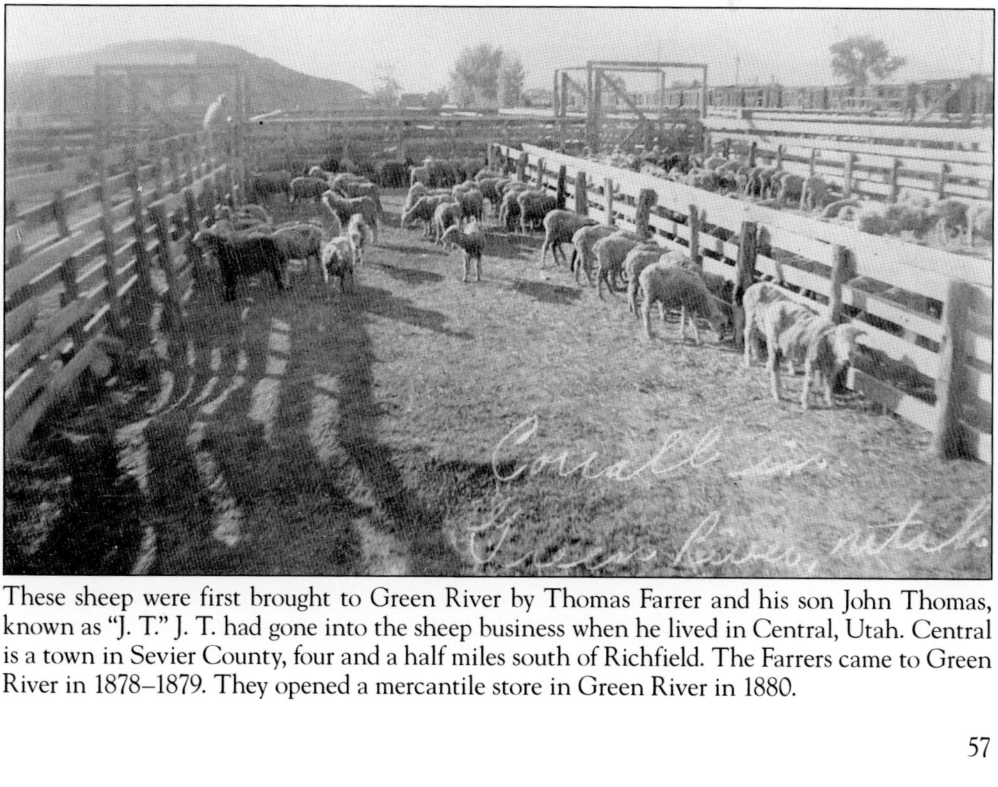

These sheep were first brought to Green River by Thomas Farrer and his son John Thomas, known as "J. T." J. T. had gone into the sheep business when he lived in Central, Utah. Central is a town in Sevier County, four and a half miles south of Richfield. The Farrers came to Green River in 1878–1879. They opened a mercantile store in Green River in 1880.

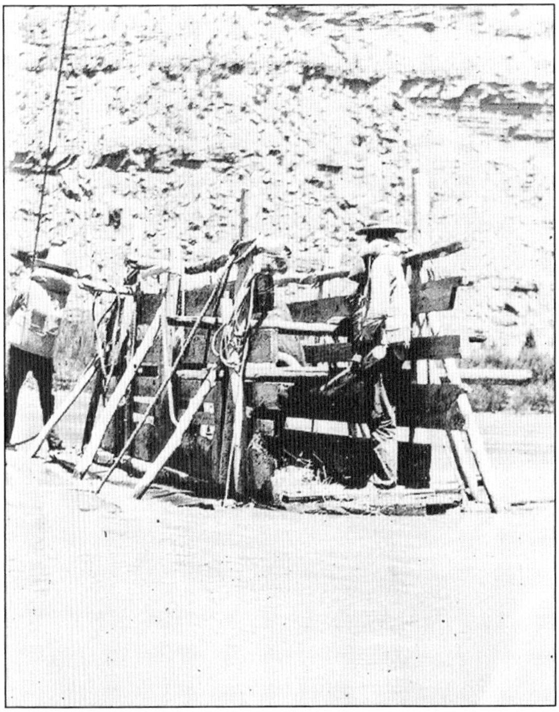

This Hereford bull is being ferried across the Green River near Florence Creek. Florence Creek heads at Florence Springs in the McPherson Range, on the East Tavaputs Plateau, 40 miles north of the town of Green River. Today the ranch is part of the Uintah-Ouray Indian Reservation. This land has a colorful history, including sheep men, cattlemen, outlaws, and Native Americans. The man is only identified as McPherson.

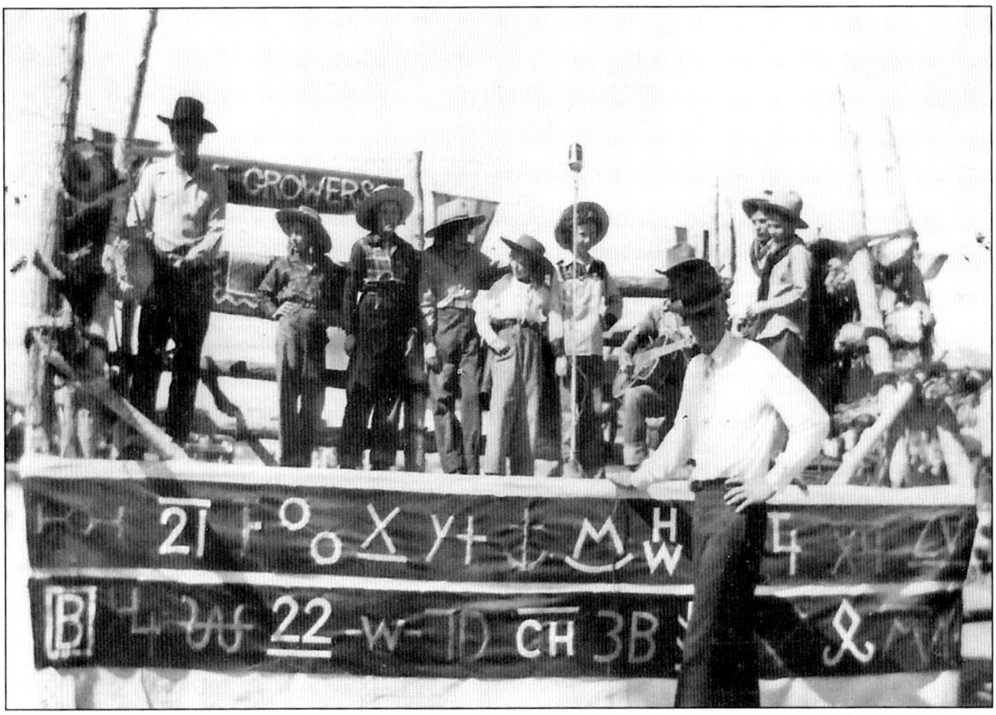

Three of the brands represented on this float belong to the Farrer family. One brand belongs to Preston Nutter, the first person to ship cattle out of Green River on the old narrow-gauge railroad. Bill Grissom, Carlos Wilcox, and Henry Wilcox all have their brand represented on this float. Andy Moore eventually bought the Grissom brand.

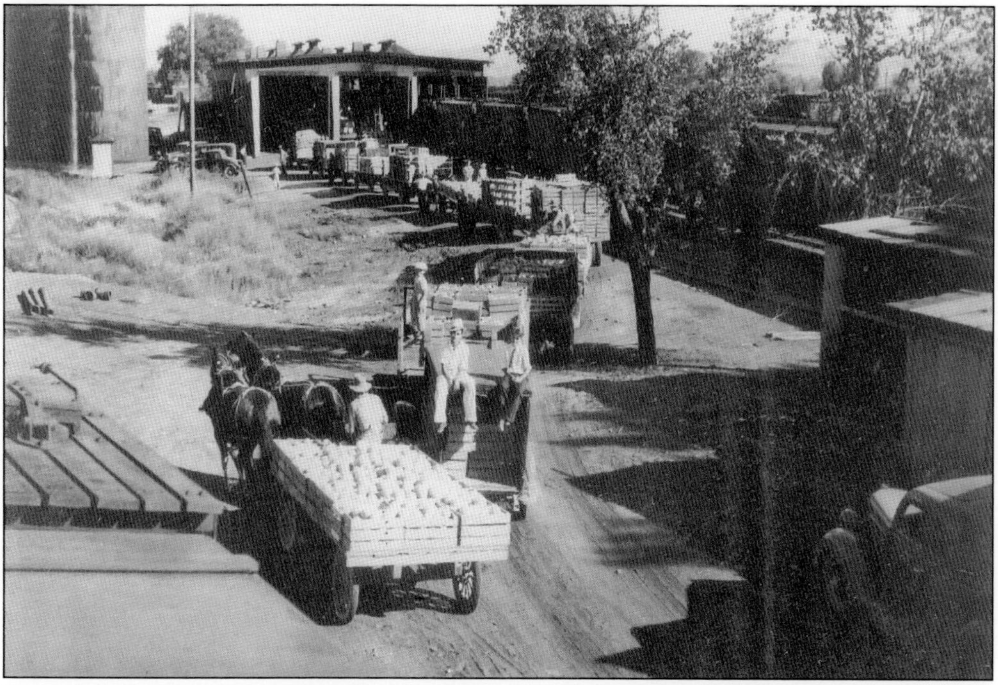

The melon packing shed at the railroad roundhouse is pictured about 1940. Malcolm Politano Jr. is in the center facing the camera on the back of the truck. Politano's first job was working at the roundhouse. It was his job to paste the labels on the melon crates.

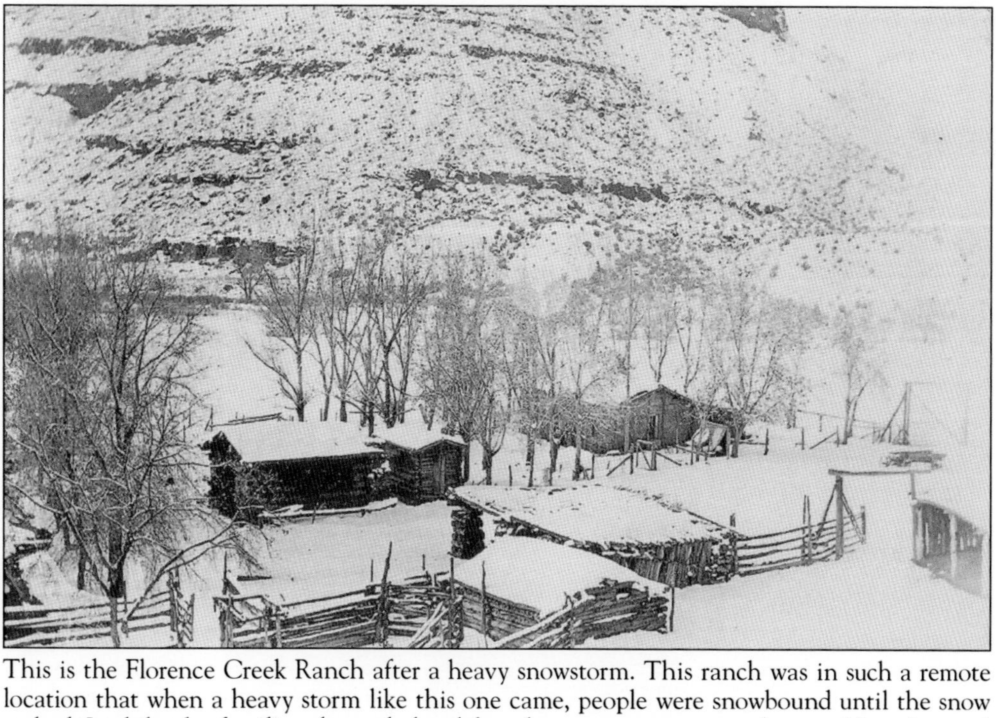

This is the Florence Creek Ranch after a heavy snowstorm. This ranch was in such a remote location that when a heavy storm like this one came, people were snowbound until the snow melted. Luckily, the families planned ahead for a heavy snowstorm, so they could get by until the snow melted.

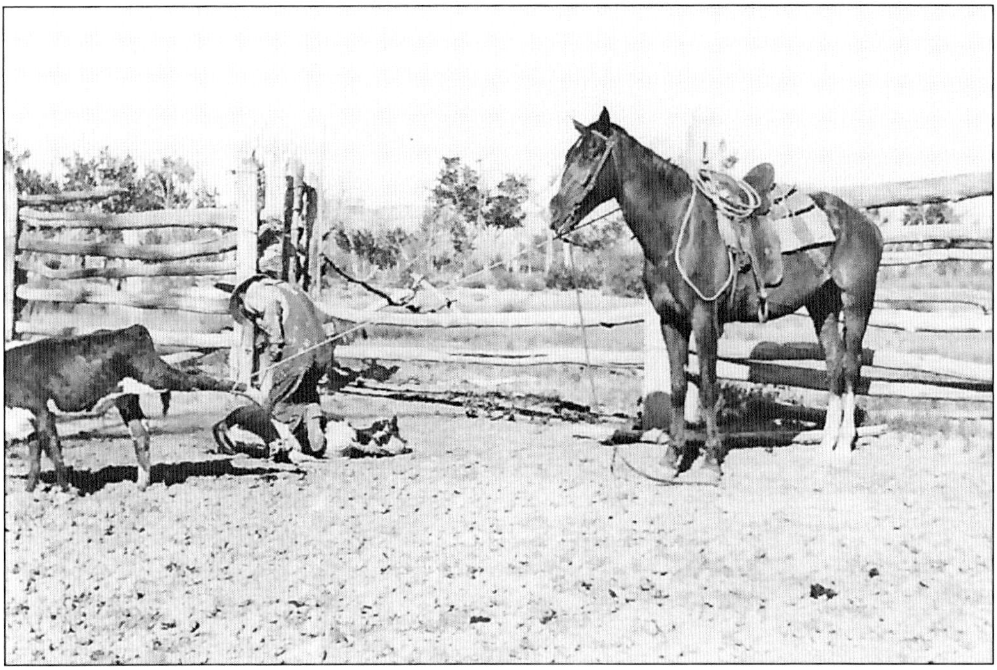

In the days prior to squeeze chutes, the only way of taking care of the cow's physical needs was to rope it and lay it down on the ground. It is straining against the rope on its leg and also the horse being used to keep the cow a little more immobile. The man in the photograph is unidentified.

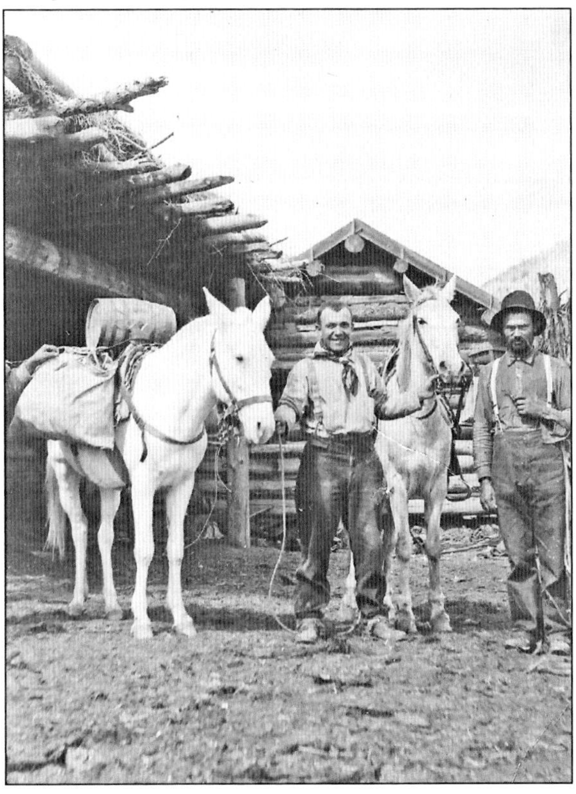

These men are prepared to camp for a day or two. The "barrel" on the back of the white horse was the predecessor to the modern-day sleeping bag. Looking at the buildings around them, it is uncertain whether these were the homes for these men or a place to camp away from home.

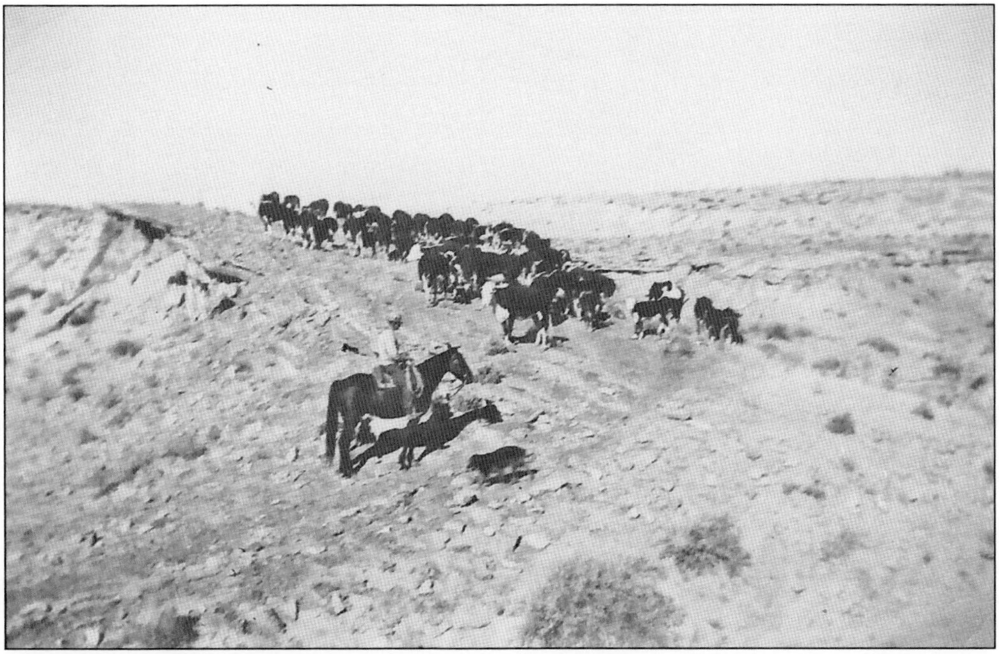

This man is trailing cattle out on the desert. Cows are stubborn animals and do not always want to go where they are being headed. Feed and water for the cattle was sparse, and the terrain was rough to walk on. Stops for watering would be planned out in advance before setting out to range the cattle or bring them back home.

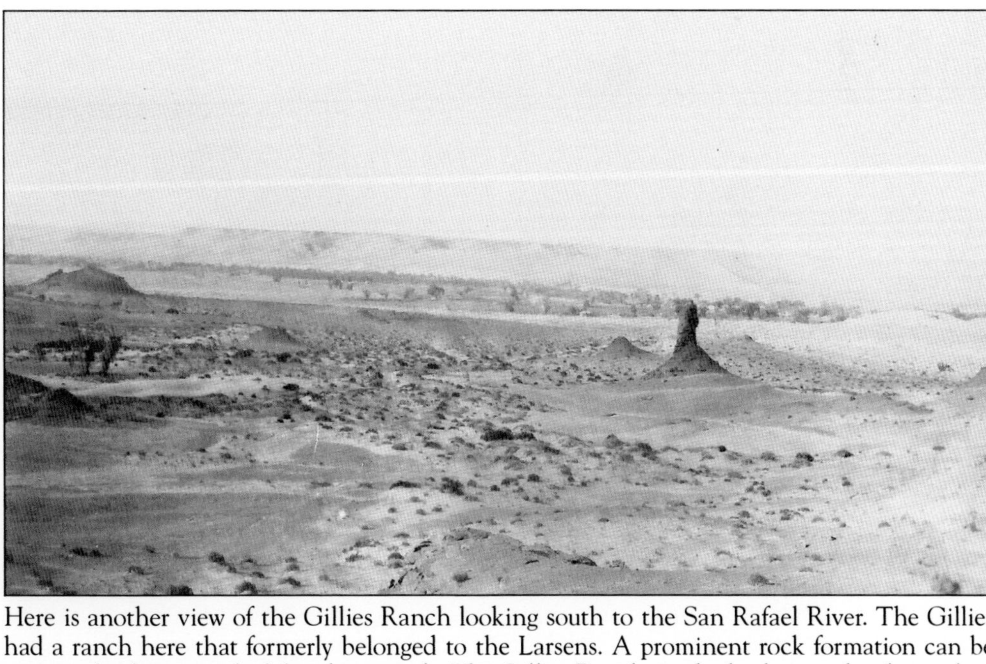

Here is another view of the Gillies Ranch looking south to the San Rafael River. The Gillies had a ranch here that formerly belonged to the Larsens. A prominent rock formation can be seen in the foreground of the photograph. The Gillies Ranch, in the background, is located on a dirt road off of Highway 24.

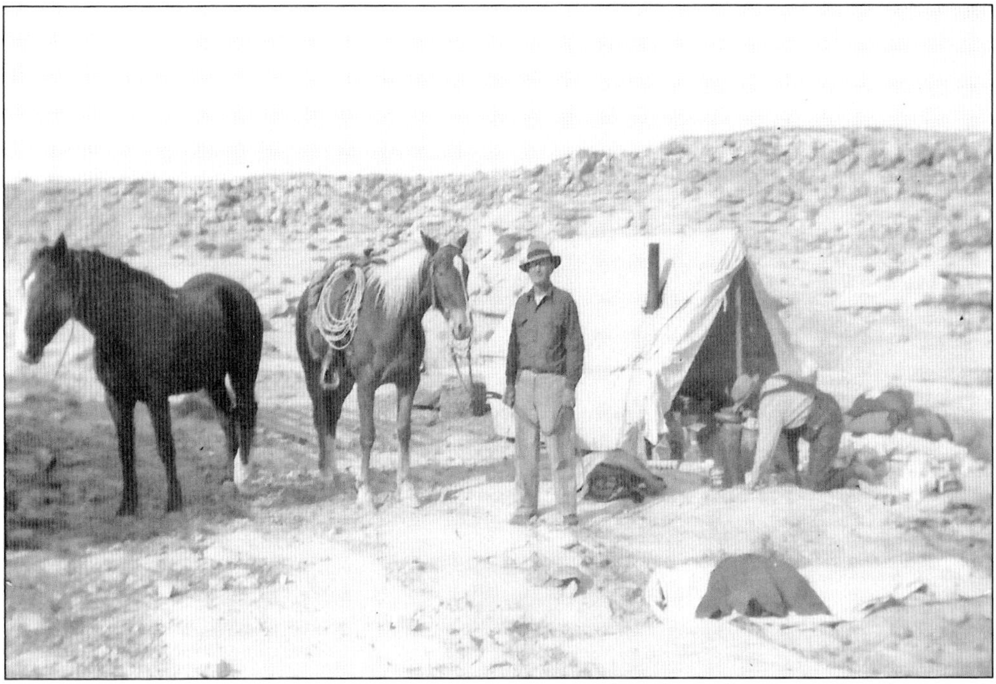

Here is the typical view of a cow camp out in the deserts of Utah. Both men in this photograph are unidentified. Part of camp was making sure the tent was tied down adequately since Green River is known to have some fierce winds during the spring months.

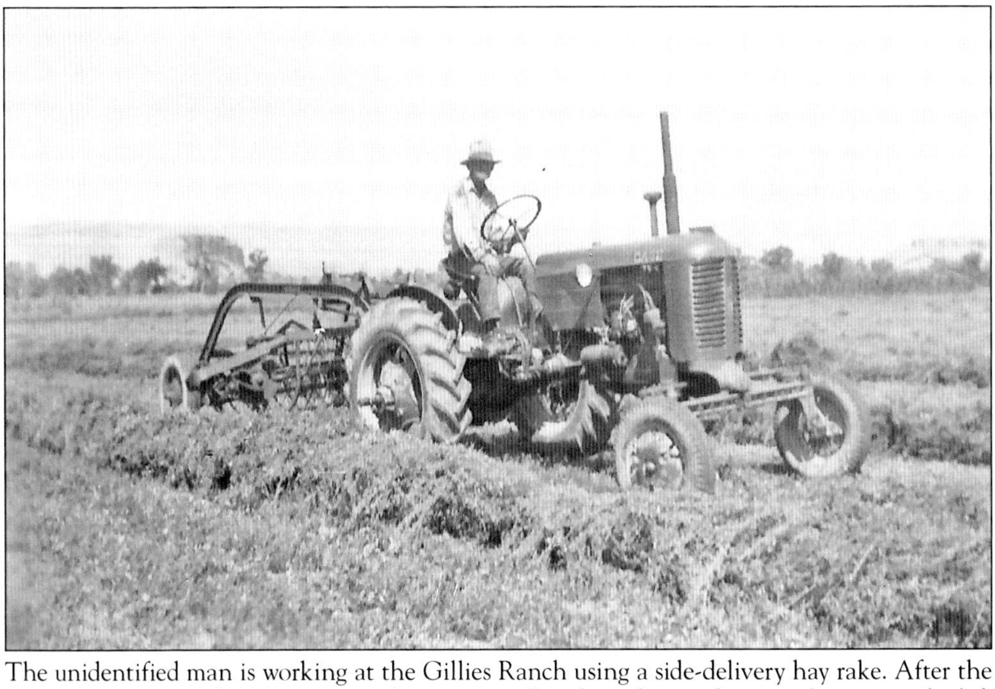

The unidentified man is working at the Gillies Ranch using a side-delivery hay rake. After the hay is mown, it is gathered into a windrow, a strip of cut hay; the windrow can be seen to the left of the side-delivery hay rake. Next the hay would be gathered into bales for sale or left as loose hay, which the farmer would use to feed his animals.

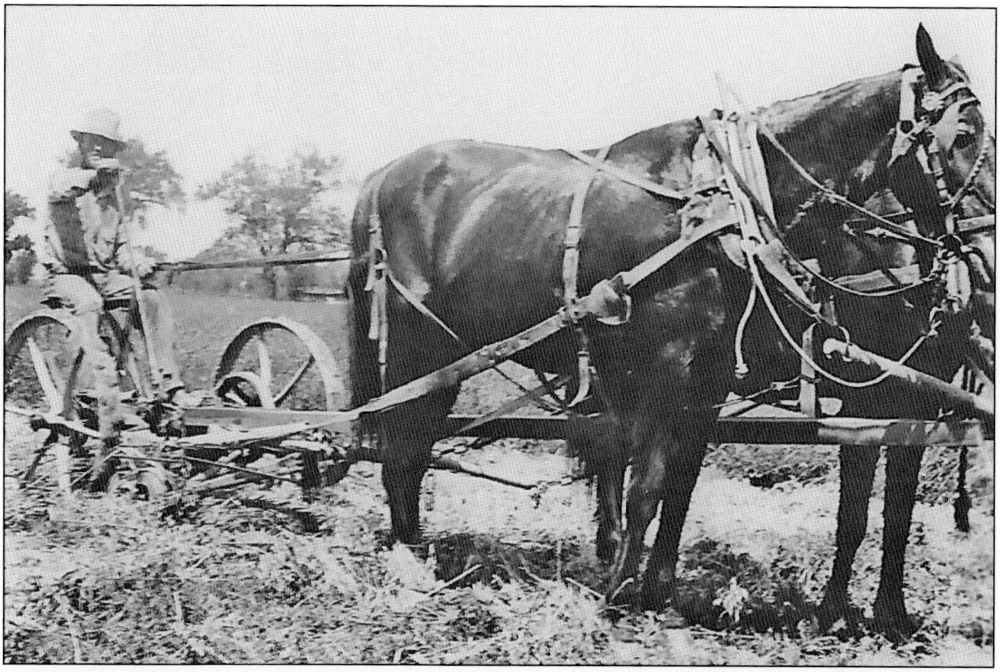

This unidentified man is using a hay mower while working at the Gillies Ranch. The mower cuts the hay, allowing the side-delivery hay rake to gather it together. At this time, a hay mower could probably cut 10 acres of hay a day. The lever is used to raise the cutting bar above the ground to change locations in the field he is cutting, so he won't re-cut his crop.

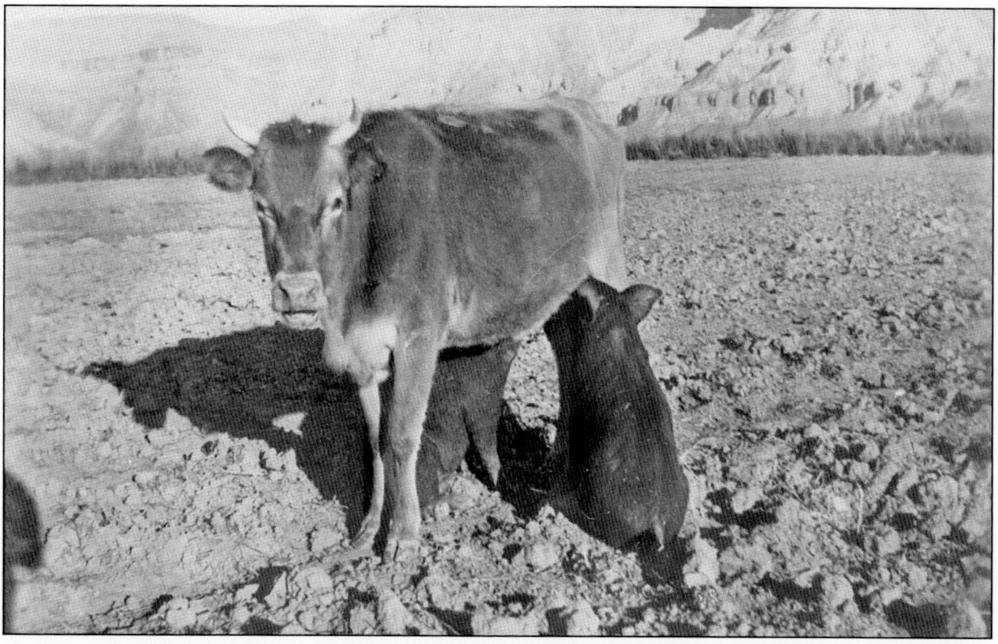

Utah is a dry desert state, so residents get liquid refreshment from whomever and wherever they can. These young pigs can see no other source of hydration nearby, so they go to the only source of milk they can see. The cow must be used to this happening since she does not seem to mind the pigs getting a drink.

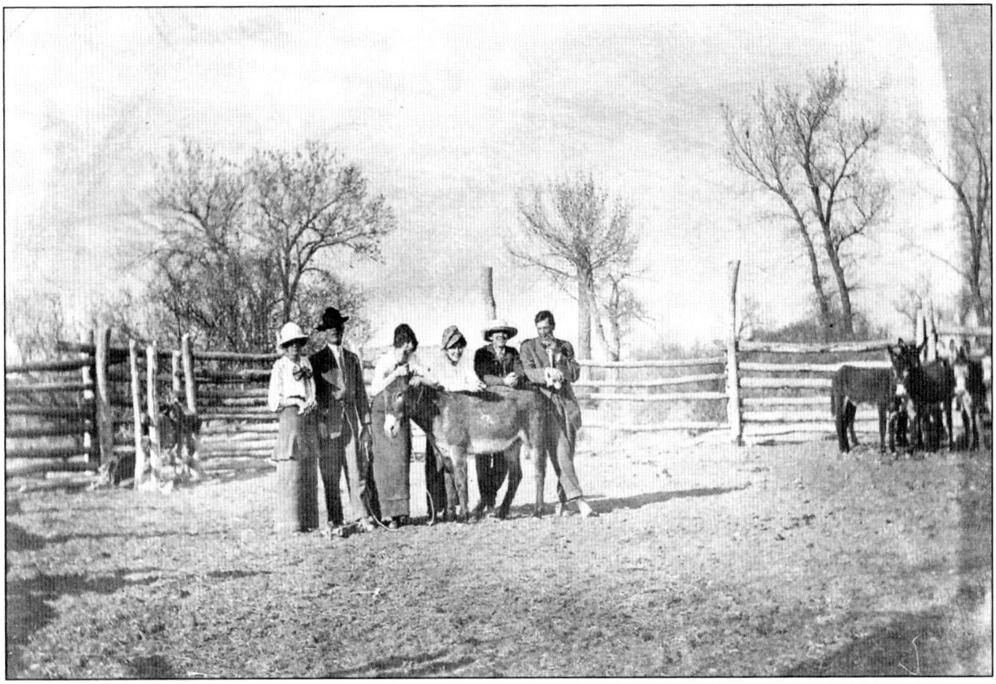

None of the people are identified in this photograph. What is identifiable is the wild burro being held by all the folks. These wild burros were left over from the days of the Spanish explorers. At one time, they were so prevalent around Green River that many were either killed or adopted.

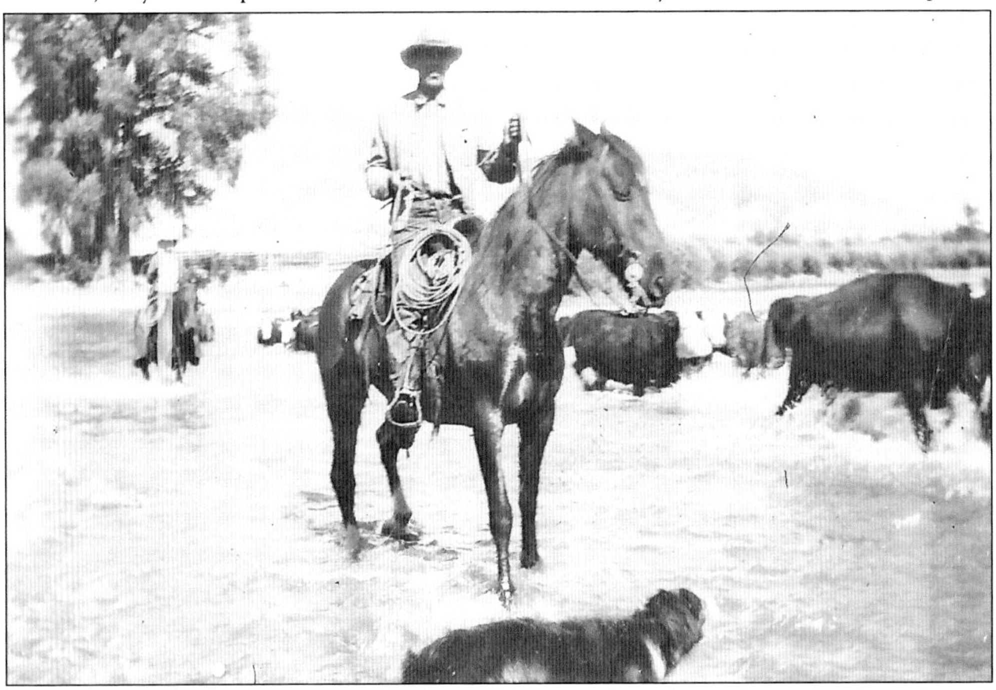

Herding cattle can be a full day's work depending upon where the cattle need to be at the end of the day. It is especially difficult to get them to move on when they have the San Rafael River to play in. The men in the photograph are unidentified.

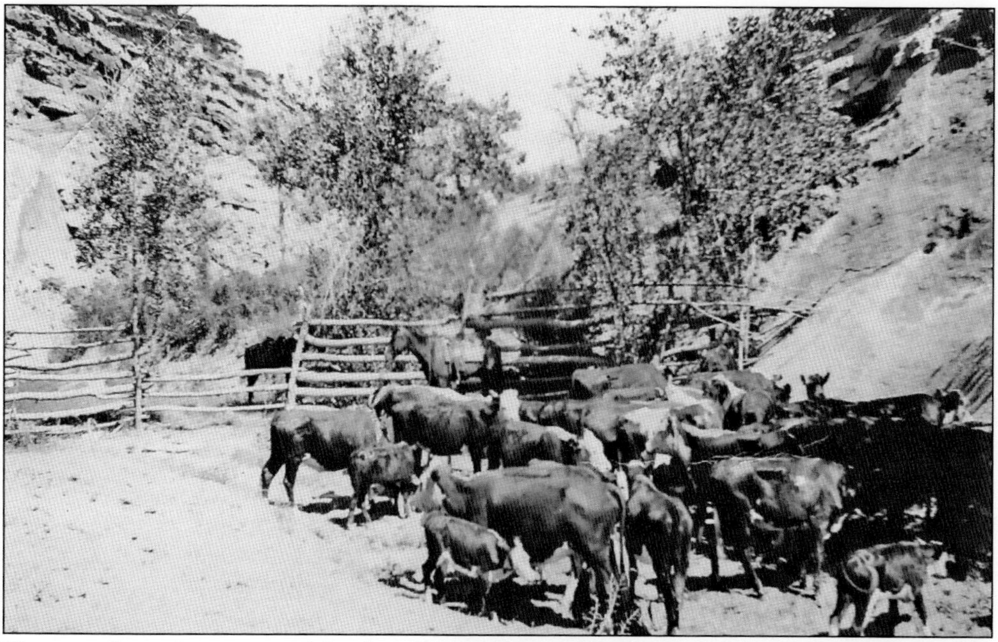

These cattle are being ranged for the summer. To range cattle means that while the weather is good, the cattle are left on the rancher's property for the summer months to find their own food. They are always collected before winter sets in. Look at the fence the cows are surrounded by; it is handmade by the trees, which were numerous enough to be cut down and make the fence.

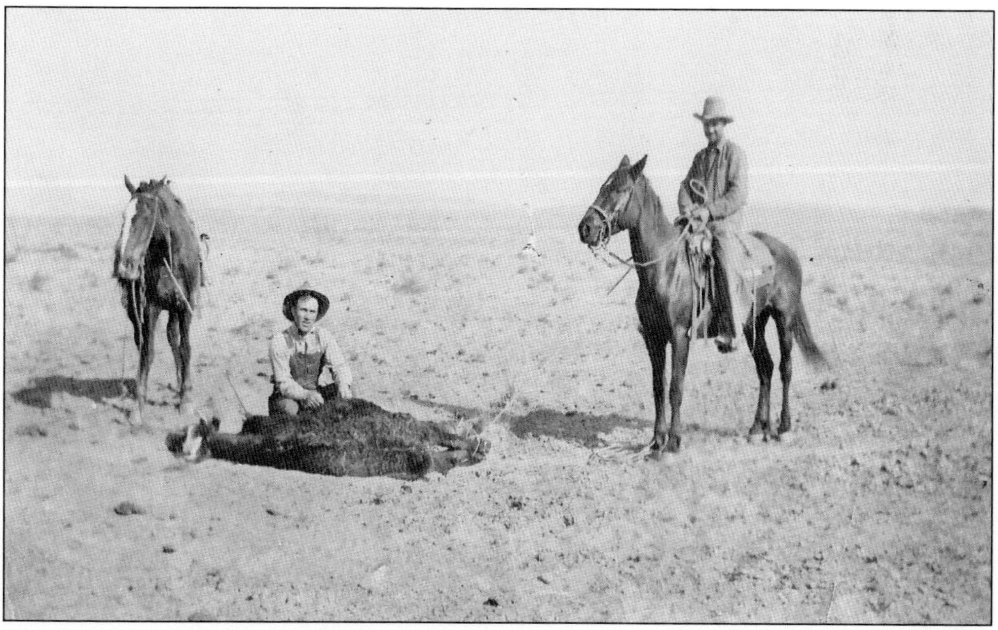

Branding out on the desert in the days before squeeze chutes meant ranchers had to rope the cow and tether it to the strongest thing in the area to prevent movement; in this case, it is to the two horses. None of the men in this photograph are identified.

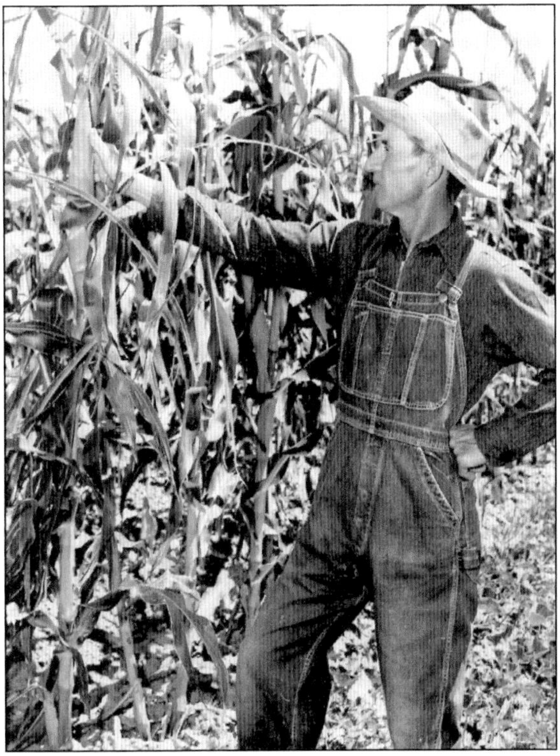

Roland Pierce Thompson checks on his corn crop. Careful watch must be kept to ensure that the red spider and other insects do not destroy the crop and that sufficient water is maintained for good growth. Green River is a great place for growing corn. Corn loves heat; the hotter it is the better. And Green River can easily reach up into the 100-degree ranks several days in a row in the summer.

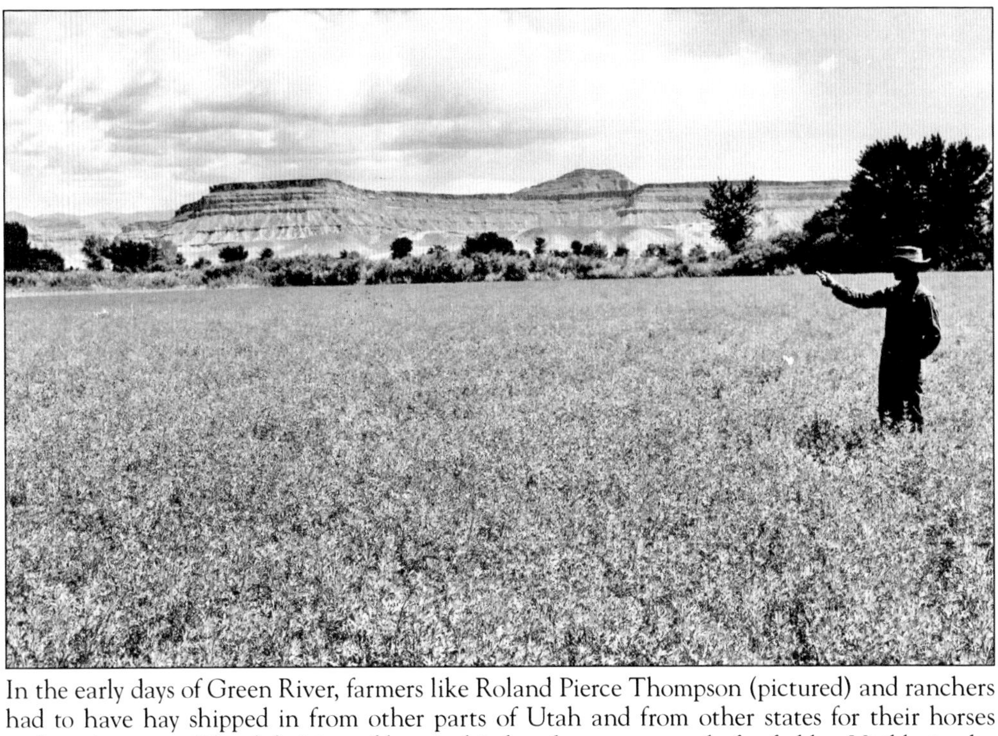

In the early days of Green River, farmers like Roland Pierce Thompson (pictured) and ranchers had to have hay shipped in from other parts of Utah and from other states for their horses and cattle to eat. The definition of hay is dried and cut grass made for fodder. Visible in the background are the Bookcliff Mountains.

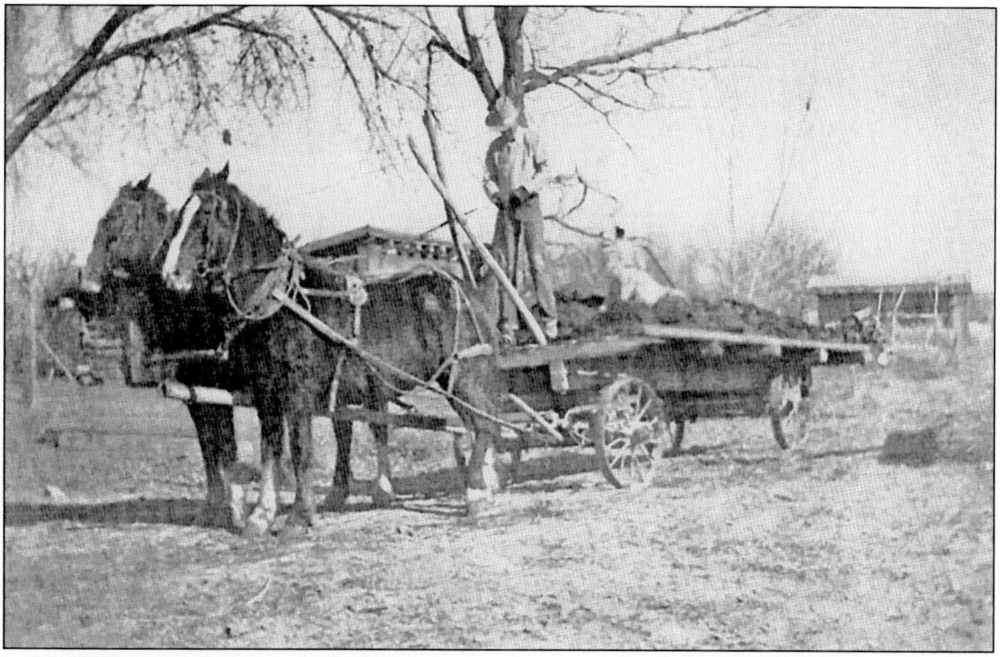

Lorin Wilson stands on the bed of a wagon on the west side of the Green River. He has a dog and a load of manure in the wagon. The manure was probably spread on his fields. Notice the metal tires on the wagon.

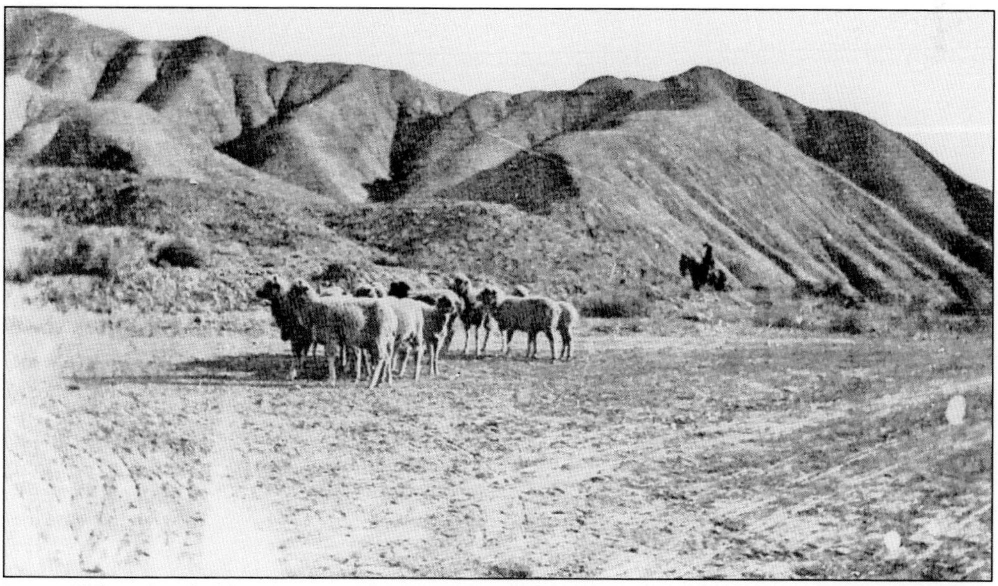

Lorin Wilson herded his sheep on the east side of the Green River. Not many of the sheep seem alarmed at the camera, since most of them have their backs to it. The man in the photograph is Dan Thompson from Elgin, Utah. Food for the sheep looks like a scarce commodity.

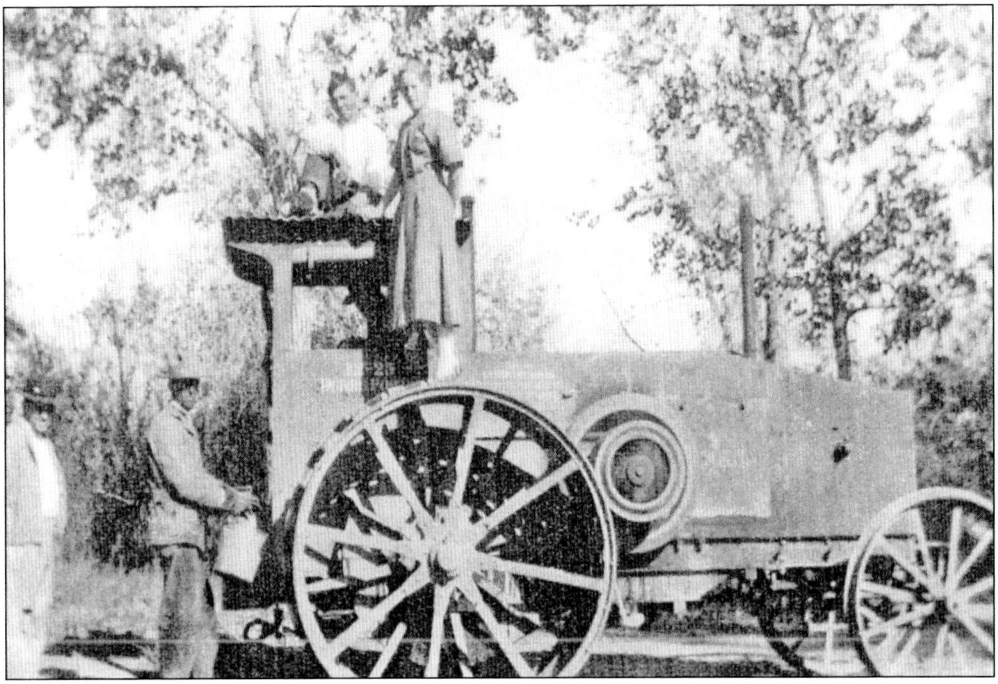

Here is the first tractor in Green River. It looks like an early steam engine. The couple standing on top of the tractor is unidentified, but they are likely the proud owners of the tractor. The man standing to the left of the tractor is also unidentified.

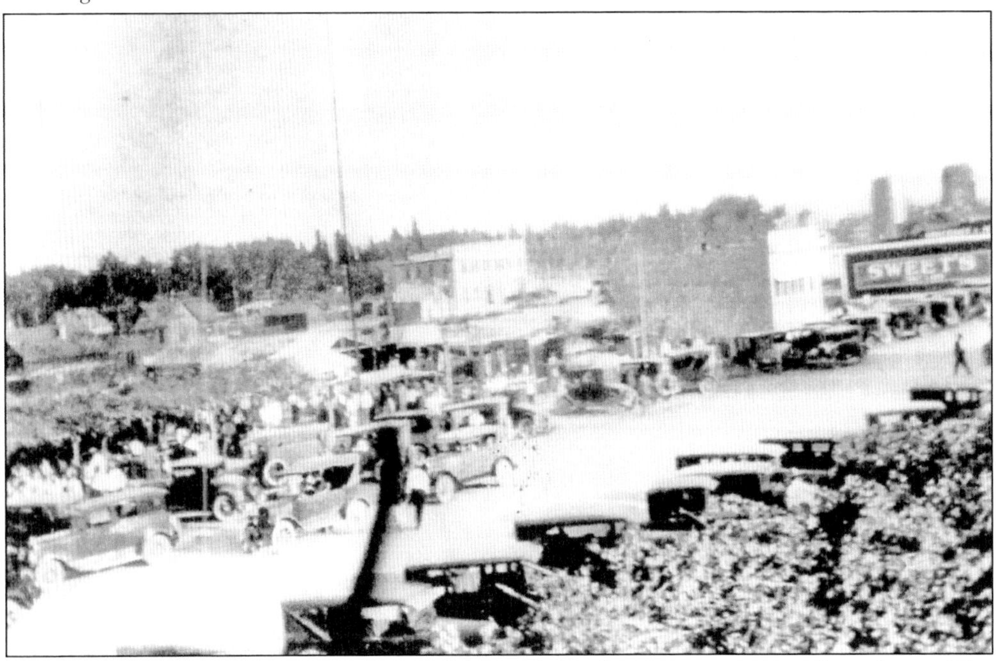

This photograph was taken from the top of the Beebe and Sons' store on Broadway Street. The many cars are gathered because a Fruit Festival was going on in Green River that day. The Fruit Festival was the early forerunner of the Green River Melon Days, which celebrated its 100th birthday in 2006. At this festival, other fruits were featured besides melons, including peaches.

Four

TRAINS, PLANES, AND WAGONS

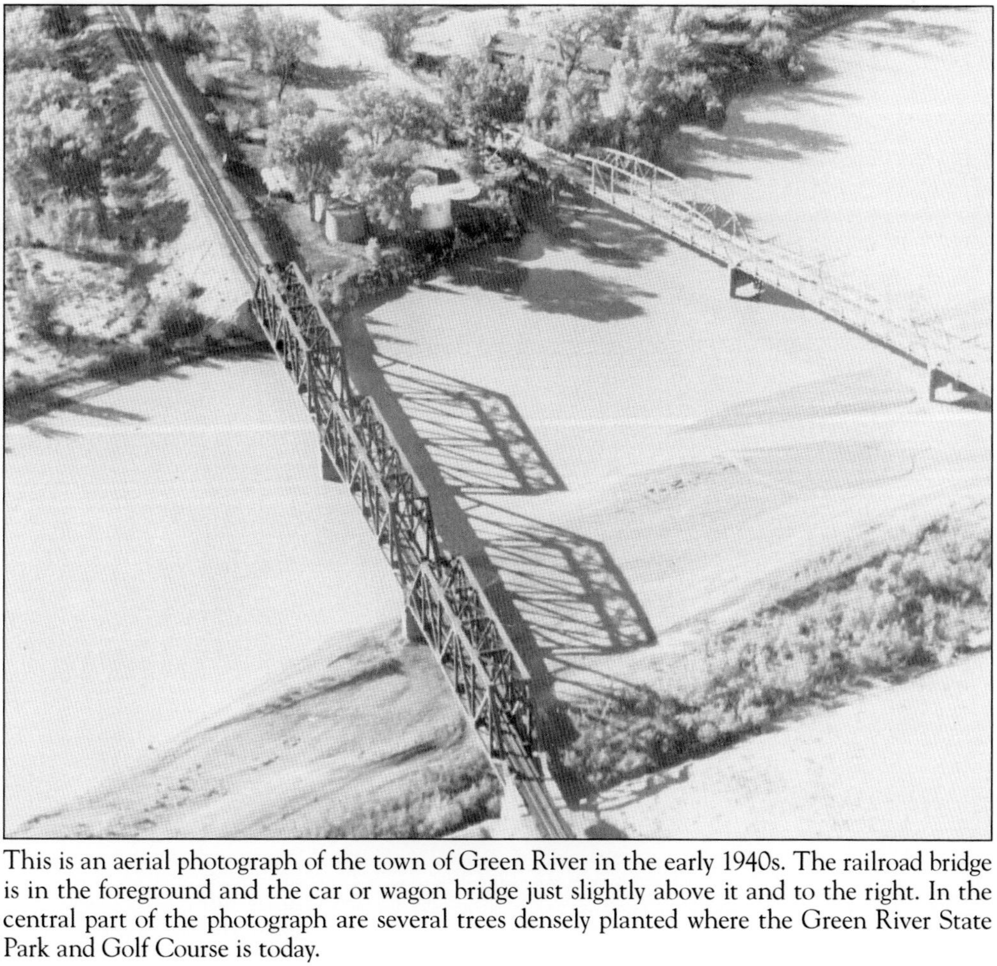

This is an aerial photograph of the town of Green River in the early 1940s. The railroad bridge is in the foreground and the car or wagon bridge just slightly above it and to the right. In the central part of the photograph are several trees densely planted where the Green River State Park and Golf Course is today.

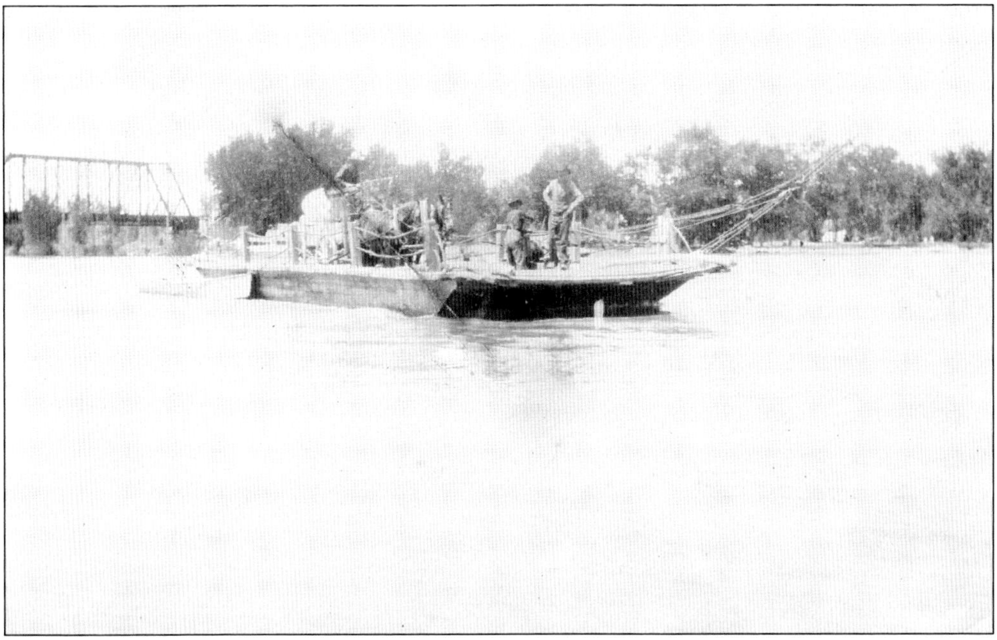

Matt Hartman was a family friend of John Thomas "J. T." Farrer. When Farrer bought the ferry in Green River, Hartman was often the operator. Hartman came from Switzerland and met J. T. in Utah. They were both in their early 20s and were friends their entire lives. The ferryboat would haul livestock and people across the Green River. Photographed above on the boat are, from left to right, Herman Dahling (on the wagon), Ira Sutton (seated), and Matt Hartman (standing). The photograph was taken in 1886. All the men were early residents of Green River.

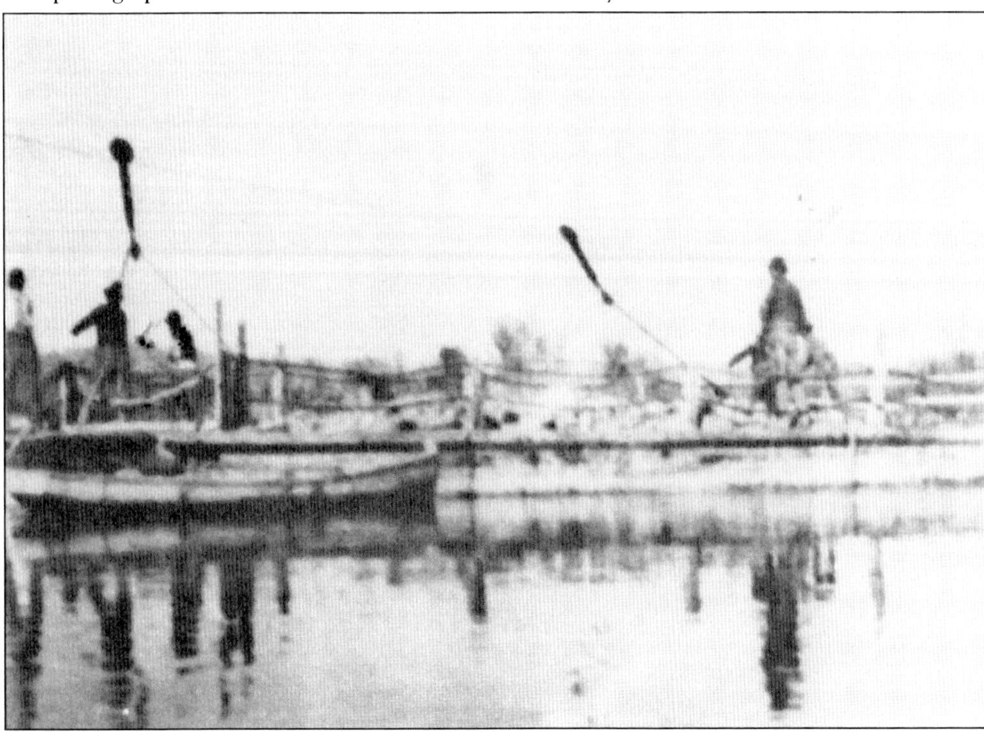

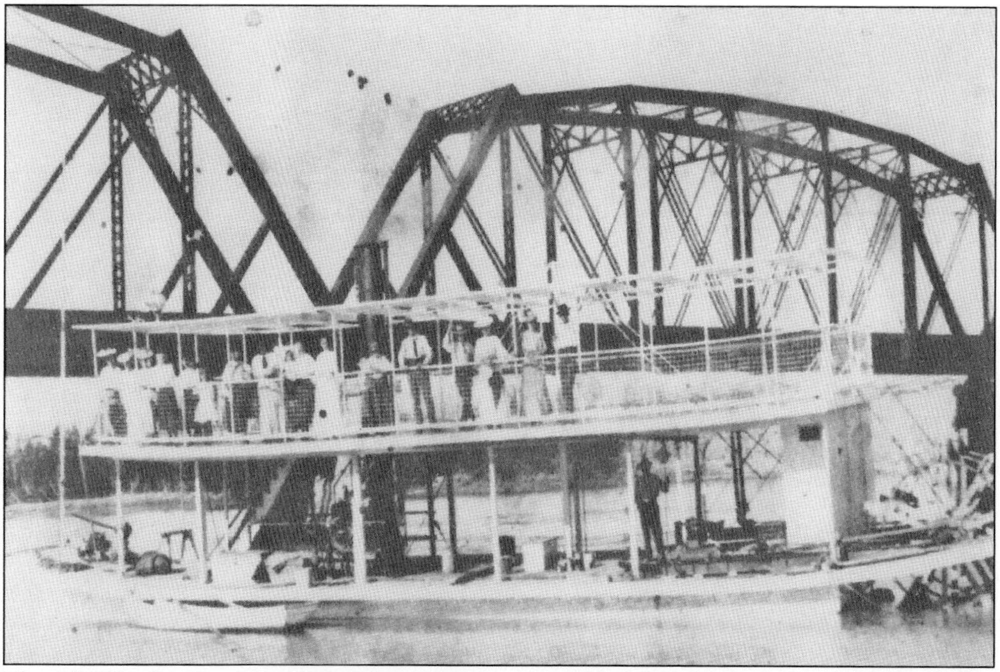

The *Cliff Dweller* was commissioned in 1905. It was believed that the steamboat would take the place of wagons in delivering mail and merchandise from Thompson Springs, Utah, to San Juan and Grand County. Residents of Green River were said to be elated at the prospect of water travel because it would make Green River a supply stop for many river excursions.

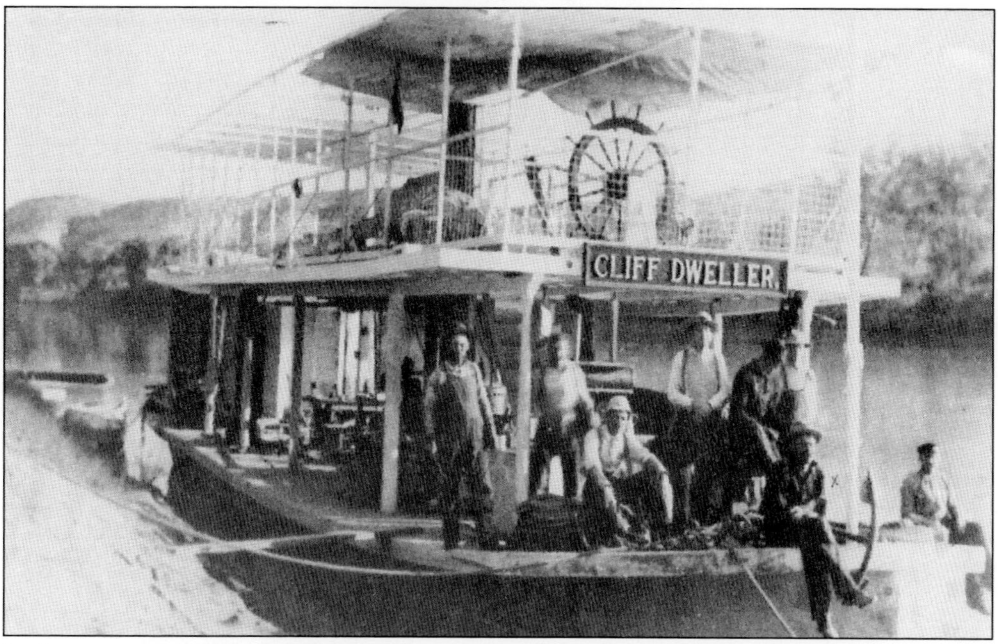

In the summer of 1906, the *Cliff Dweller* was to make a test run down to the confluence of the Green and Colorado Rivers. It was hoped that soon after this pleasure boat business began, Green River would become nearly as large as Salt Lake City. Capt. Henry T. Yokey is at the lower far right of the photograph.

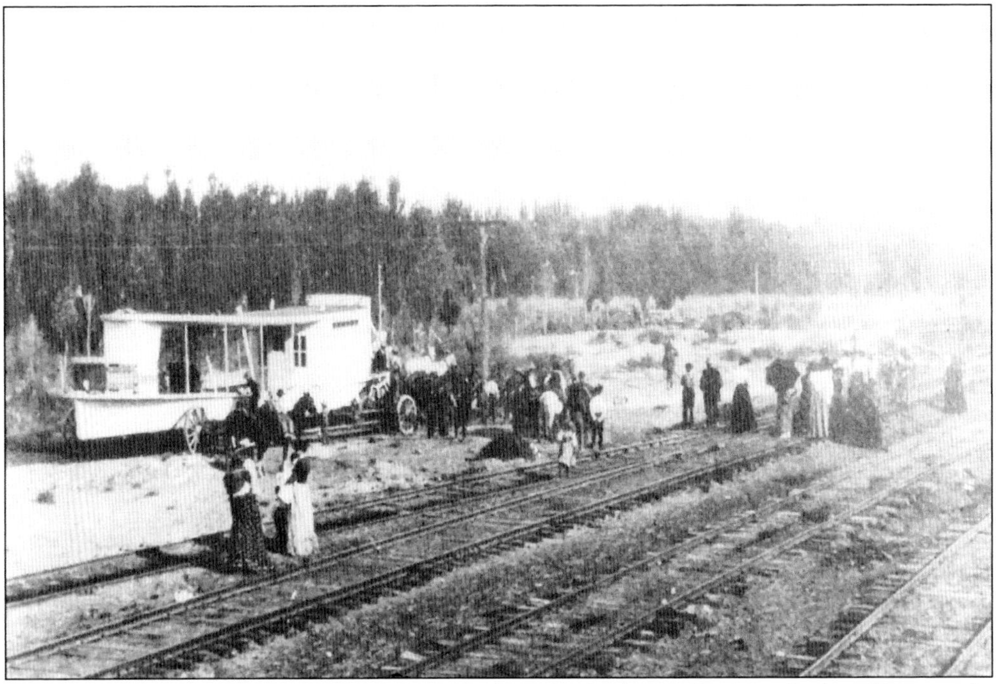

The *Undine* was on its way to the river to be launched. The *Undine* weighed 19,500 pounds. It took eight teams of horses to push the boat into the river until it was floating on its own. Residents of Green River and Elgin were both on hand to see the launching. The *Undine* made several trips on the Green and the Colorado Rivers. Life did not end well for the *Undine*. It crashed on the rocks 10 miles above Moab when the crew tried to pull the boat up over the cataracts using a towline. The hull of the *Undine* lodged on the rocks five miles above Moab and remained there for nearly 20 years before high water finally carried it away.

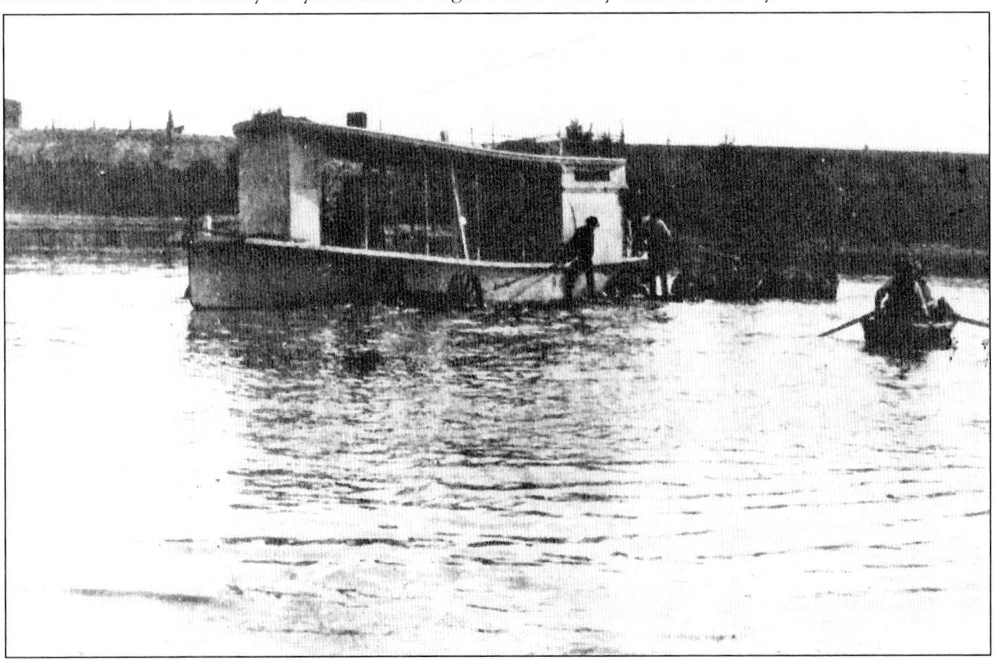

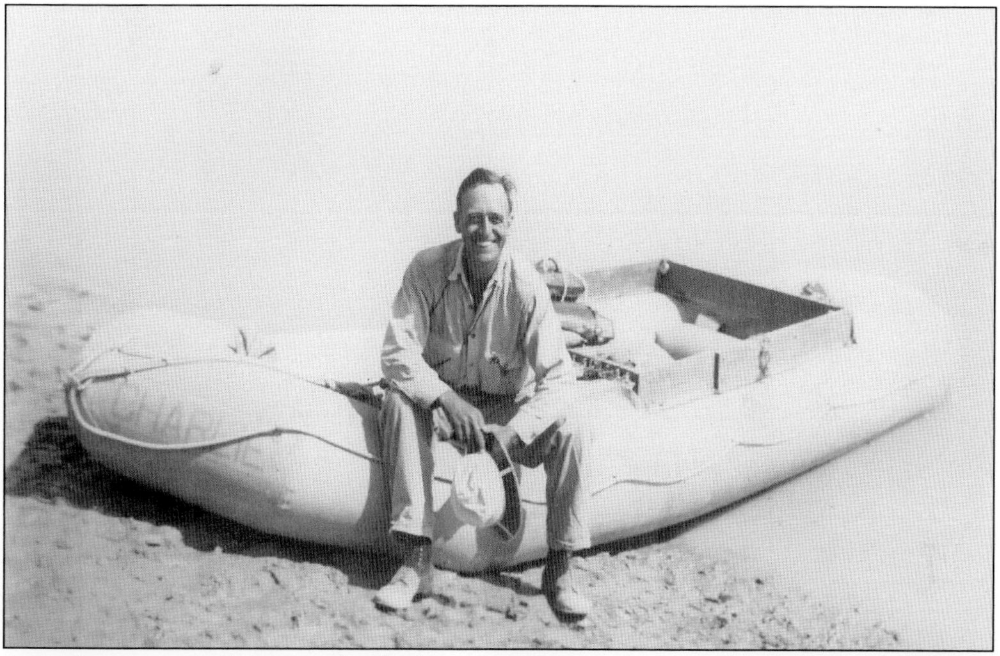

Amos Burg is pictured above with *Charlie*, the first inflatable raft to float the canyons of the Green and Colorado Rivers. The boat was named after Charles Walker, a friend of Amos Burg, who helped him contact B. F. Goodrich, who built the raft out of vulcanized rubber material. Walker also put $200 toward the trip down the Green and Colorado Rivers.

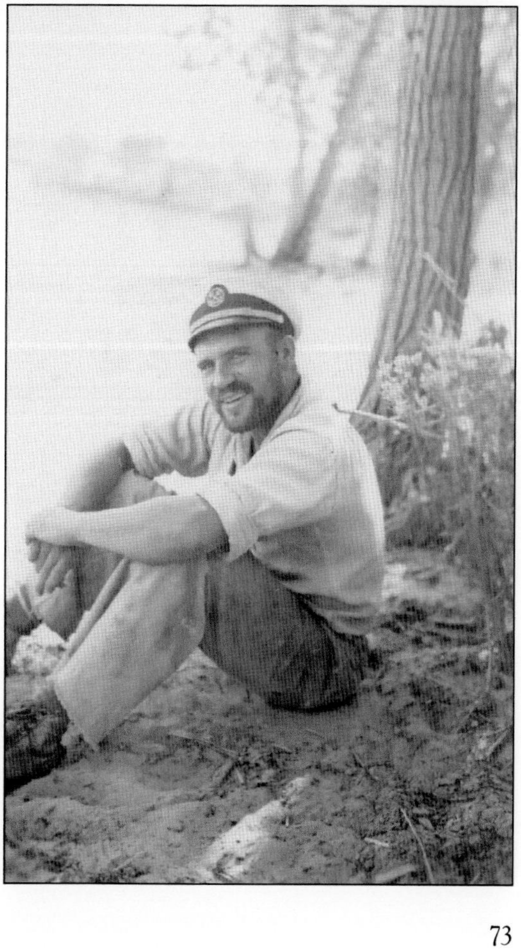

Buzz Holmstrom, like Amos Burg, was a resident of Oregon and, also like Amos Burg, had a fascination with the river. While the two were planning the trip down the Green and Colorado River, it was decided that Holmstrom would row the boat and Burg would photograph the expedition. On August 26, 1938, they launched from Green River.

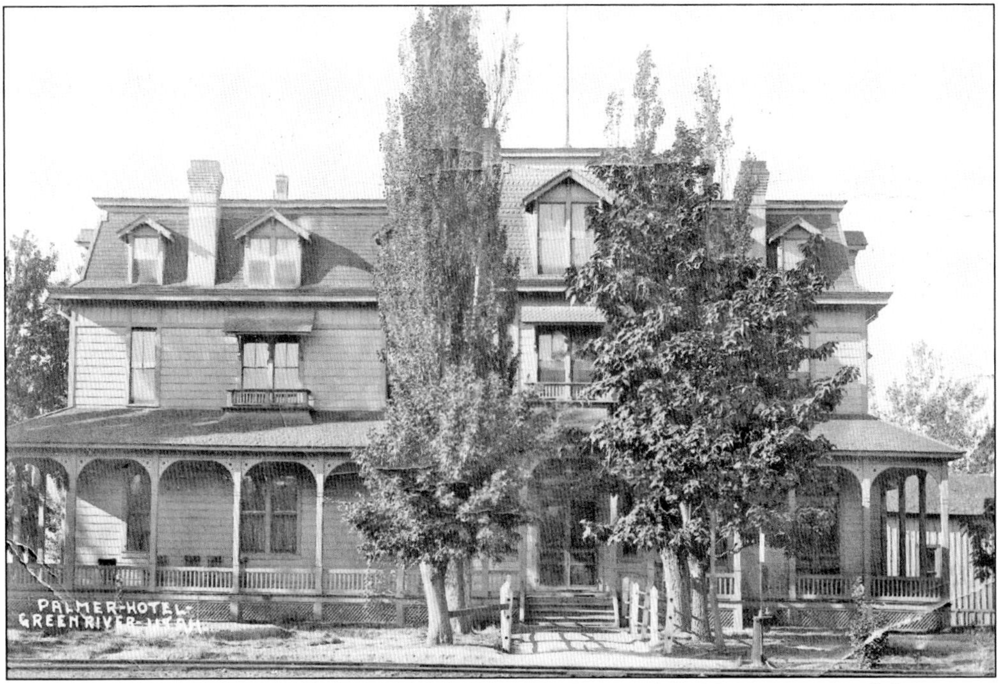

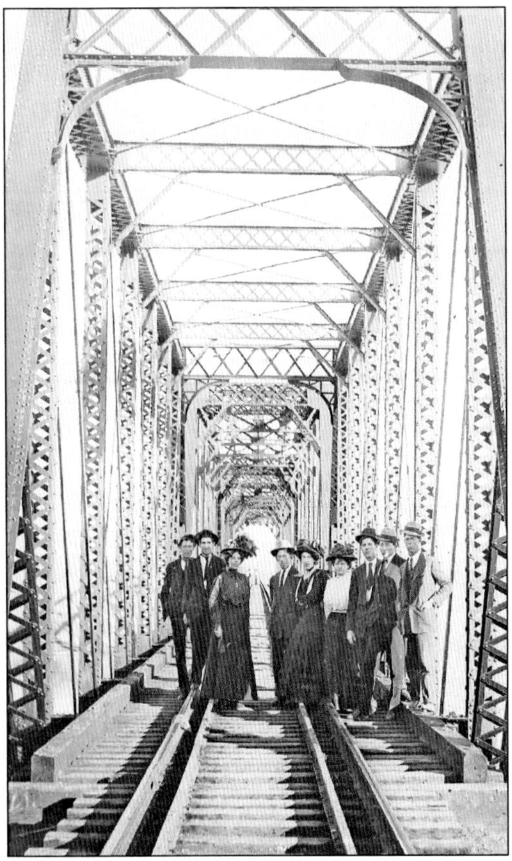

Early in railroad history, trains did not have cars for eating and sleeping. To make these accommodations for passengers on the train, houses were built along the railroad track. The Palmer House was named for Gen. William Jackson Palmer, the man who founded the Denver and Rio Grande Railroad. The Palmer House in Green River was built in 1883 and was demolished in 1924.

Una Gillies is the youngest girl in this photograph on the Green River Bridge. One of her brothers is third from the right. Susanna Gillies is also in the photograph. The rest are unidentified. They are celebrating the opening of the standard-gauge rails of the railroad bridge.

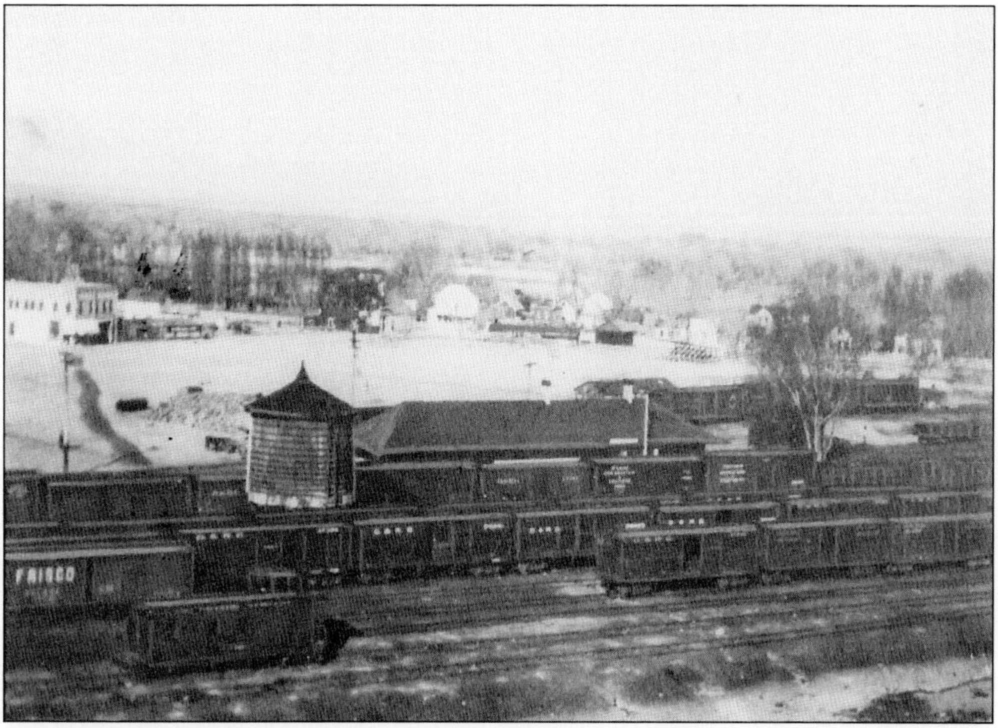

The Green River and the rail yards are seen in 1912; the roundhouse and water tower are in the foreground, with the Metropole in the left background. None of the buildings listed in this photograph are still standing. Some of the homes seen in this photograph are also gone. In the early 1980s, Green River's population began to decrease.

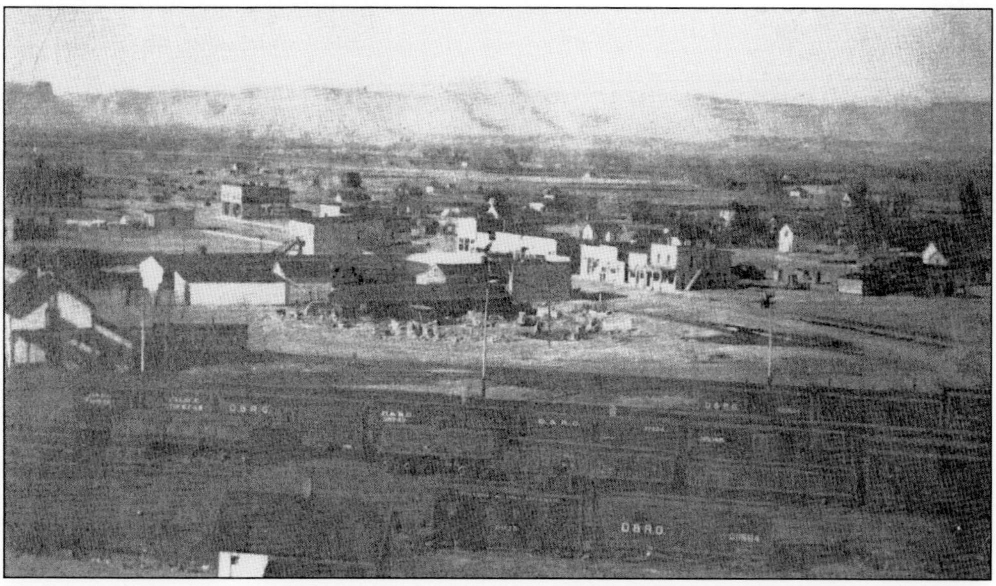

To the west (above) is another view of the rail yards and Green River. Some of the buildings are still standing; the Midland Hotel has recently been refurbished and is now used as a residence, but the owners have kept the Midland Hotel sign on the building. What was the Politanos' store is now the community center. A few other changes have also been made.

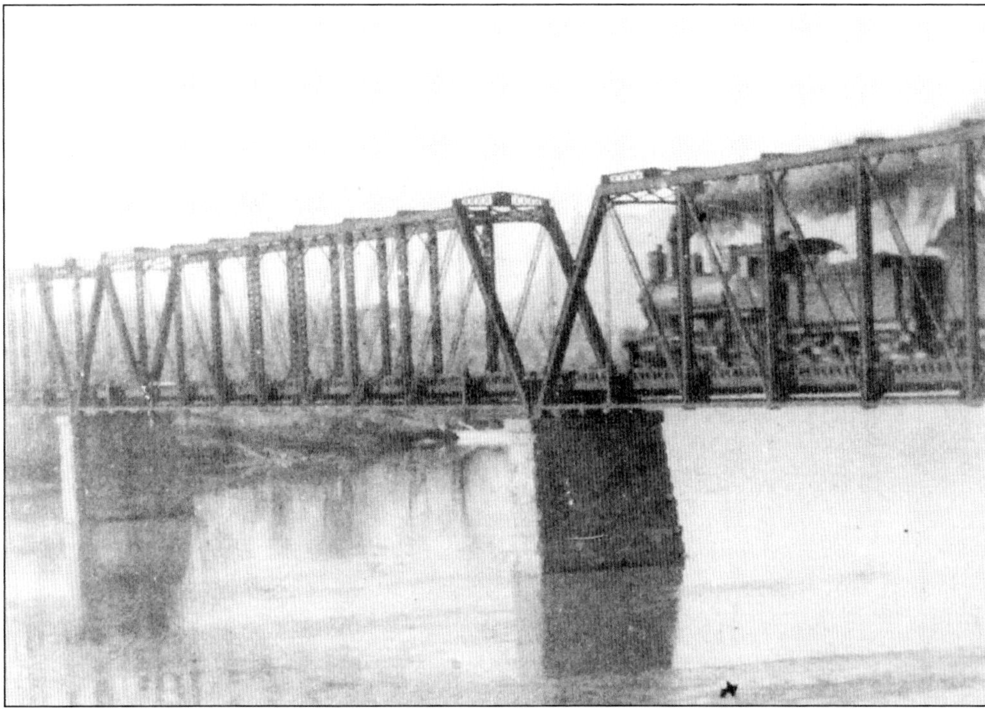

The railroad bridge in these photographs is from two different eras. In the photograph above, it can be seen that the railroad bridge is made up of wooden trestles. Repairs were made on several occasions, but finally, it was updated to the concrete and steel trestles seen in the photograph below. Though it is not known exactly when the bottom photograph was taken, it was after 1931 because that is the year the wooden trestles were replaced. The railroad bridge obviously had lots of use. In both photographs, trains pass over the bridge.

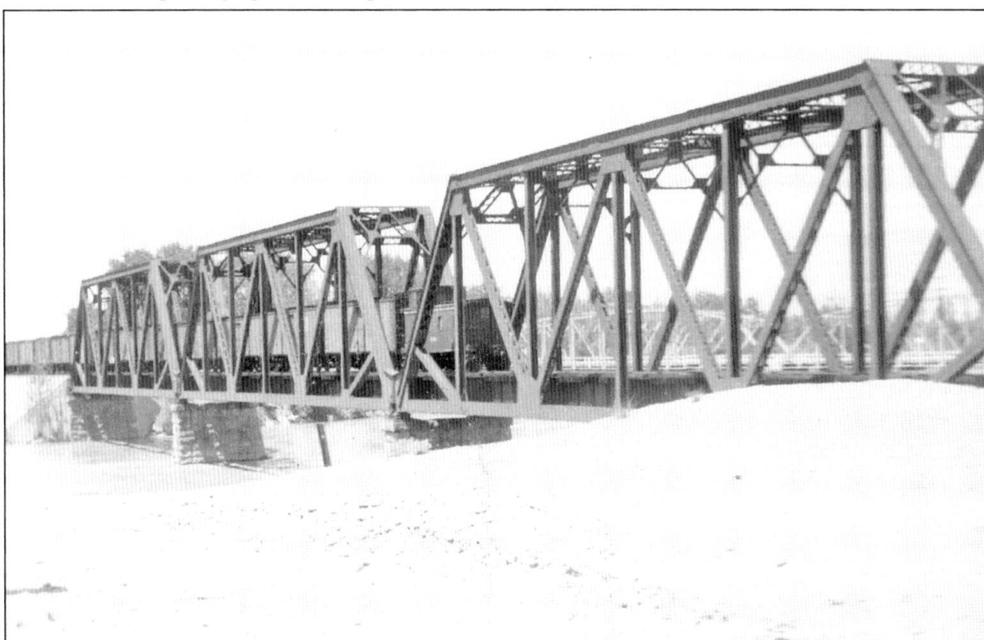

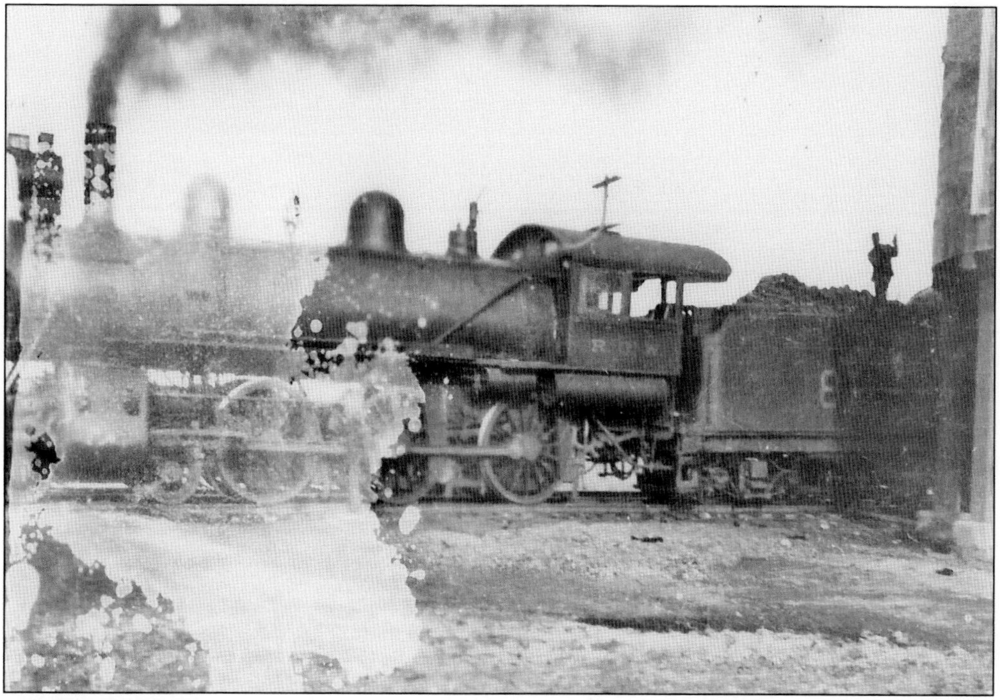

The Denver and Rio Grande Railroad has had a long history in Green River. Unfortunately, the car in the photograph below had an unexpected meeting with a train. It is not known whether the people surrounding the train were survivors of the collision or passengers on the train; they all seem well dressed, as if they were going to attend a party. The photograph above is an older one of a train passing through Green River. The first passenger train ran through Green River on April 23, 1883, with Jim Beal as the engineer.

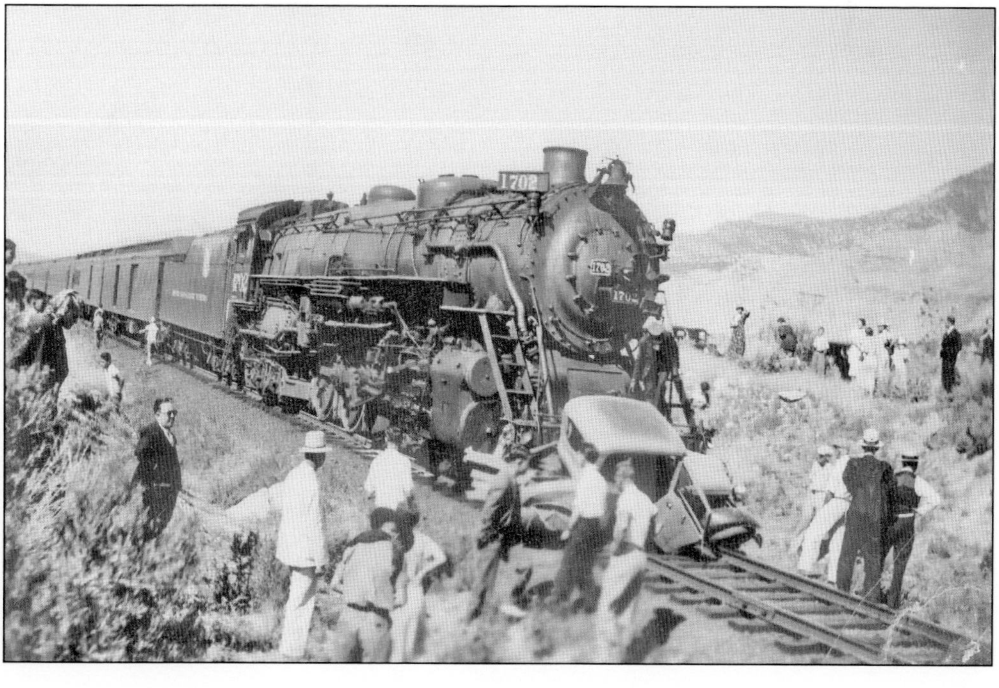

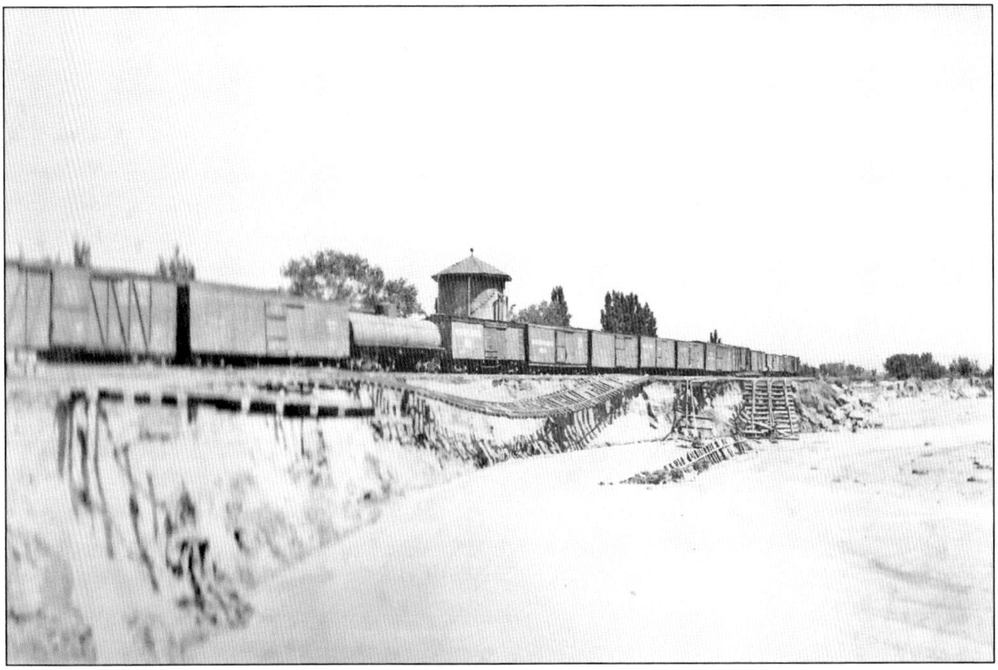

The Saleratus Wash is south of Green River. These photographs came to the Green River Archives courtesy of Annette Barnes, whose father-in-law, Ralf R. Woolley, took them in the 1920s on an expedition as he was passing through the area. They show how much damage a flood caused. The railroad ties are visible, strewn around the ground where the force of the water moved them. In the far left is the water tower.Below, all the water that had not receded yet can be seen. In the background on the far right is the Palmer House.

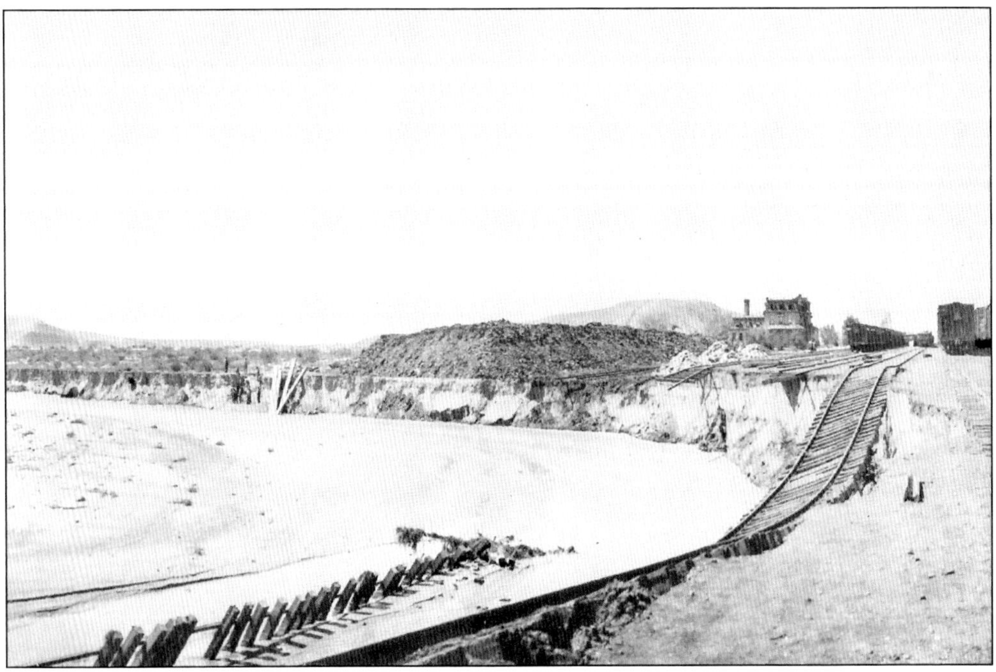

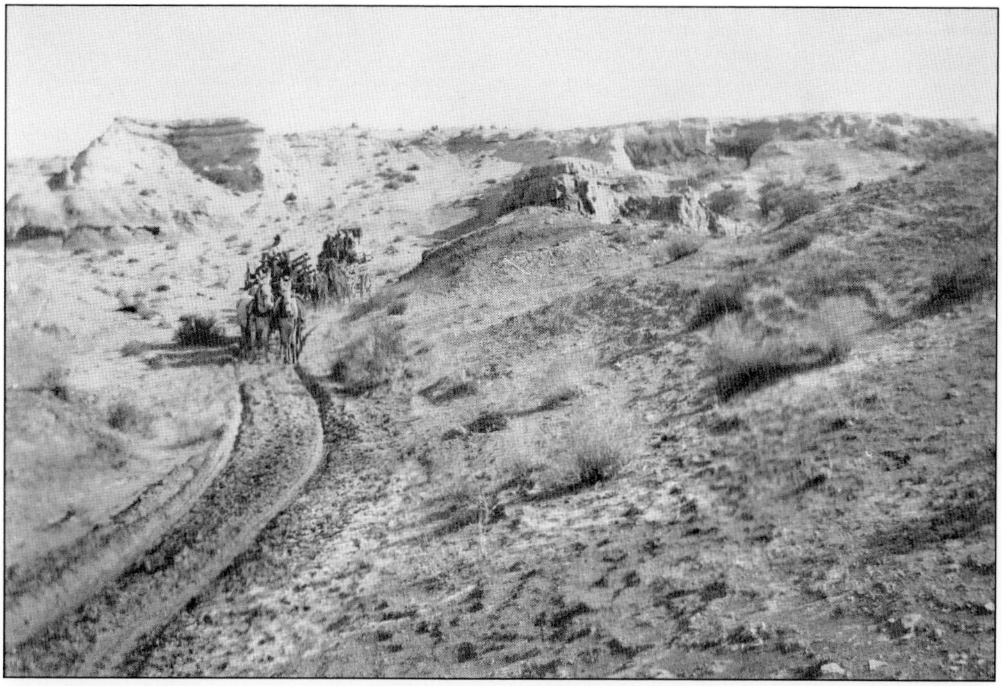

The Gillies family is in the San Rafael desert. The wagon shown was the only mode of transportation at that time, and it is piled high with all of their belongings. The ruts on the road are visible, so it clearly was well used, but the road still must have made for a treacherous ride.

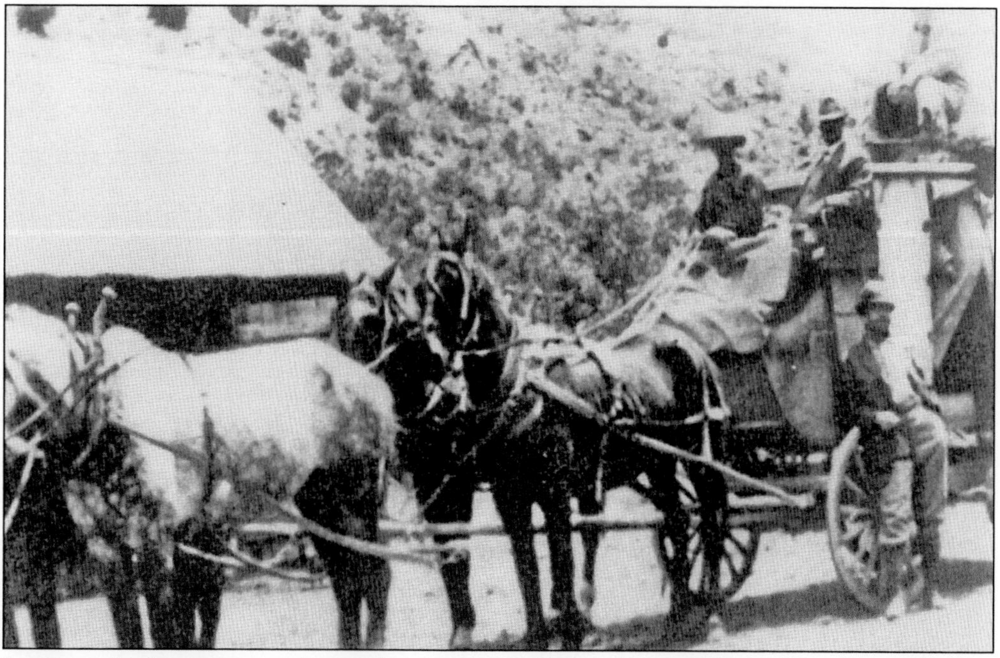

In the early days, stagecoach travel was at times faster than regular wagons. An additional advantage of the stagecoach was that it allowed for travel in inclement weather and for extra company. The passenger on top of the stagecoach is well dressed for being outside of the stagecoach among the dust and weather.

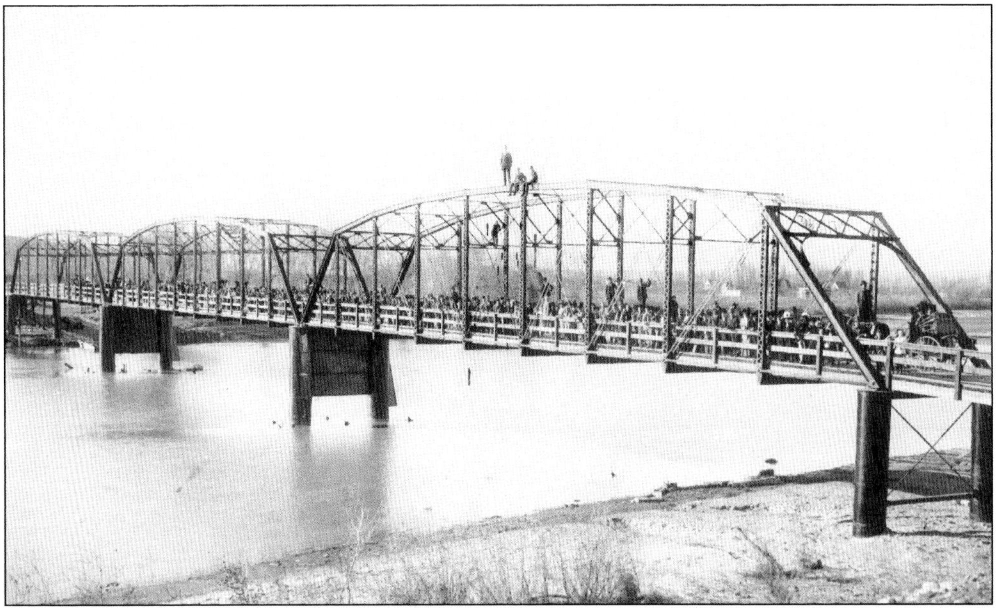

There was a celebration held in 1910 when the first lane of the bridge was opened and ready for use. The bridge dedication took place in December 1910. In other photographs of the dedication, people can be seen eating the Winter Queen melon. Winter Queen melons stored well in cellars and basements, allowing people to have fresh fruit in the winter

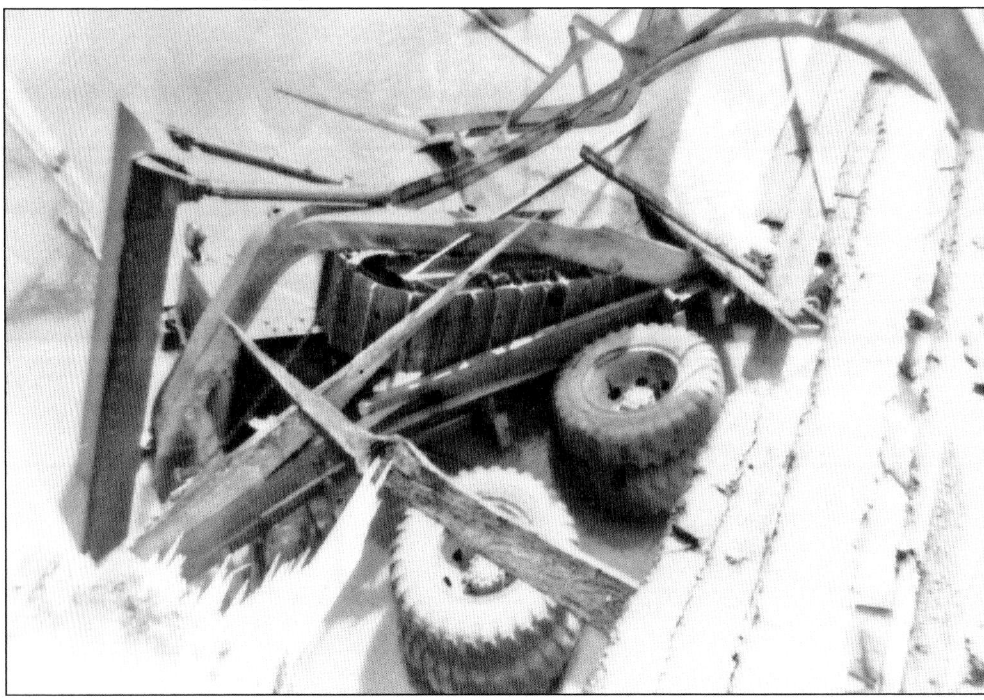

On July 30, 1946, the bridge collapsed when a large semitrailer truck loaded with a caterpillar tractor fell into the river. It was estimated that the truck and tractor weighed nearly 24 tons. The Ashforth Transfer Company, owner of the truck that crashed, was able to retrieve the truck and tractor from the river.

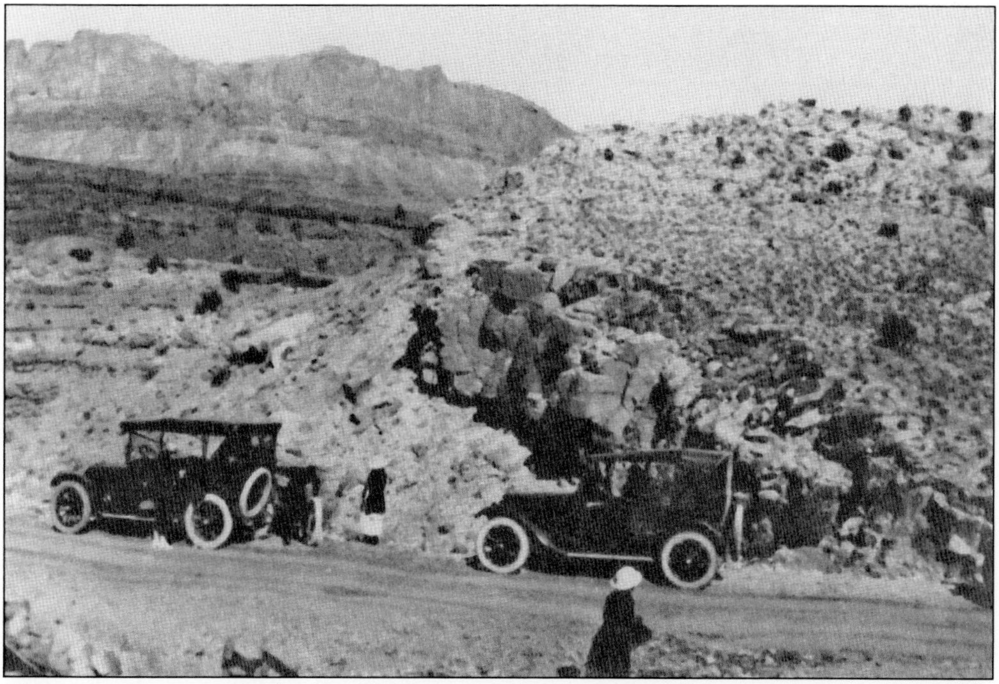

These two cars are stopped at Jessie's Twist, a road just a few miles outside of the town of Green River. Farther along this road is Hatt's Ranch. If one looks carefully on the road near Jessie's Twist, fossilized oyster shells can be seen.

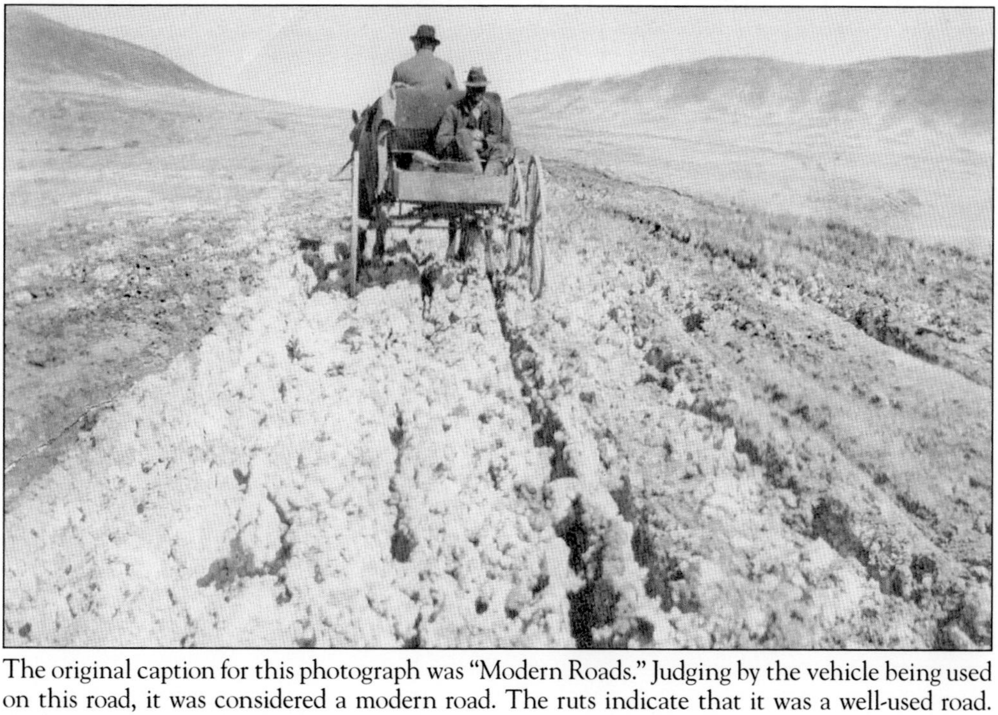

The original caption for this photograph was "Modern Roads." Judging by the vehicle being used on this road, it was considered a modern road. The ruts indicate that it was a well-used road. Both men are probably grateful for the hats they are wearing, since they cannot turn on the air-conditioning in their vehicle.

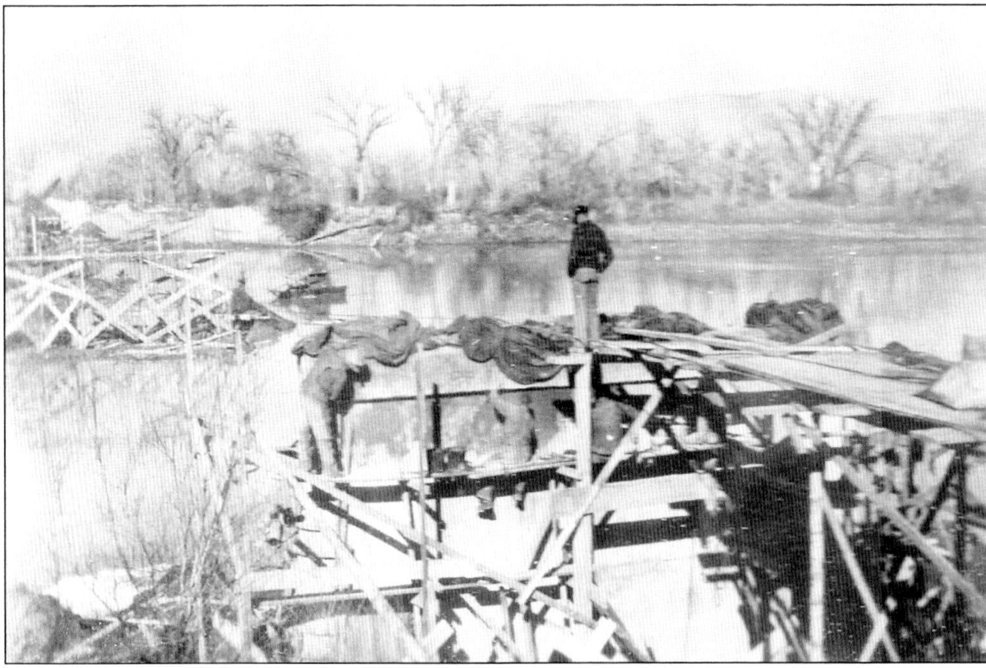

Here is one of the few photographs the Green River Archives has of when the bridge was being built. It looks like dangerous work, walking along the thin scaffolding, at any minute possibly falling into the Green River below. Two men are there, one working on the pilings and the other inspecting the work that had already been done. The bridge was opened to traffic in 1948.

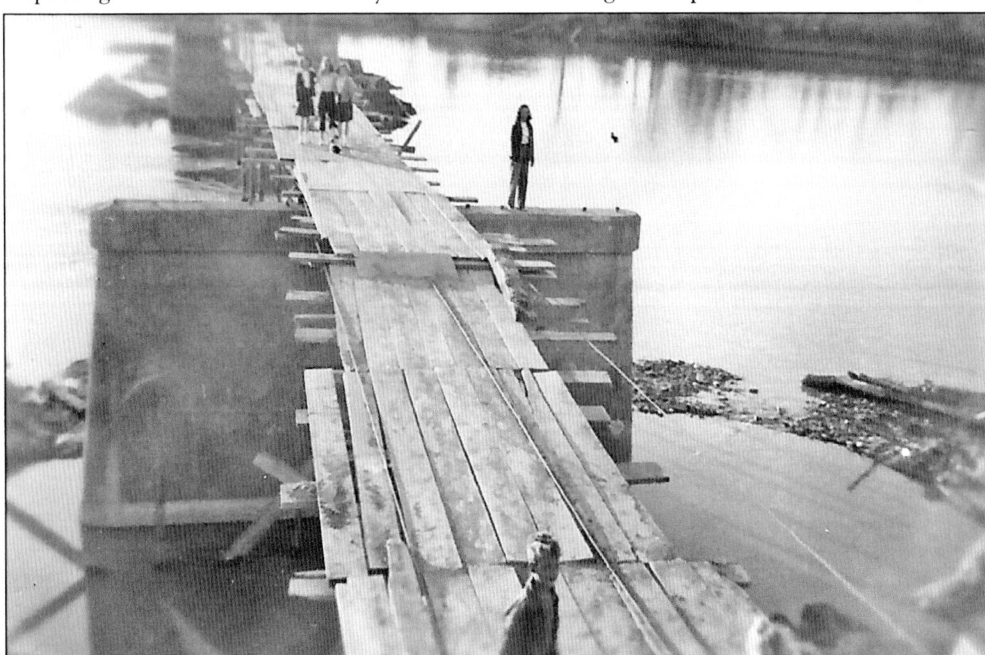

Obviously, the bridge is not open to traffic yet because three young girls are walking side by side as another individual looks on. When this bridge was built, the homes of several Green River citizens had to be moved to make way for the bridge.

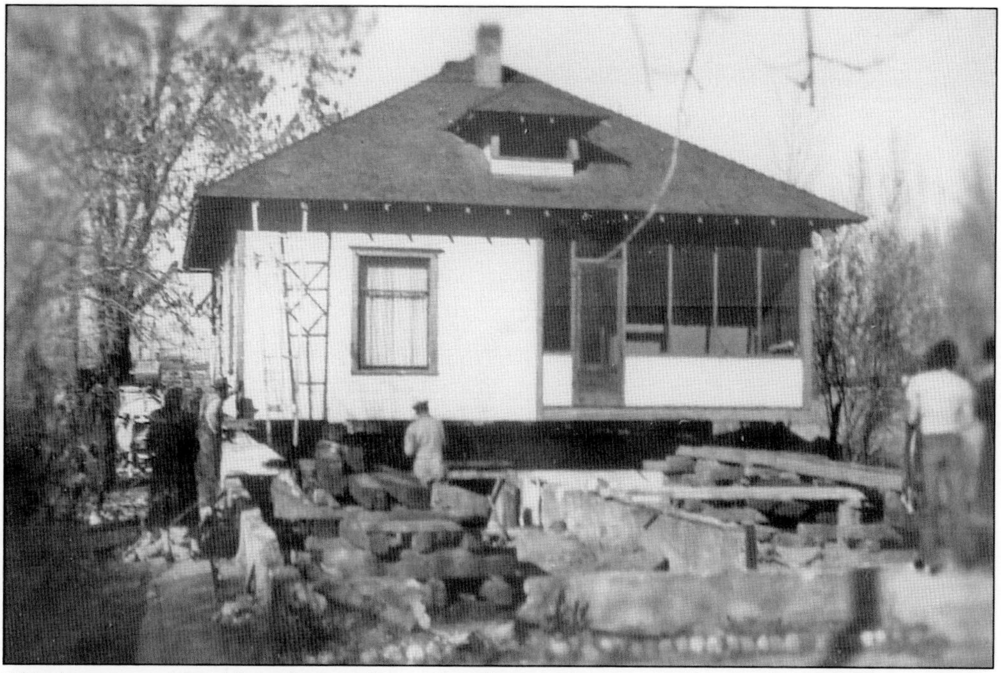

This house was Harold Anderson's home. It is being moved to make way for the wider road; the cribbing underneath the house was used to move it. The Andersons were one of the few families lucky enough to only have to move their home to another part of their property. It was moved about 100 feet north of where it had previously been.

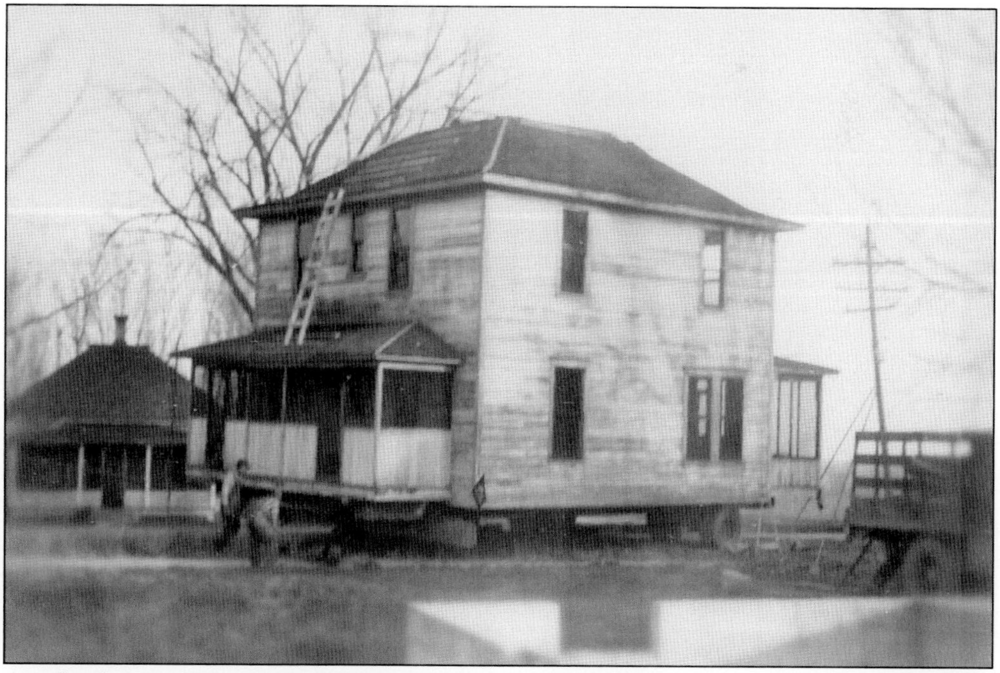

Another home, this one belonging to the Martin Maharry family, had to be moved off of their property to make way for the bridge. It was moved to Long Street. In later years, it was owned by the Dennie family. The bid to build the bridge was granted to T. C. Rowland of Salt Lake City.

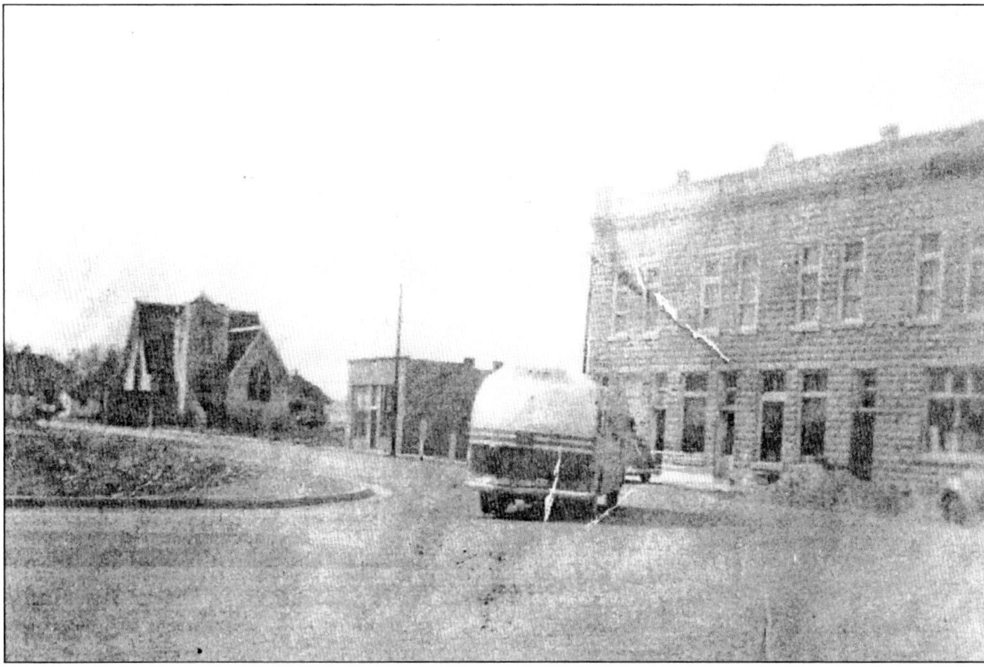

This is a scene of Green River showing some of the landmarks of the town. It was taken from Main Street looking toward the west. On the right-hand side of the street are the old bank building and the Bible Church, both of which are still standing. The Bible Church has had different religious affiliations use the building over the years, but it is still open every Sunday.

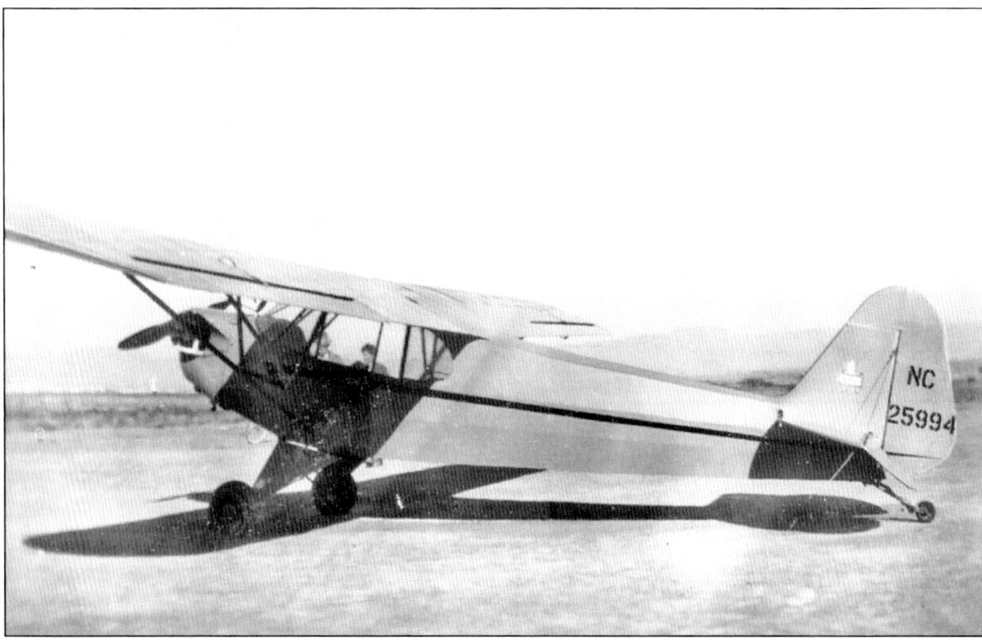

This airplane either just came in from a landing or is preparing to take off. A couple stands on the other side of the plane, possibly getting ready to depart. Green River had an airport for several years, with few changes of ownership during the past two decades. The airport began as a simple landing strip about 1920 on private land owned by Samuel B. Wilson.

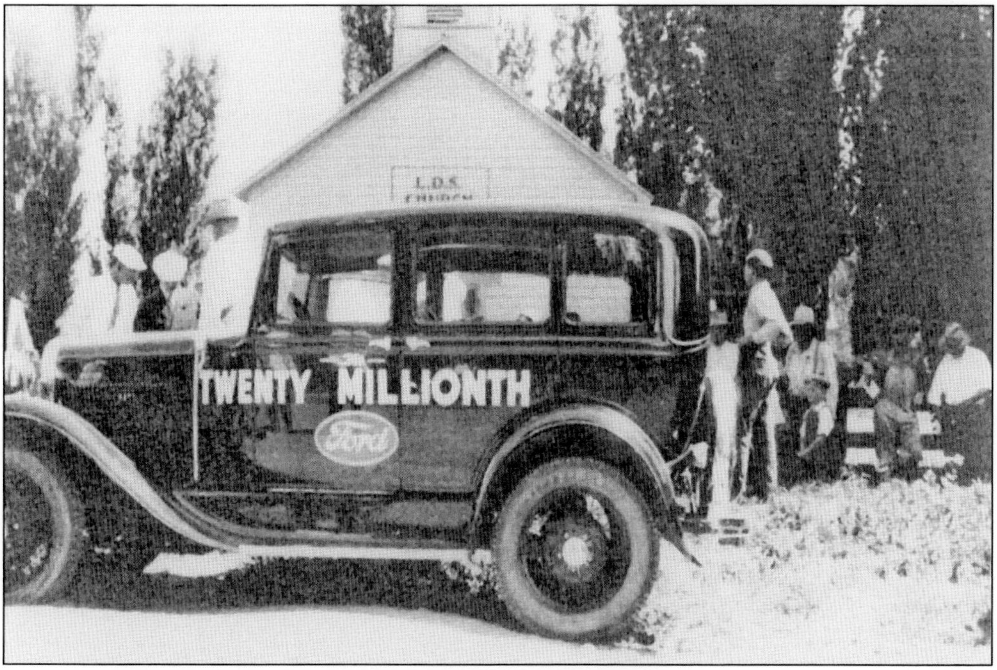

The 20-millionth Ford came off the production line on April 14, 1931. The car was the first Slant Windshield Town Sedan and was the most photographed Model A in history. It traveled from coast to coast and made several stops in Utah. It is shown at its stop in Green River. Although it was believed that the car was destroyed in a fire, it was found in Michigan, where it was originally bought.

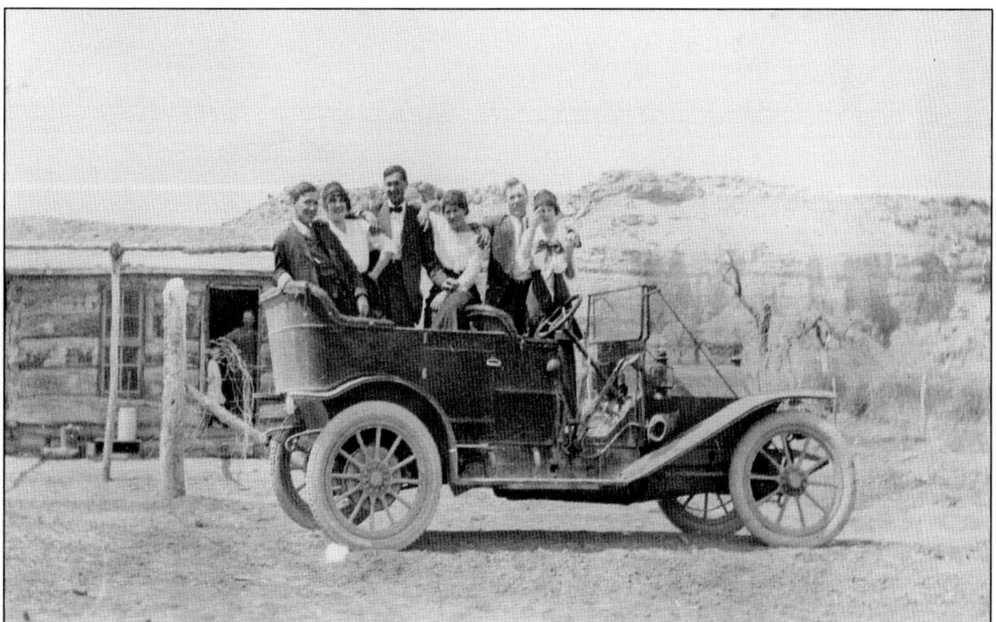

At the Gillies Ranch are Robert K. "Bob" Gillies, Lydia Gilles, Joseph S. Gillies, Johnnie James, Atta Cottrell, and Ann Gillies. The group looks like they are on the way to a fun adventure in what appears to be an early convertible.

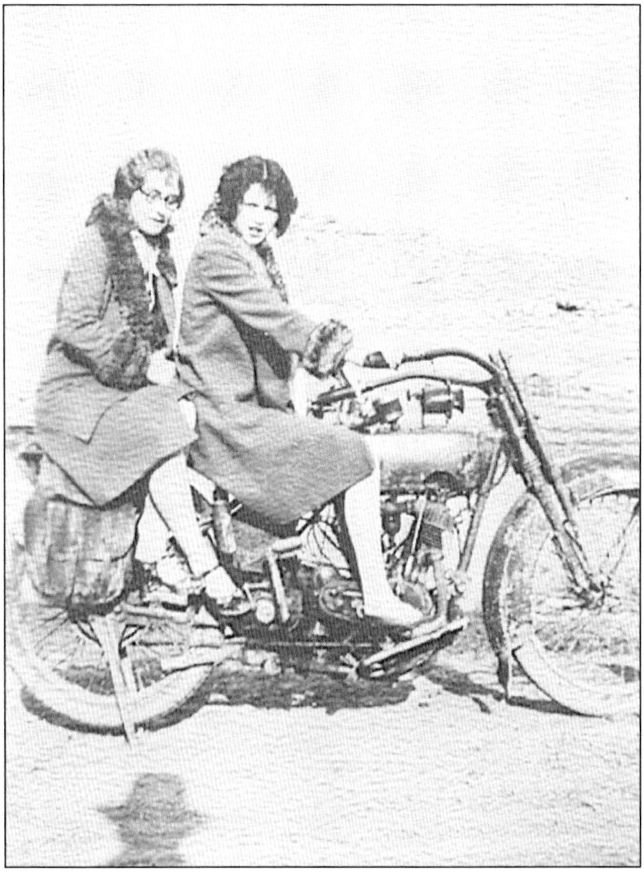

Sylvia Harris (Ekker) is the passenger on a friend's motorcycle. The photograph was taken in Valley City, where Harris taught school for one year. Valley City is now a ghost town located in Grand County; it is 5.5 miles south of Crescent Junction, Utah.

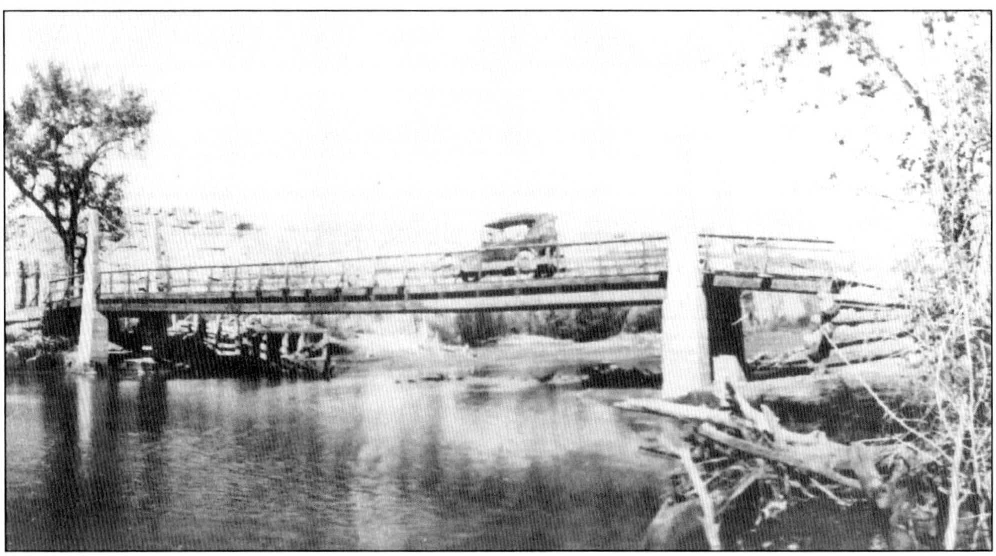

This photograph shows the San Rafael Bridge over the San Rafael River. Spanish Franciscan friars named the San Rafael River after the Archangel St. Rafael—the angel of the spirits of men, the Healer, and one of the four angels who stood around the throne of God. It is early in the bridge's history, judging by the vintage of the car driving across the bridge.

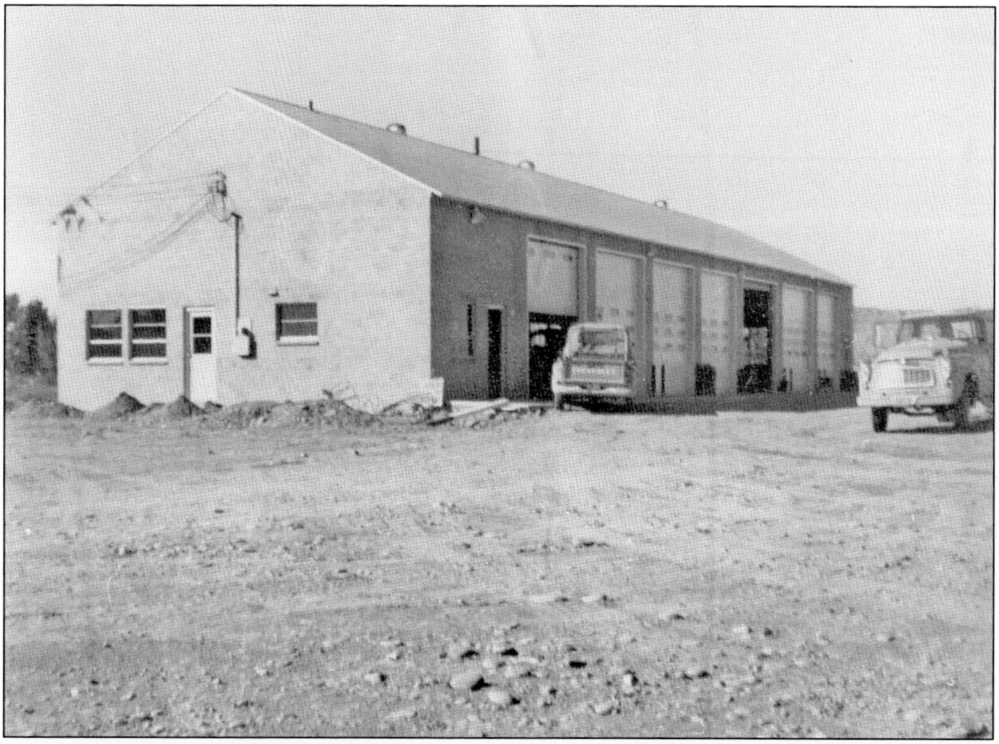

The Utah State Road Shed is located on Main Street in Green River. The shed was originally located in Elgin, Utah. When it was moved to its current location, the shed was built on five acres of the old riverbed. Inside the building are trucks, road equipment, showers, and restrooms for the employees' use.

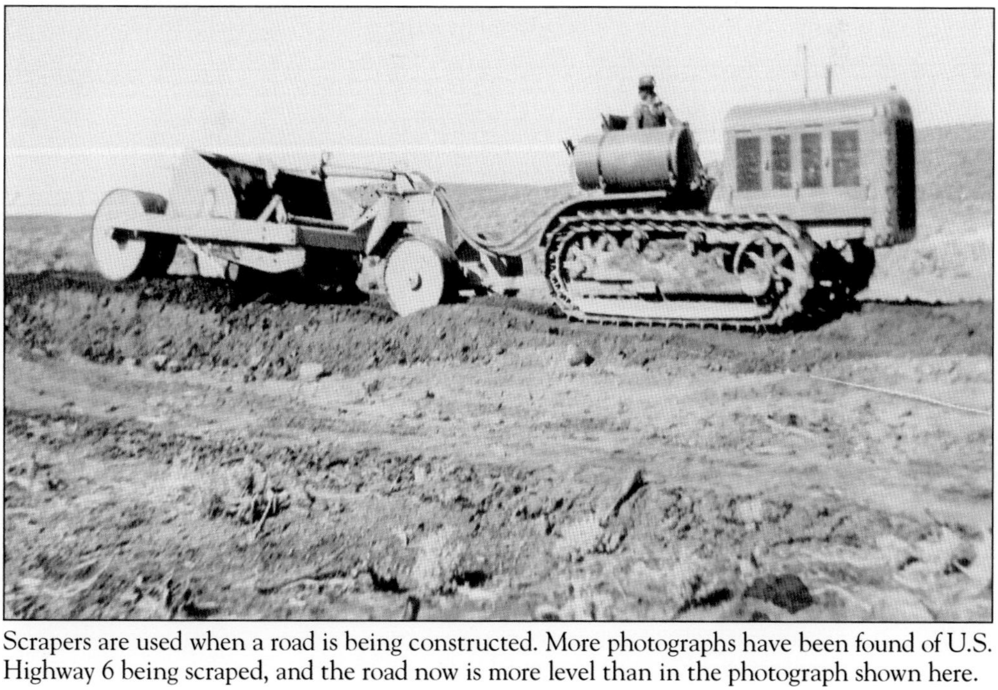

Scrapers are used when a road is being constructed. More photographs have been found of U.S. Highway 6 being scraped, and the road now is more level than in the photograph shown here.

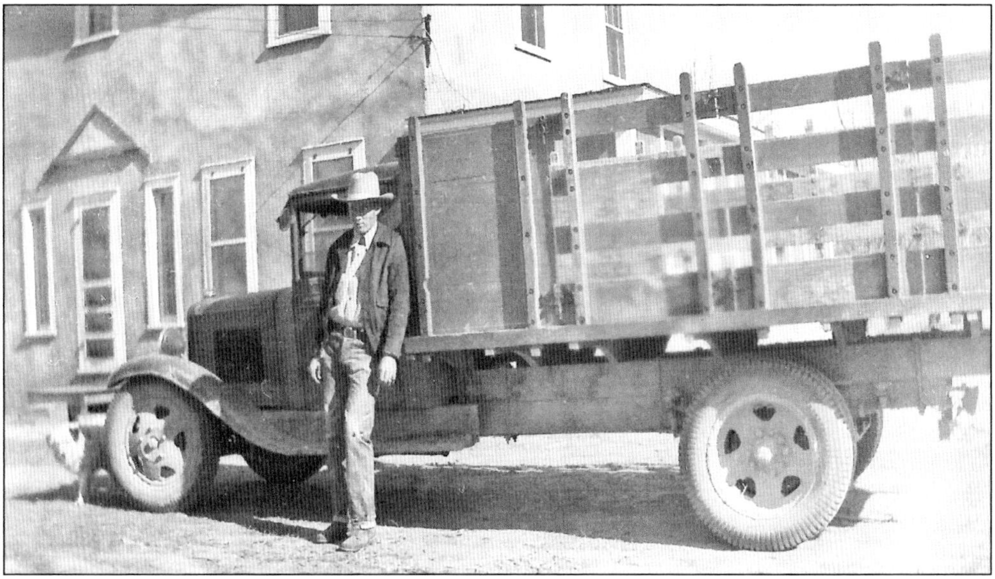

Francis Wilson is standing in front of a useful farm implement, a truck. The trucks on a farm are used for everything from hauling crops like corn or hay to market, to moving animals like sheep, cows, or horses when they are to be sold or are injured and cannot move on their own.

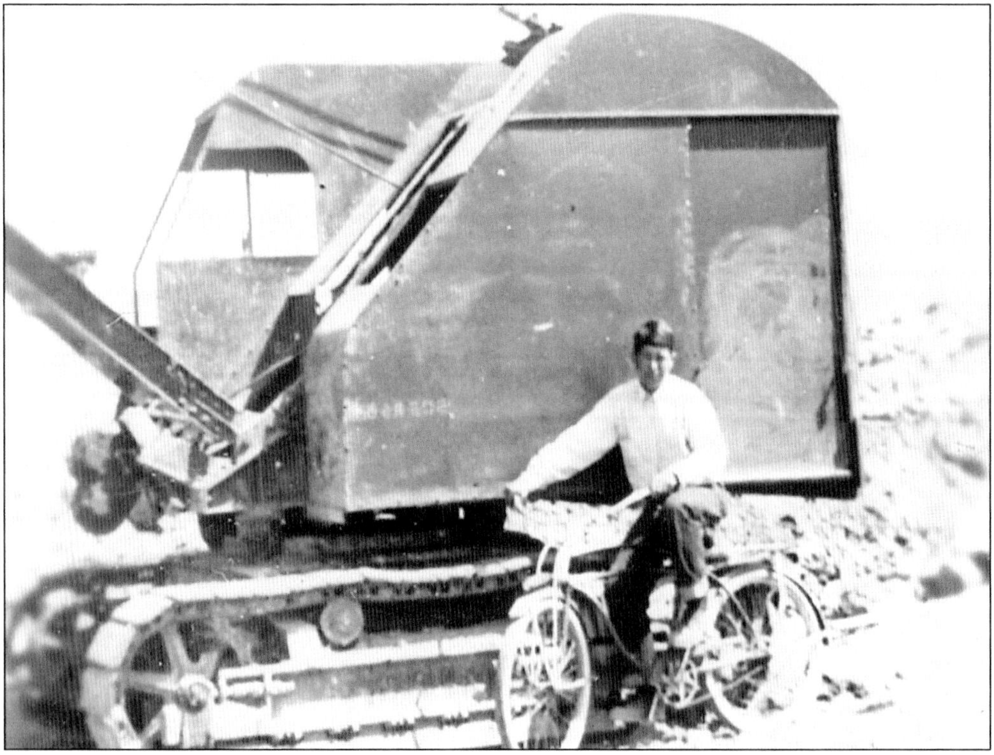

Jay Marsing is photographed on a bicycle in front of a tractor. The tractor had a large bucket in front of it. Not all residents of Green River had access to farm equipment. Agriculture is still part of Green River's economy today, but it is not as prevalent as tourism. Marsing must have been impressed with the large machine and so wanted to be in a photograph with it.

Five

HOMES, BUILDINGS, AND BUSINESSES

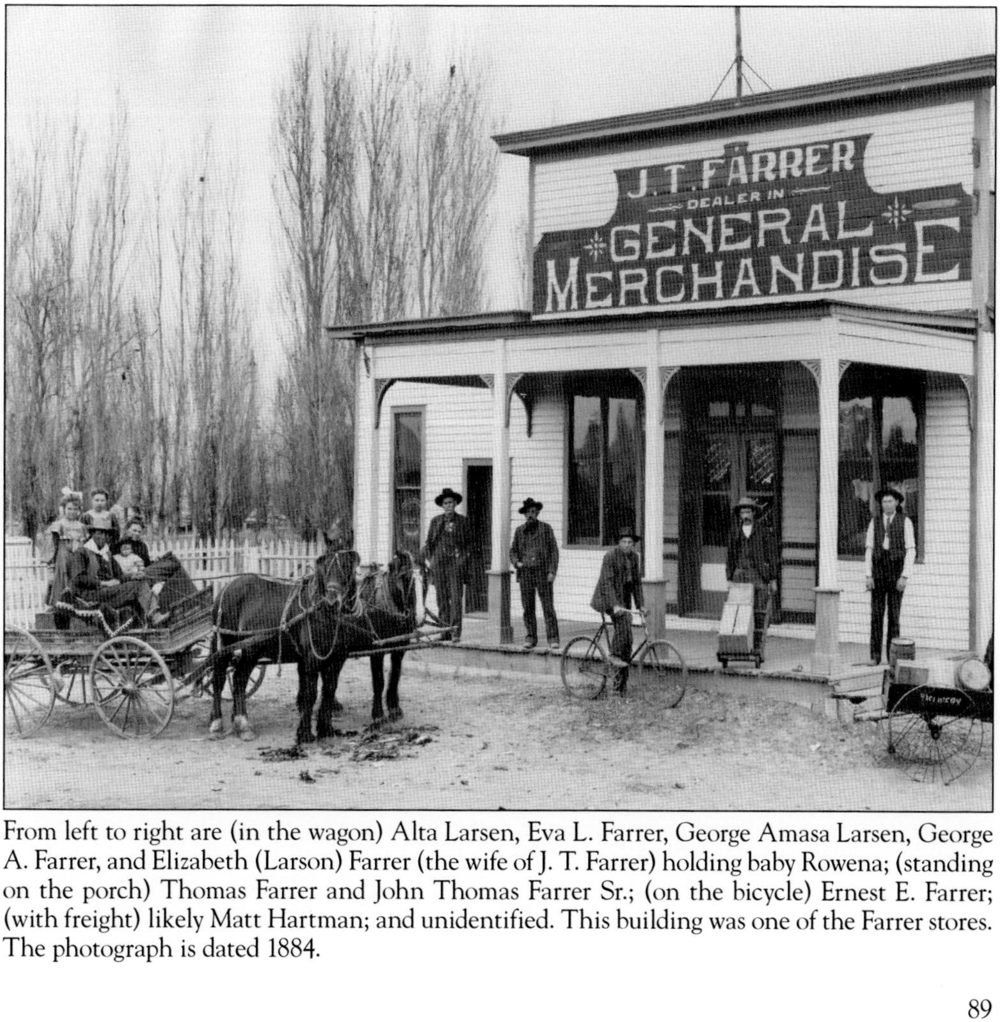

From left to right are (in the wagon) Alta Larsen, Eva L. Farrer, George Amasa Larsen, George A. Farrer, and Elizabeth (Larson) Farrer (the wife of J. T. Farrer) holding baby Rowena; (standing on the porch) Thomas Farrer and John Thomas Farrer Sr.; (on the bicycle) Ernest E. Farrer; (with freight) likely Matt Hartman; and unidentified. This building was one of the Farrer stores. The photograph is dated 1884.

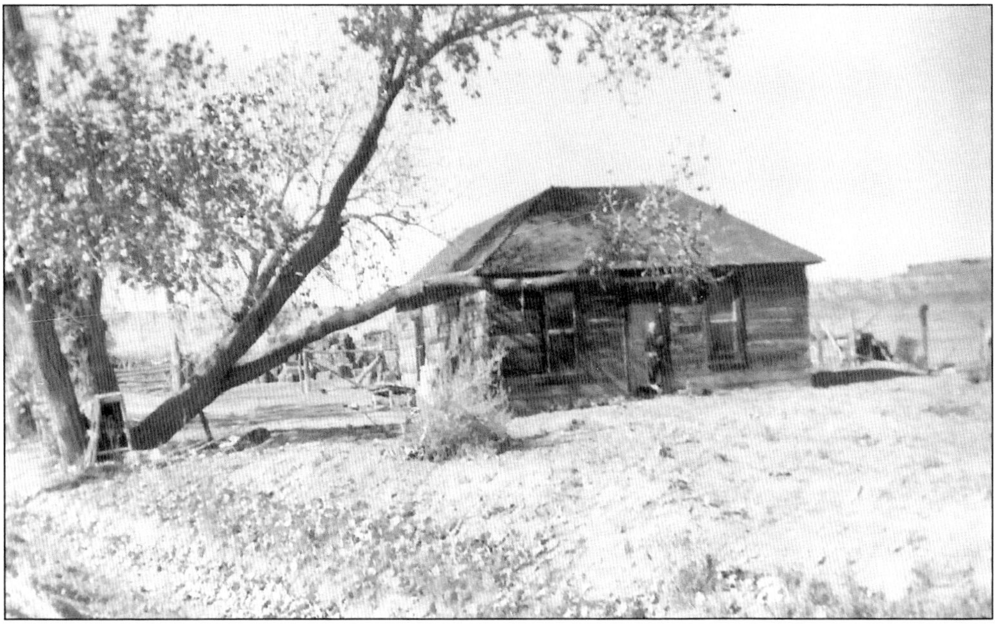

This is one of the homes located on the Gillies Ranch along the San Rafael River. The ranch had many buildings, of which several were used as homes. The Gillies family was quite large; there was a need for space for all the children and their friends. Several of the buildings are still standing out in the San Rafael desert.

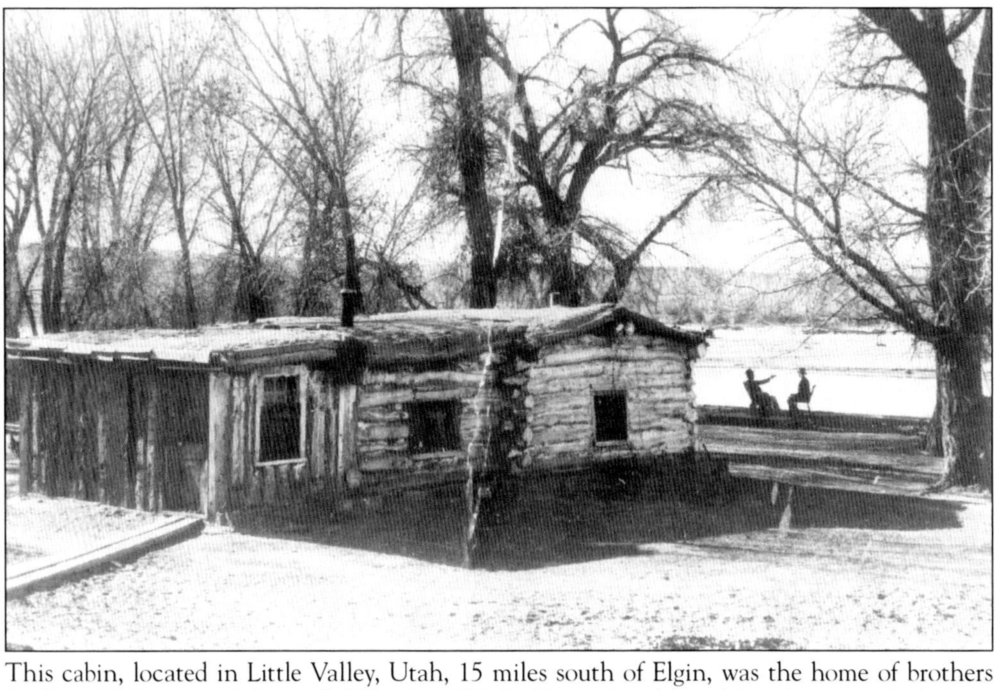

This cabin, located in Little Valley, Utah, 15 miles south of Elgin, was the home of brothers Arthur, Wallace, and Roswell Wheeler. While living in this cabin, they installed three waterwheels for irrigation and planted alfalfa and fruit trees. After Arthur and Wallace left for the Yukon River country, Roswell Wheeler lived as a recluse. He died in a fire in 1920 in what some considered mysterious circumstances.

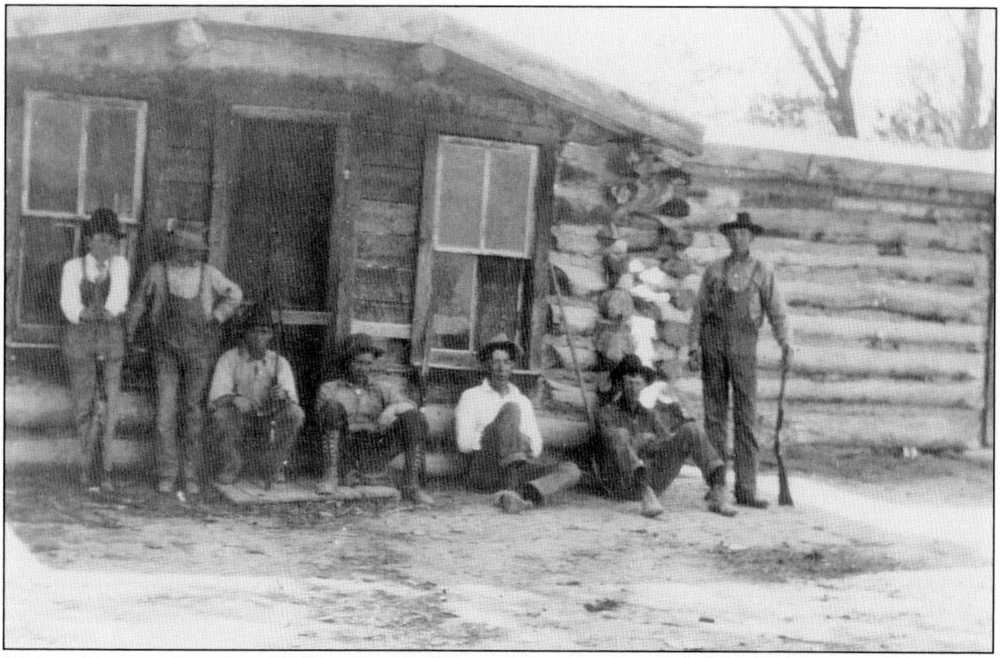

This cabin was found at Willow Bend. None of the men in the photograph are identified. It appears they have come in from a day of farming and are exhausted. Willow Bend is located farther up North Long Street. There are some houses remaining up in Willow Bend, but only a few are occupied.

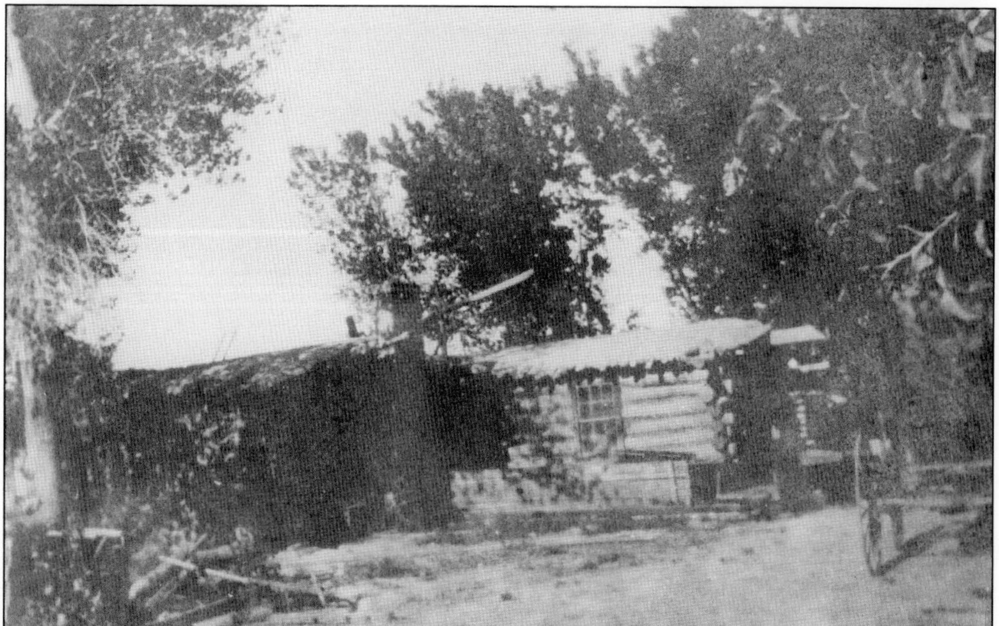

George Thurman's first home is pictured here. He later built another home on North Long Street that burned in 1985. The silo from the second home still remains. Another home was built on the land where the home had burned and suffered damage. The spot where the home was now has a greenhouse in its place.

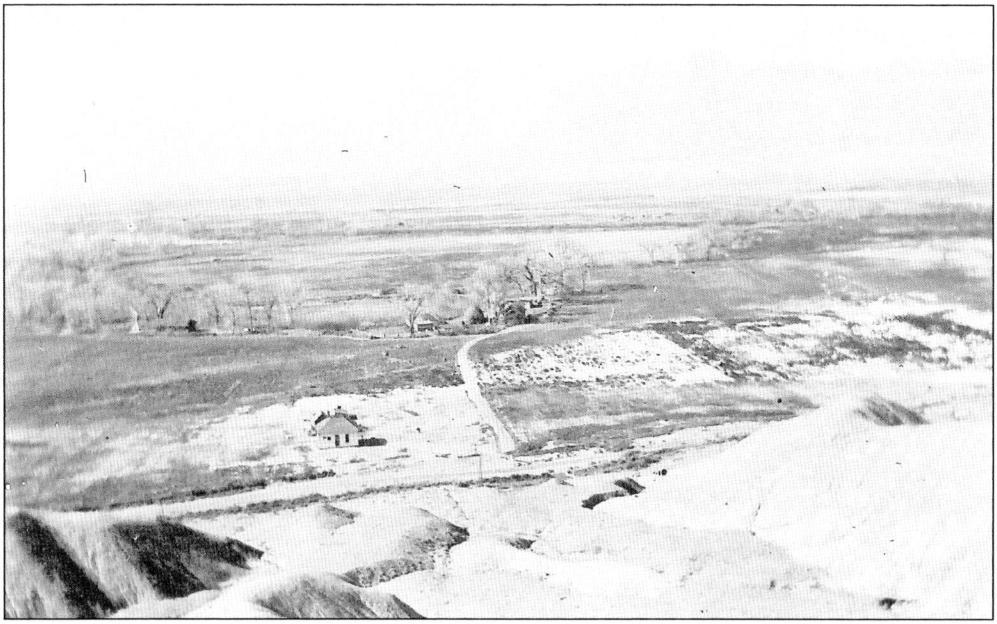

The Silliman/Wilson cabin is in the background of the photograph; in the foreground is the house built by the Wilsons, now belonging to Earline Nelson. These homes are located on Hastings Road and are distant enough from Green River not be included in the city boundaries. They are residents of Elgin.

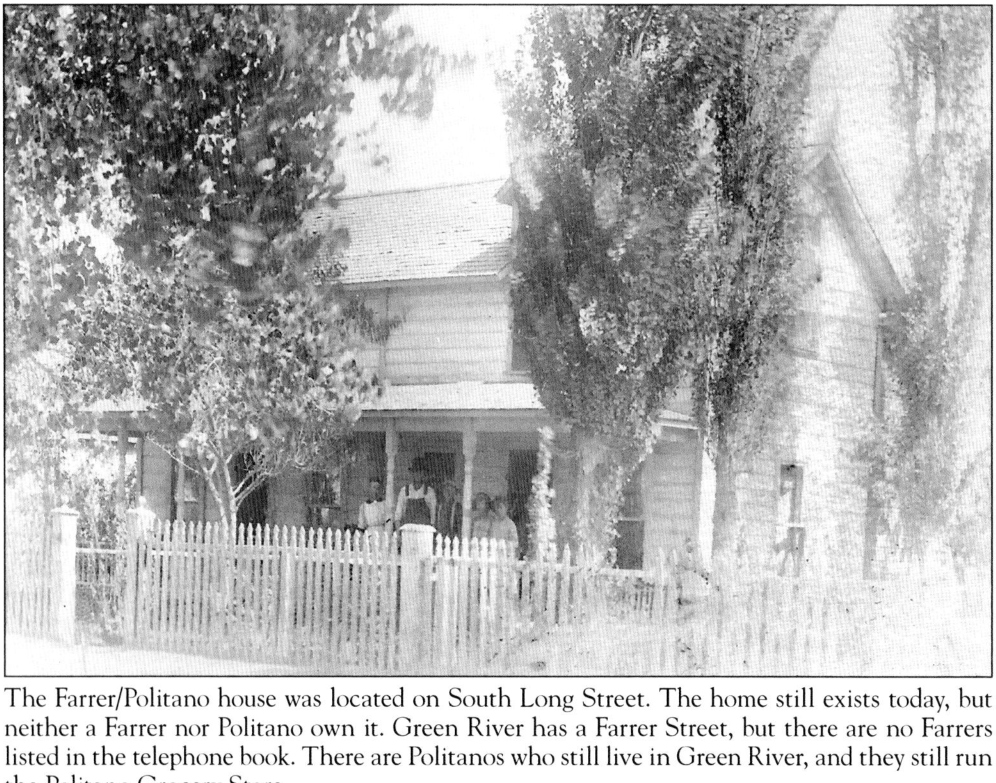

The Farrer/Politano house was located on South Long Street. The home still exists today, but neither a Farrer nor Politano own it. Green River has a Farrer Street, but there are no Farrers listed in the telephone book. There are Politanos who still live in Green River, and they still run the Politano Grocery Store.

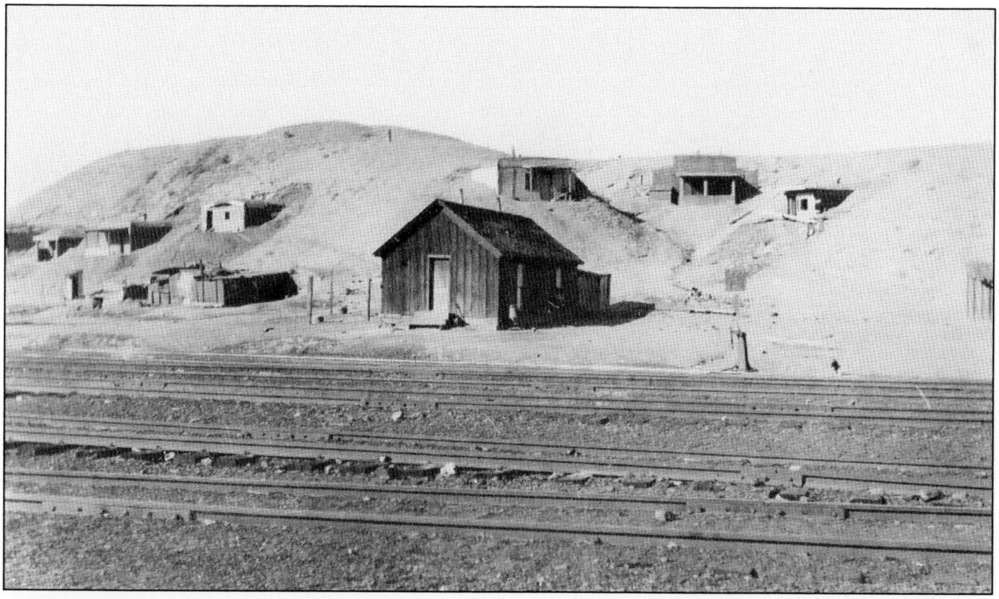

"Hill-side Villas, near Green River" reads the label for this photograph, taken about 1920 just southwest of the current railroad depot. Some of the floor materials are still visible and are the only evidence these houses were ever there. The term "Hill-side Villas" was used as a humorous label for these houses, which were quickly built.

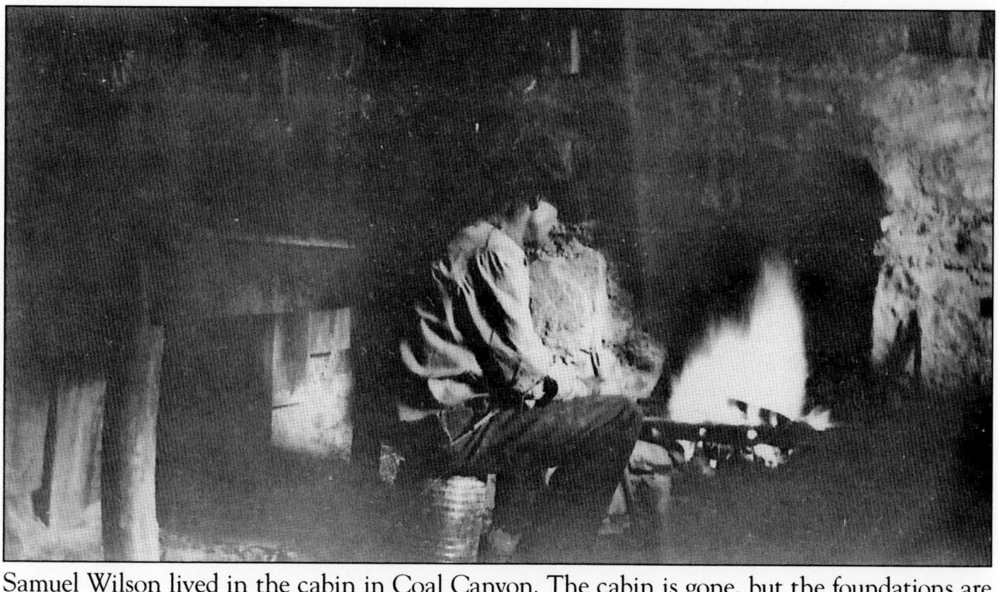

Samuel Wilson lived in the cabin in Coal Canyon. The cabin is gone, but the foundations are still visible. To get to the area where the cabin was located would take a good half-hour hike today. Coal Canyon is a dirt road just a few miles to the east of town, right off Hastings Road. There are petroglyphs and pictographs in Coal Canyon.

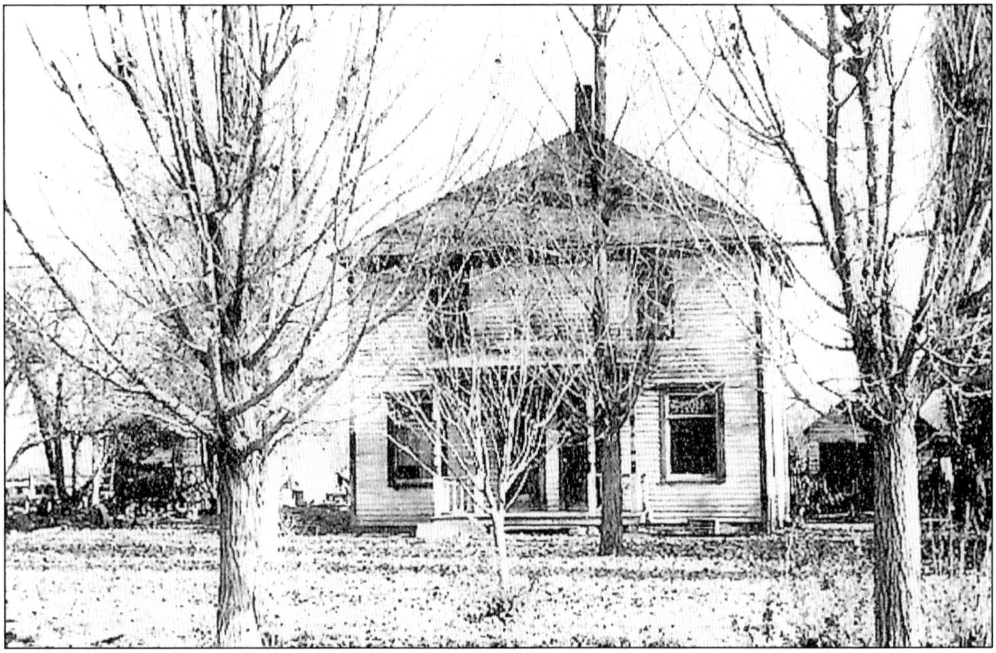

George Thurman's home was built about 1906. The house originally had two front doors. The north door led to the parlor, which used for special occasions. There were two stained-glass upper windows, which were salvaged when the house burned in 1985. The shed seen on the right side of the photograph still exists.

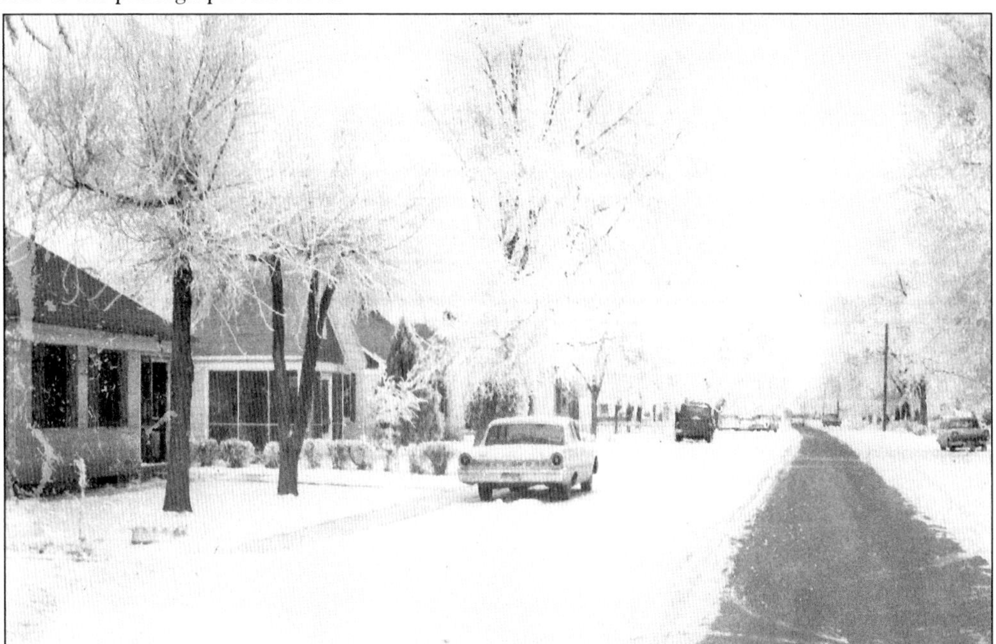

This is a photograph taken of South Long Street in winter. To the left are railroad houses. They still stand today and are privately owned. Now Green River's library is also located on South Long Street, as well as one of the first Latter-day Saint chapels in Green River, which is now used as the Senior Citizens Center.

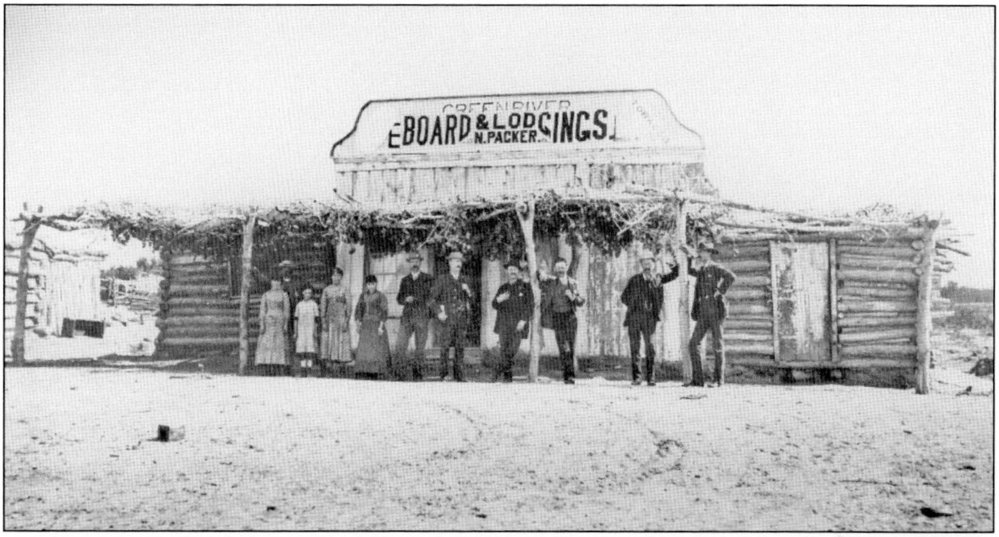

The Greenriver Board and Lodgings was one of the first "hotels" found in Green River. Today Green River's economy is based on tourism, but when this photograph was taken, there were not any other accommodations in Green River other than the Palmer House, which was built by the railroad. The proprietor's name on the sign is N. Packer. None of the people in the photograph are identified.

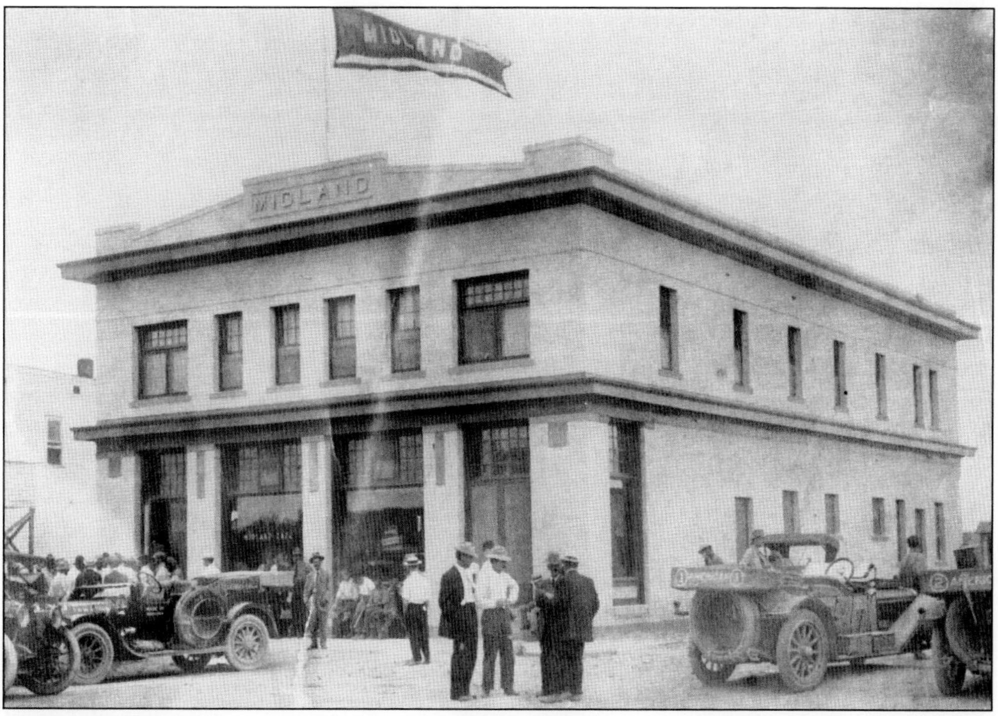

The Midland Hotel was built in 1913 by the Midland Investment Company. Two neon signs were installed in the windows in 1932. Dances for many occasions were held in the basement. The scene in front of the Midland was the occasion of the scouting trip for the Lincoln Highway; it was later decided the northern route would be better. The building still stands and is being remodeled as a private residence.

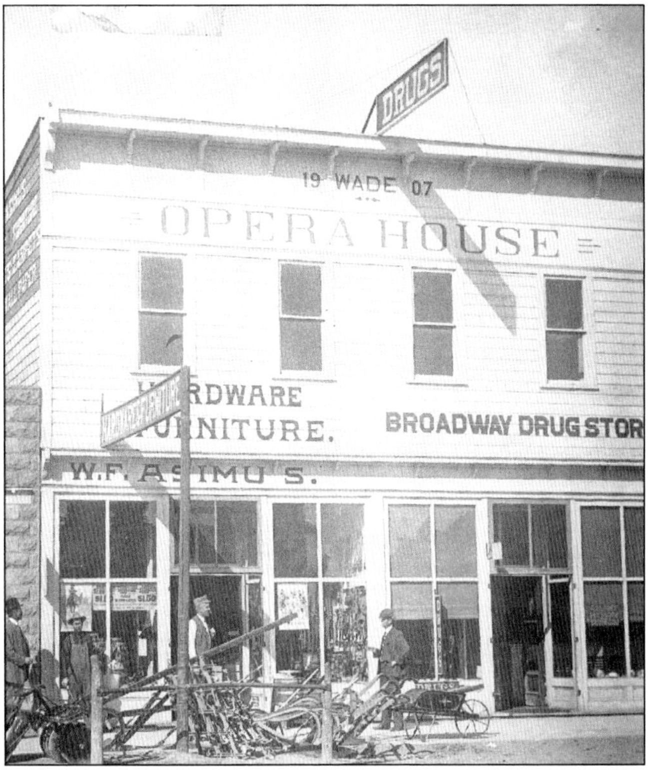

Green River had its own opera house. It was built in 1907 and was located on Broadway Street between the Midland Hotel and Frank's Pizza (the original Silver Dollar). Located on the first floor, the Lobby Saloon was advertised as "A Gentleman's Place of Amusement." Also on the first floor was W. F. Asimus Furniture and Hardware and the Broadway Drug Store. The opera house was on the second floor. The building went up in flames in 1920.

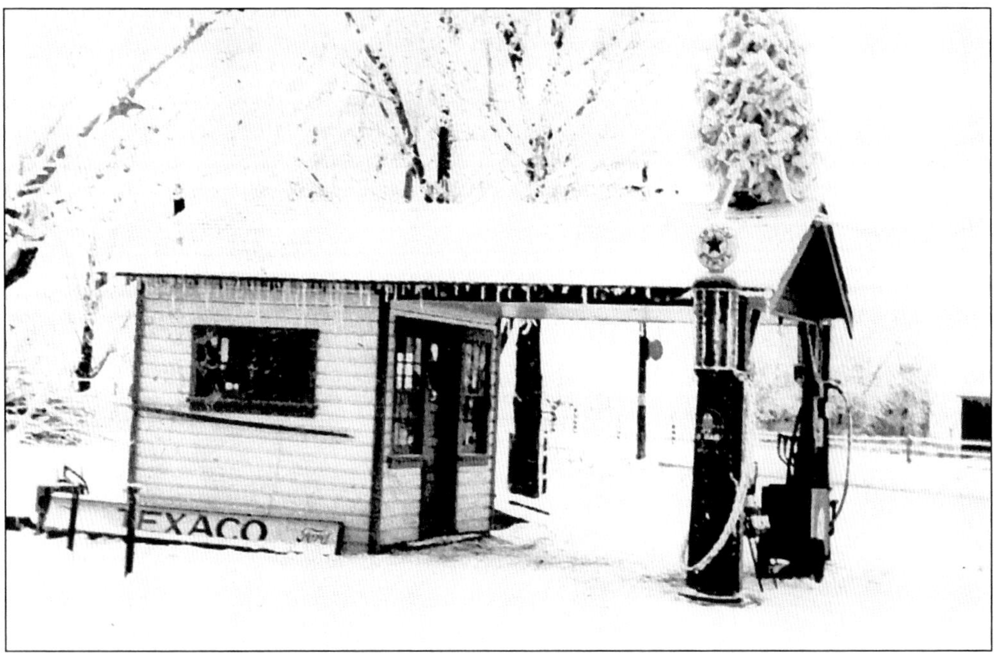

Harold "Hal" Anderson owned this station in the mid-1930s; it was his first gas station. He later built another station on this same location at Long and Farrer Streets. When the bridge collapsed in 1946 and the new station was built, it was on a new street that went through the town. Later Harold's son Gary and his wife, Frankie, operated the station after Hal's death.

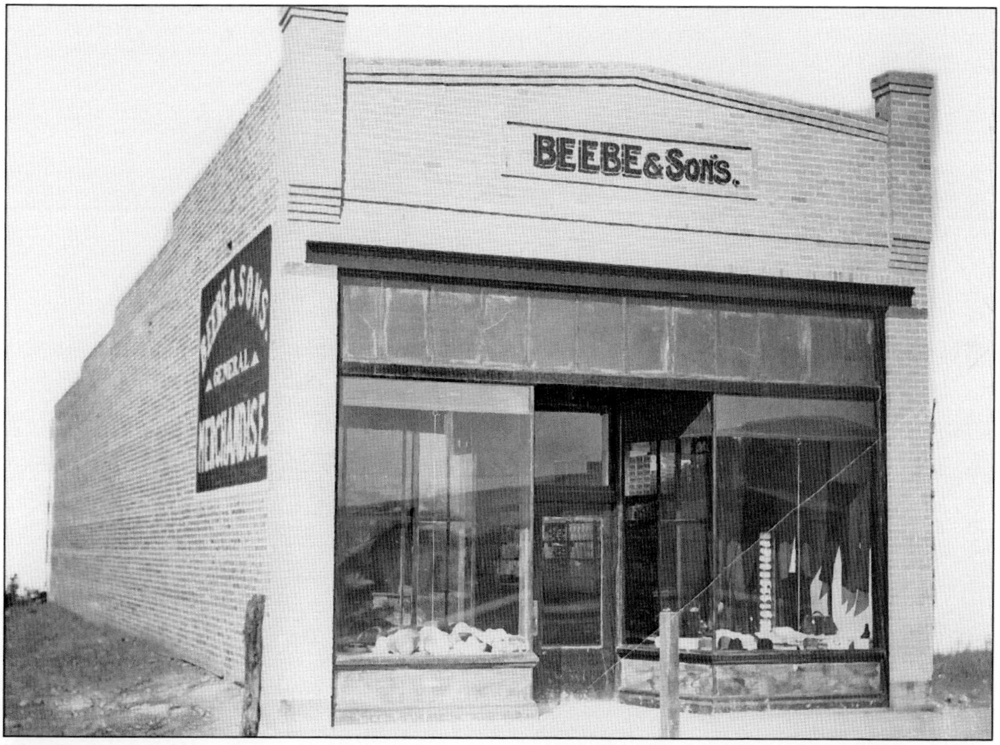

The Beebe and Sons General Merchandise store stood on Broadway Street from its construction in 1910 to 2006, when it was demolished to make room for the expansion of the Melon Vine Grocery Store. It had several owners over the years, including the Beebes, Lou Maharry and Monroe Noblitt, the Peacoks, and others.

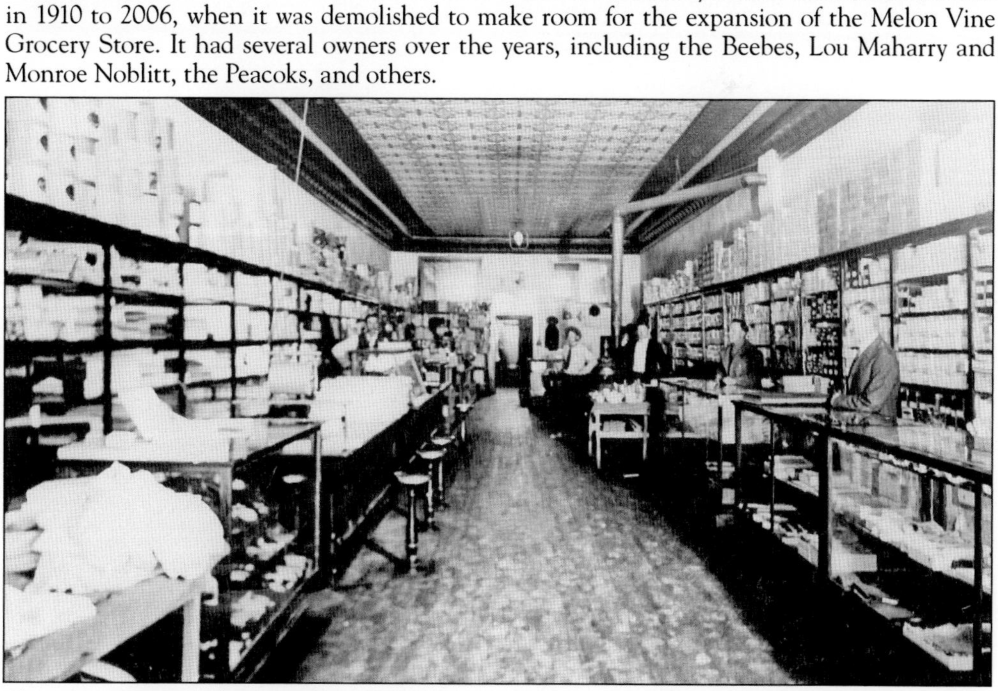
This is an interior photograph of the Beebe and Sons store. The store sold groceries and dry goods. Dry goods mean fabric to make clothes, wool hats, and scarves. Many different products line the shelves, and the wide aisle could accommodate many customers at the same time.

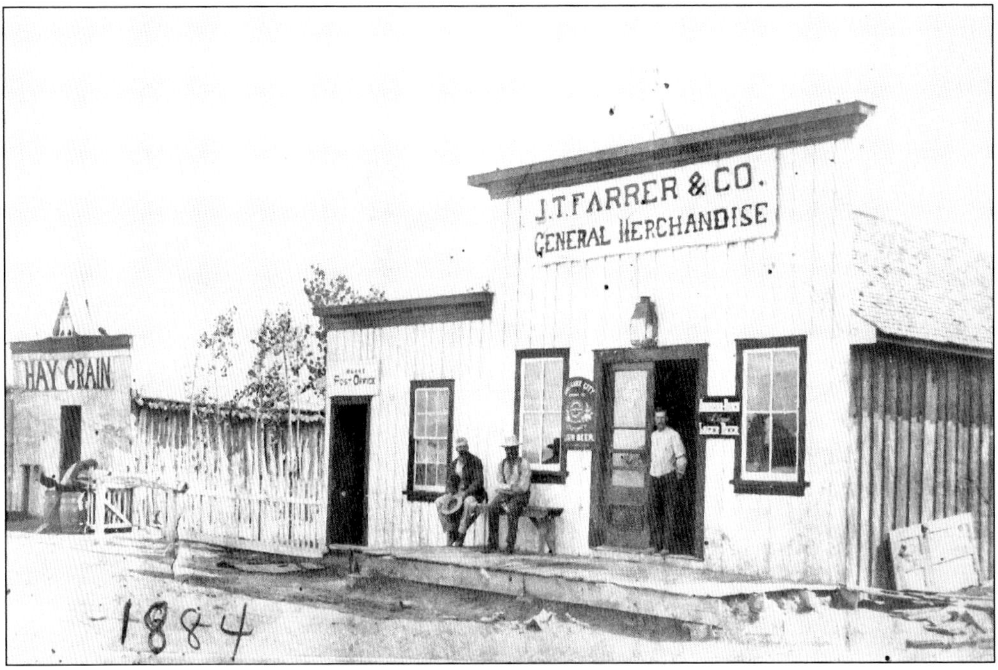

Built by Tom Farrer and his son, J. T. Farrer, in 1880, the store was a general merchandise, post office, and livery. Besides the store business, they also worked as cattlemen and sheep men. Notice the name of the post office: Blake. The town of Green River was originally called Blake, then the name was changed to Greenriver, and finally to Green River.

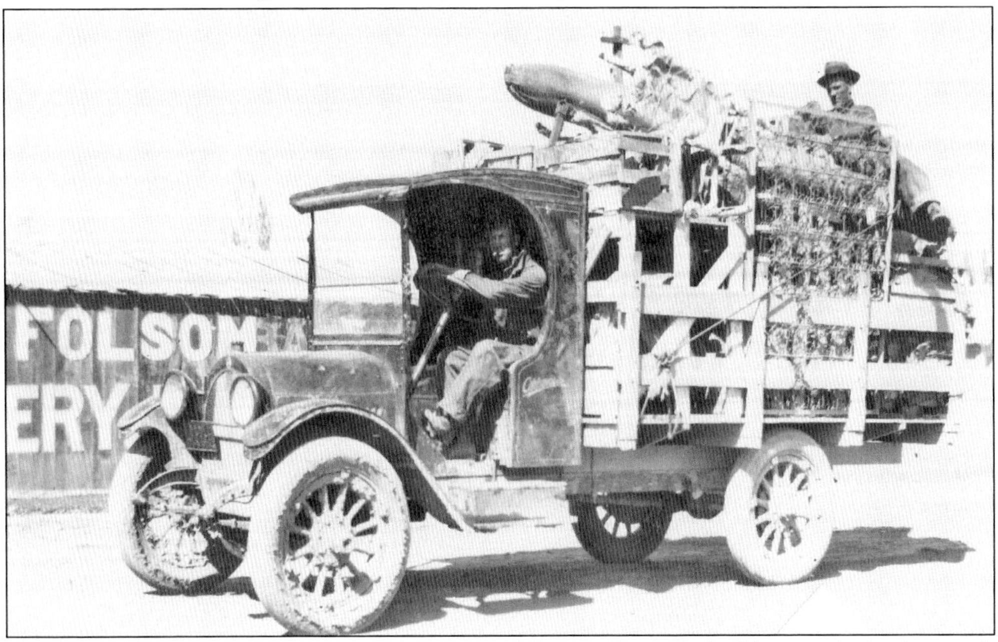

This photograph was taken in 1919. Notice part of the words on the building in the background. The name of the business is the Folsom Delivery Service. The Folsom this most likely refers to is John Folsom. John had many businesses while in Green River. One business John had been in was a water delivery system. This was in the days before water was piped into each home.

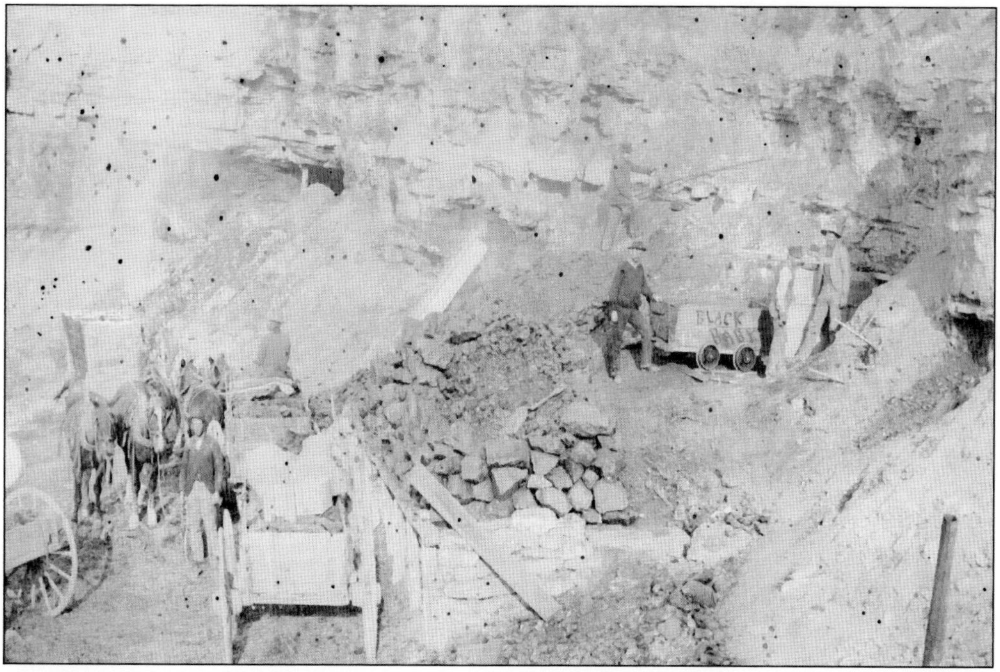

The Black Baby Coal Mine was located east of Green River up Coal Canyon. The mine car on the right has the name of the mine painted on it. The Farrers first developed the mine. In later years, it changed hands several times. The entrances to the different shafts are closed at this time.

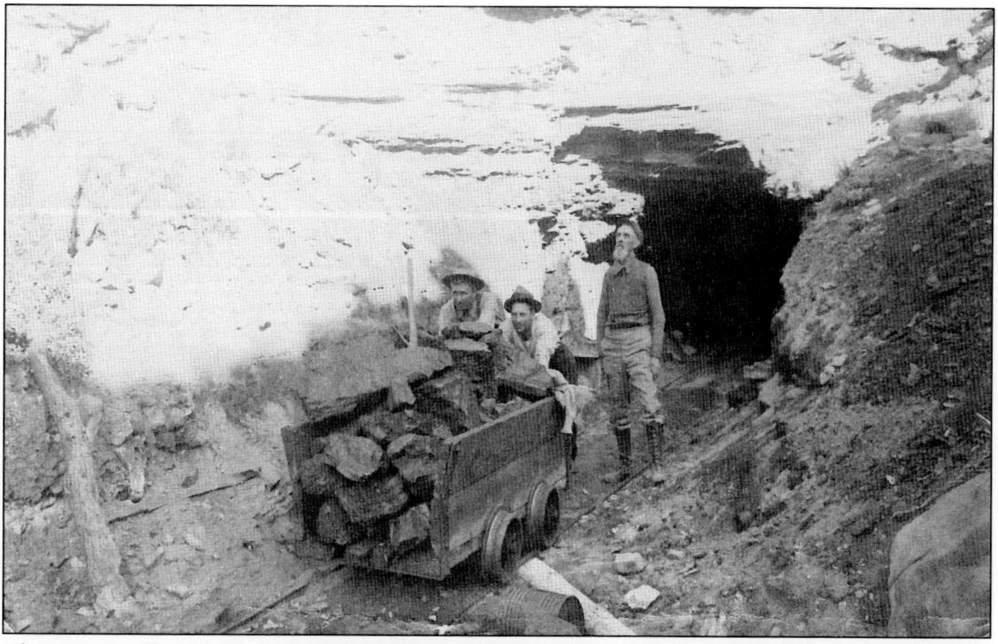

The men are (from left to right) Sam Wilson, Harry Baines, and an unidentified man running a load of coal out of one of the mines in Coal Canyon. Wilson would later own the 42 Ranch on North Long Street. The ranch was named for the turbine pumps, which lifted 42–second feet of water into the "42 canal." Wilson also rebuilt the pump house, which housed the turbines.

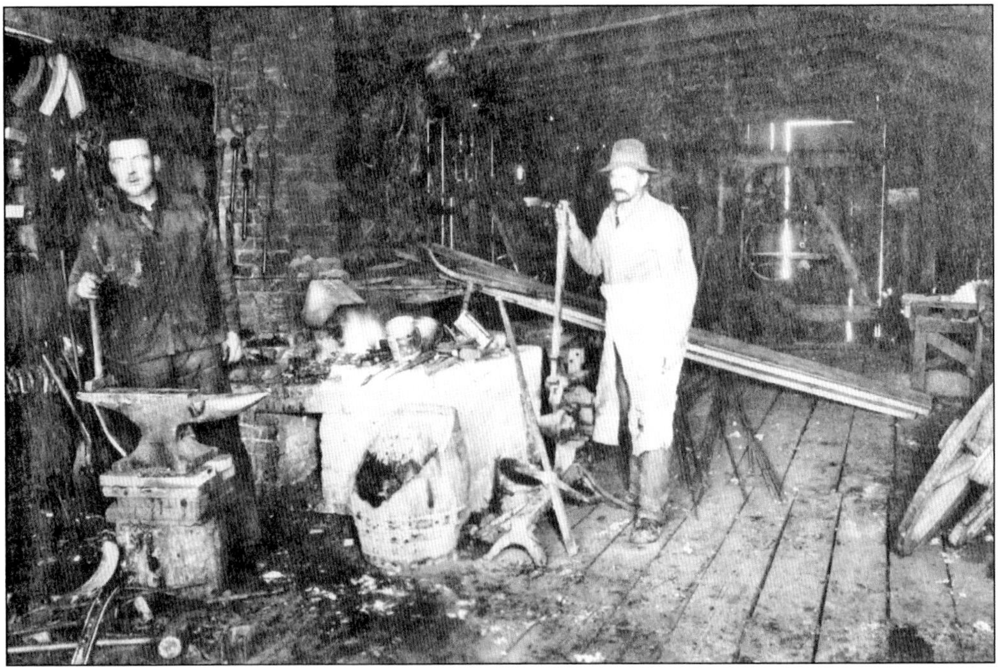

This is an interior photograph of Charles Swasey's blacksmith shop in Green River. The men are identified as Charles Swasey Jr. (left) and Chris Halverson. The Swasey name is well known in Emery County. Swasey Mountain is named for Charles A. Swasey, the father of the Swasey in this photograph.

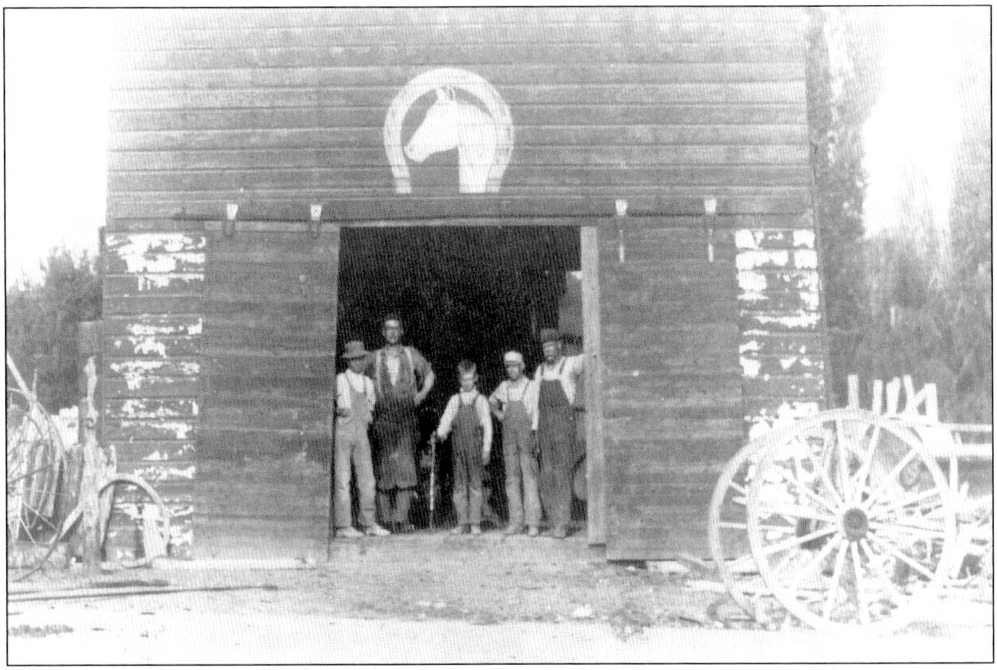

This is an exterior photograph of Charles Swasey's blacksmith shop in Green River. The identified men in the photograph are Charles Swasey Jr. (second from left) and his son Melvin Swasey (third from left). The rest of the men in the photograph are believed to be McCall boys.

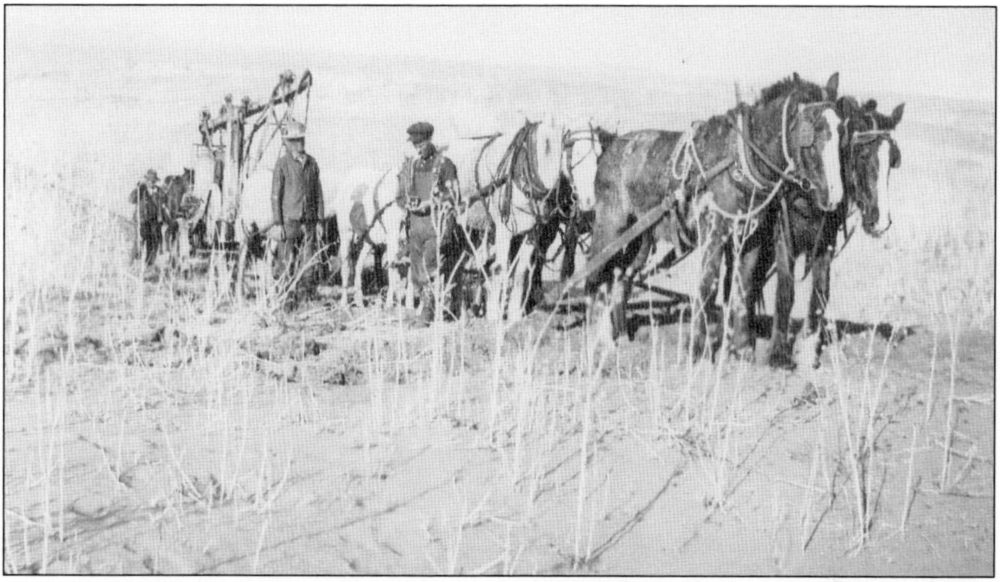

This photograph was taken about 1910 during the valley's first oil boom. In June 1910, a newspaper reported that oil was discovered at the Cook Levi well near Green River. Another flow was estimated to have given 125 to 200 barrels of oil. It was reported there would soon be five oil rigs in Green River and that a refinery would be built. One of the men photographed is Dunc Gillies.

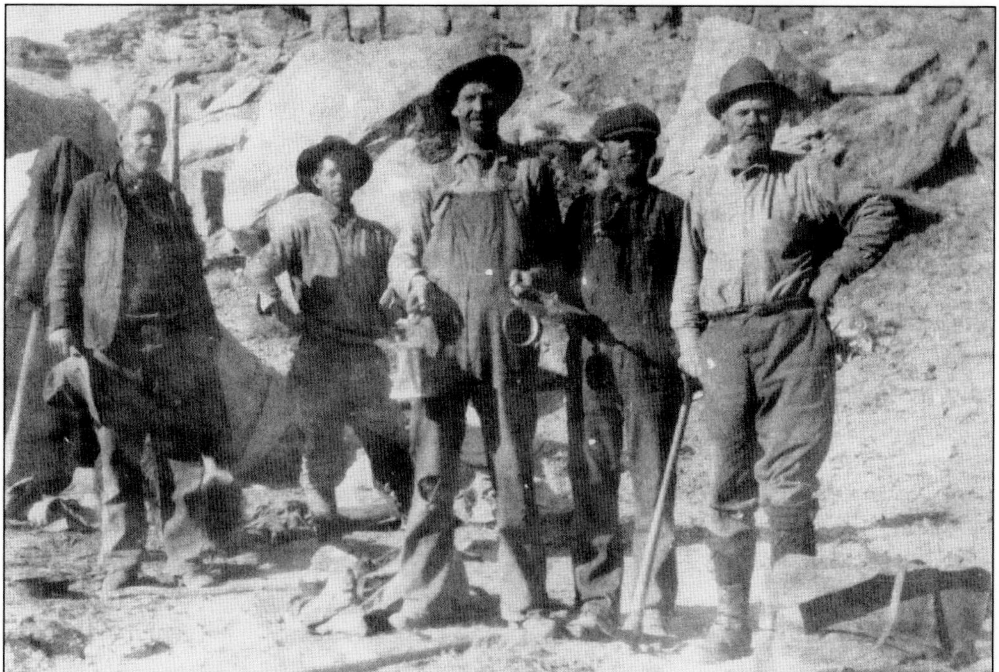

The San Rafael Reef area was mined for vanadium ore. Vanadium is defined as a silvery brittle metal. Vanadium is present in carbon, crude oil, coal, oil shale, and tar sands. In the areas around Green River, there would be many places to find vanadium because of the substances in which it is found.

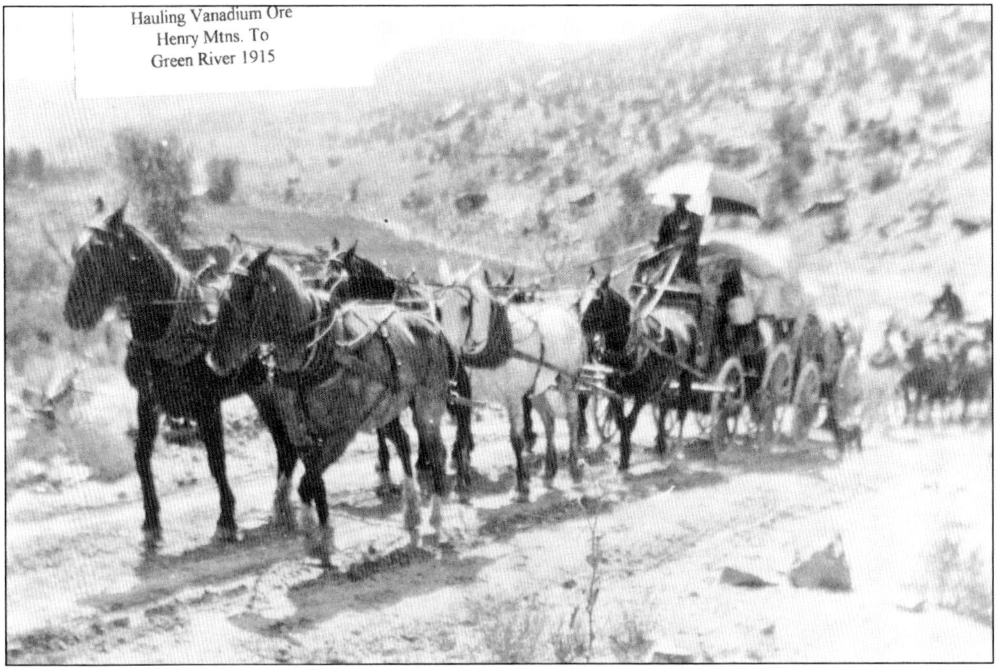

This photograph was taken about 1915. Vanadium to some degree is found in several objects, such as surgical instruments, axles, and crankshafts. It is also used in ceramics and glass manufacturing. This ore is being hauled out of the Henry Mountains to be sent to Green River. None of the men in this photograph are identified.

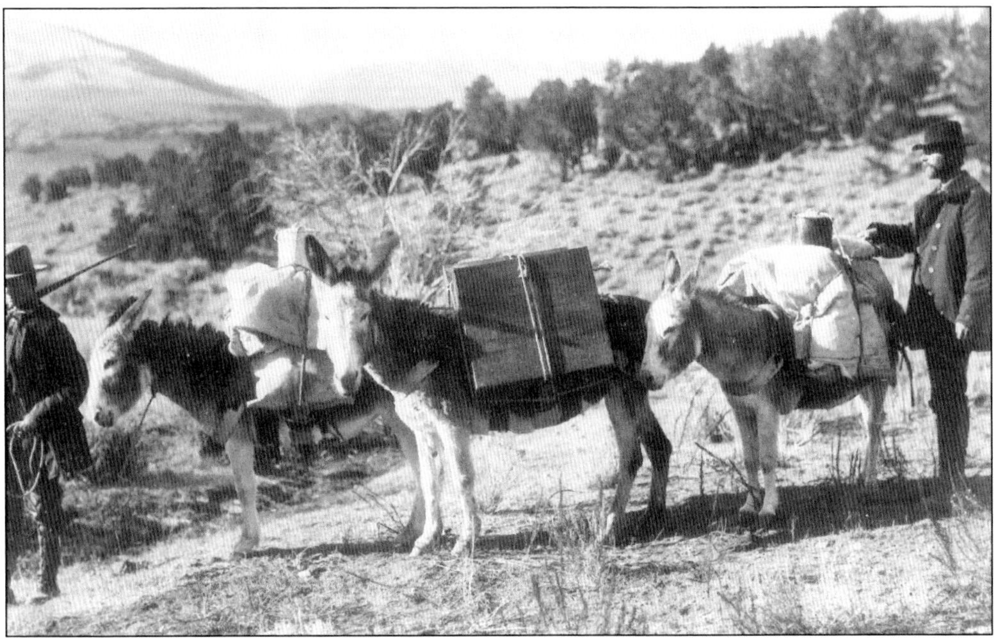

This photograph shows heavily loaded pack burros hauling supplies. Neither of the men are identified. It appears as if they are going to be camping for a day or two. Notice the bundles on the first and third burro that look like bedrolls and also the gun being carried by the man on the far left.

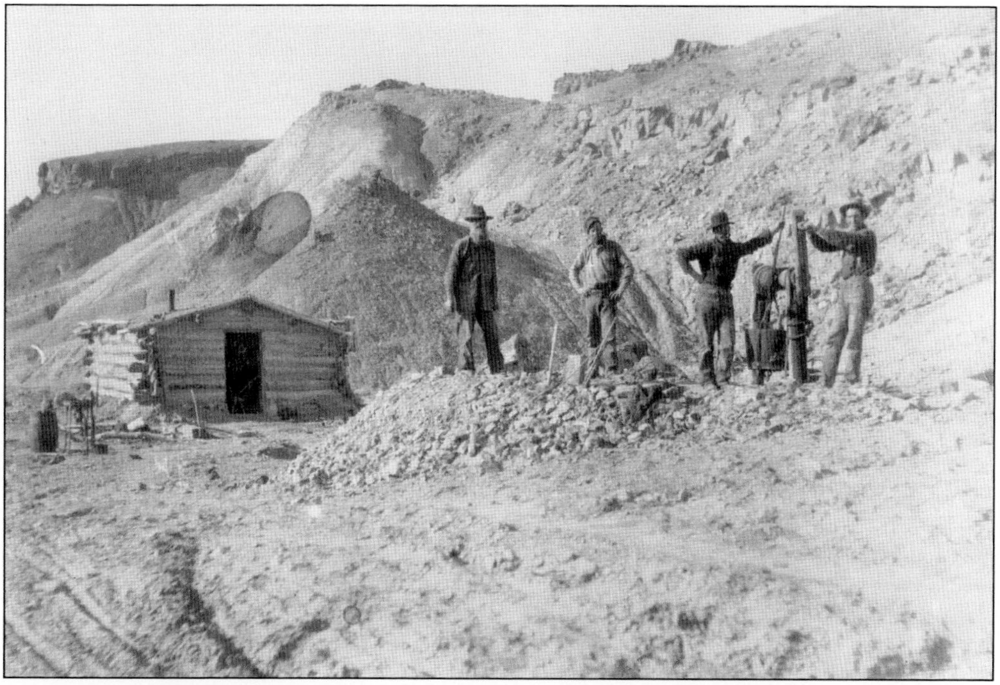

It is unknown whether these unidentified men are camping as they follow cows to bring them to summer range or whether they are mining in the area. The instrument they are leaning on would probably more likely be used in a mining operation.

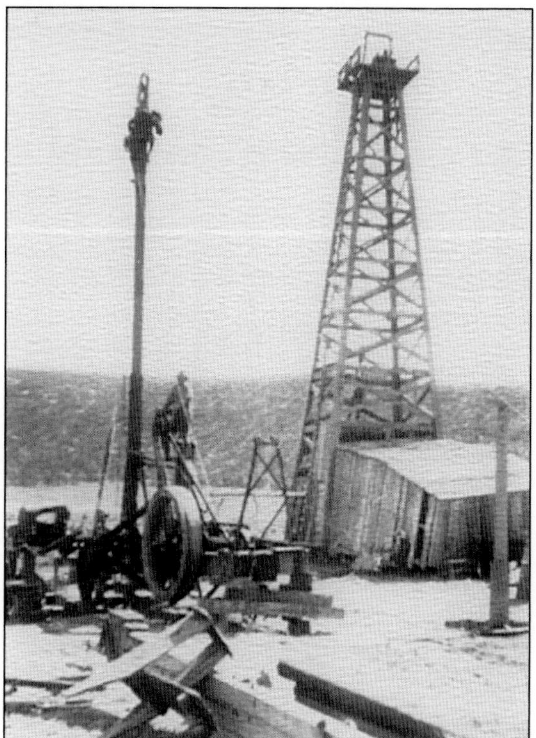

Look closely to see a man up on the pole. The original caption on the photograph says, in part, "looks like a monkey on a stick." None of the men in the photograph are identified. Ironically, what is identified is "Harry"—the name of the oil rig and water well.

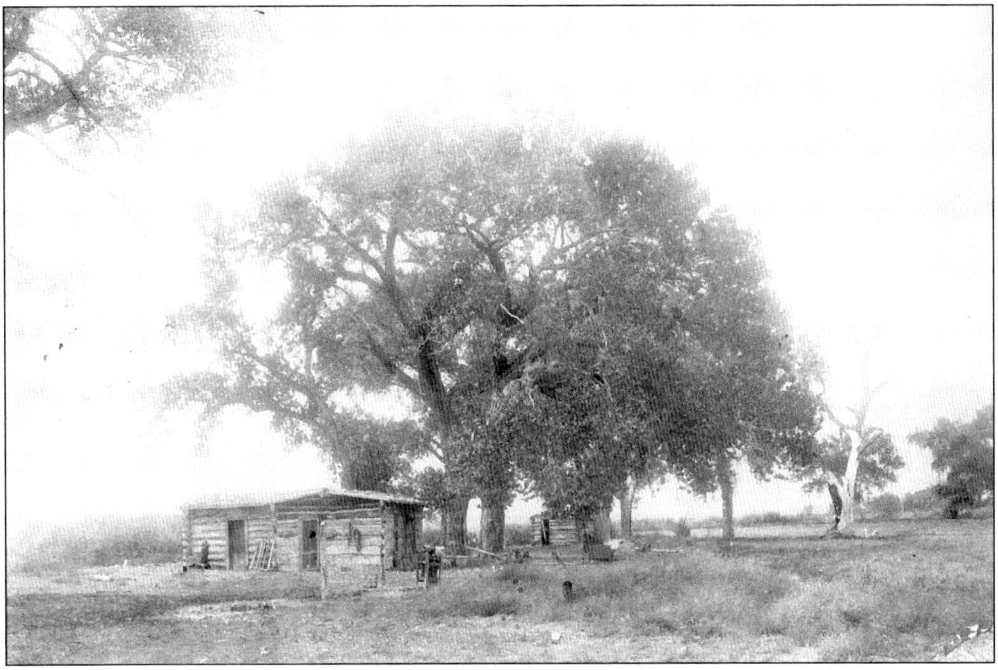

This is the Silliman/Wilson cabin. It is located on the east side of the river, north of the town of Elgin. Elgin is a suburb of Green River. It is still populated, but the population has dwindled over the years. Elgin was first developed as a siding on the Denver and Rio Grande Western Railroad. Its post office was established on March 5, 1898.

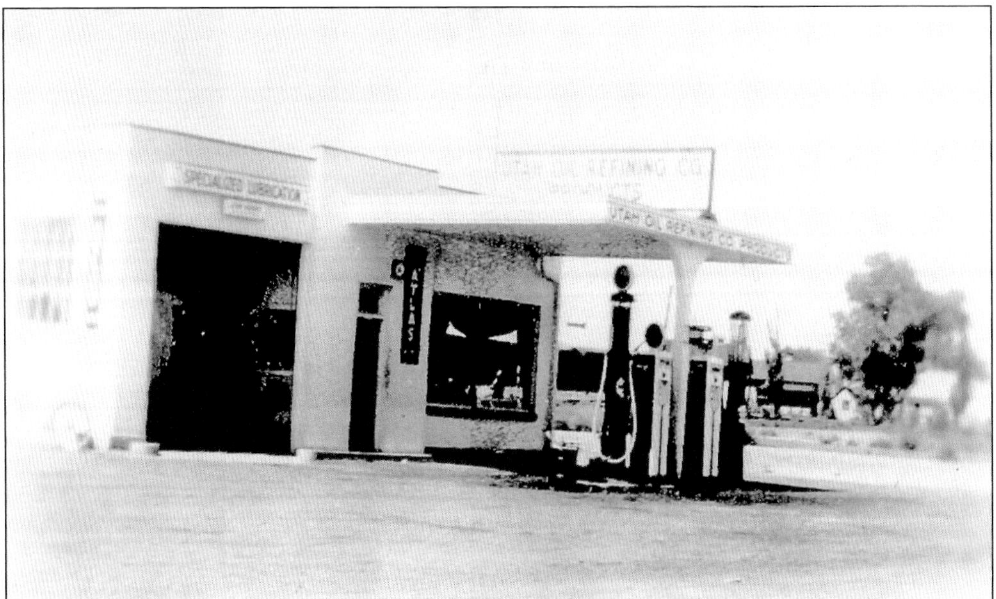

This building has served many purposes. When this photograph was taken, it was a gas station. The black areas on the photograph, on the garage and ground behind the gas pumps, are where the vulcanized tire repair system exploded. The building was demolished in 2007 because it was falling apart.

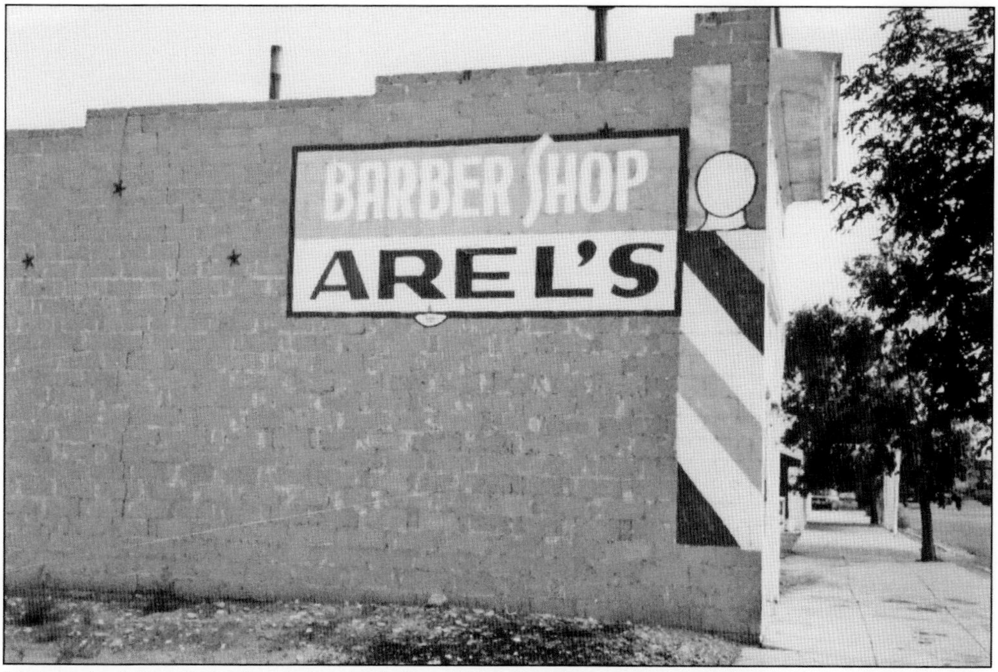

This is Arel Hunt's barbershop. Arel shared this building with his wife, LaRue. LaRue was the operator of LaRue's Beauty Shop. They were located on Broadway Street in Green River. For almost 50 years, Arel was the only consistent barber in town. There were others, but they came and went. Arel lived in Green River until his death in 2002.

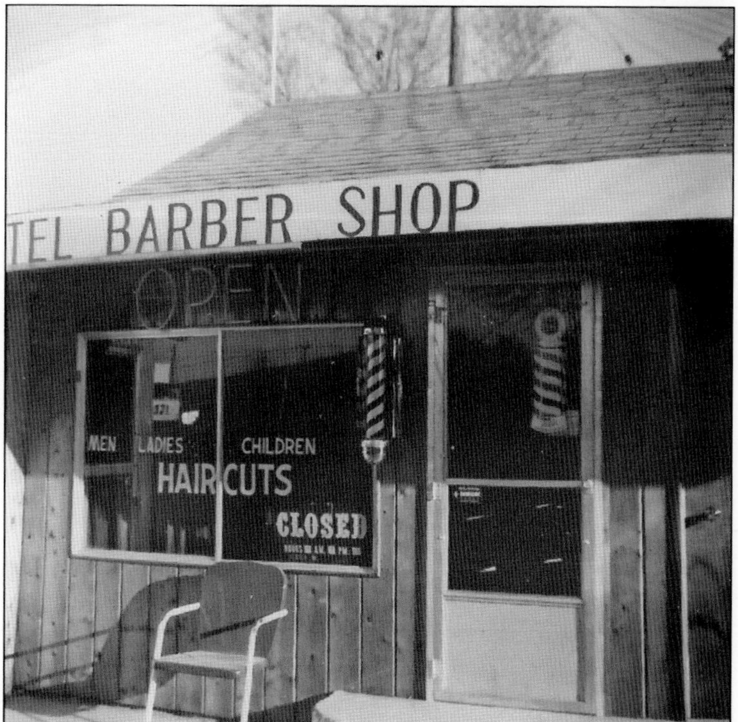

This is a photograph of Stott's Barber Shop, located on Main and Long Streets. It was in a small building in front of the Stott Motel. Max Stott was the barber in his family, and his father, Isaac Stott, was the man who built the Stott Motel. In later years, Max and his wife, Marian, operated the motel.

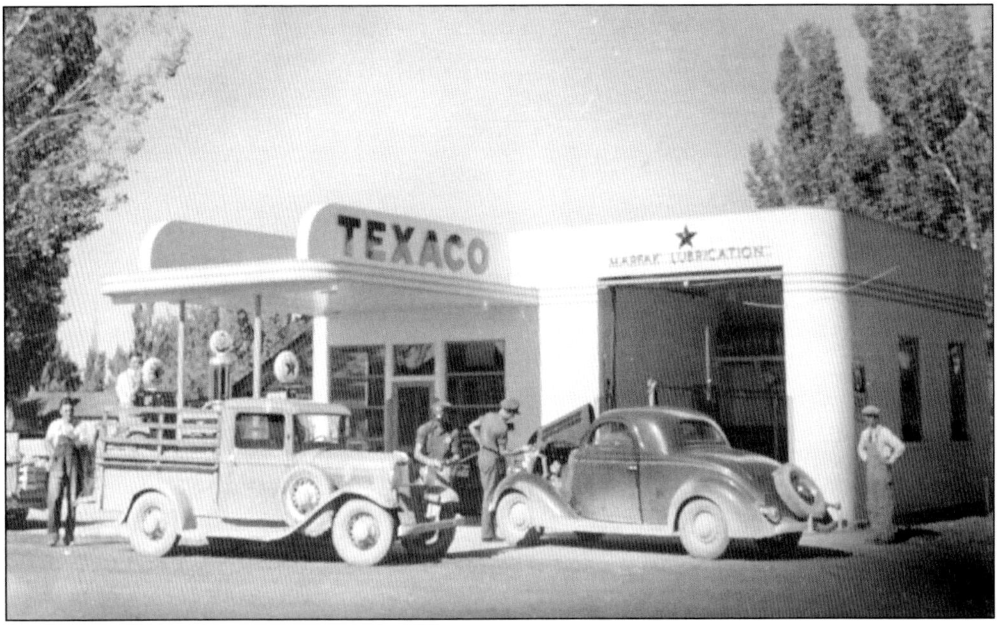

This is Hal Anderson's second station. This station was located on the corner of Farrer and Long Streets. Local residents referred to this intersection as "Thompson's Corner." Anderson's son Gary and his wife, Frankie, are now the operators of the business on Main Street. Gasoline is no longer sold here.

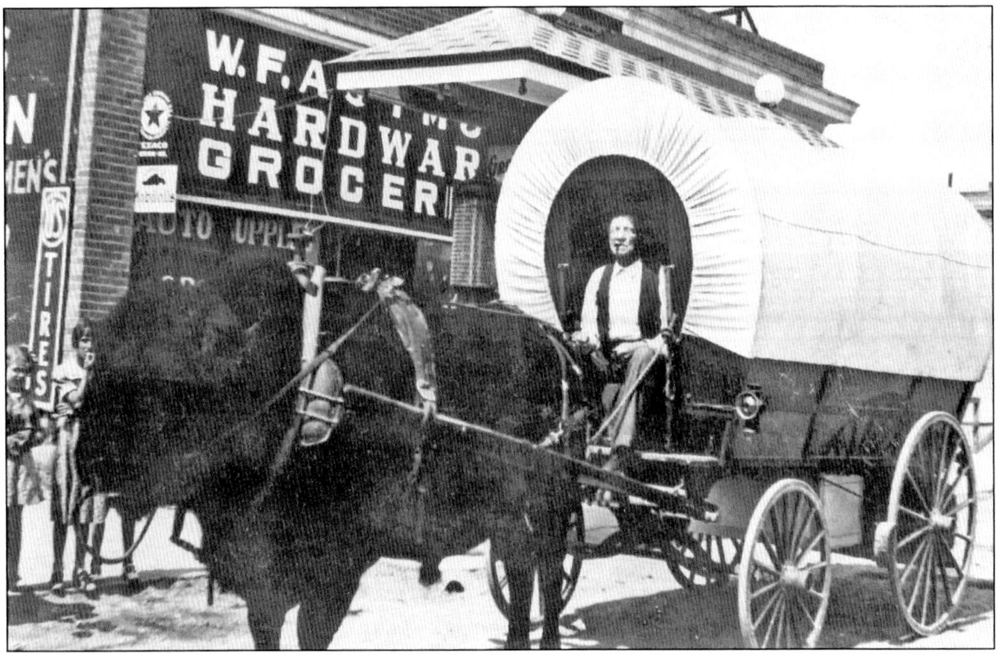

W. F. Asimus Hardware and Grocery was located on Broadway Street. The business existed under this name from 1909 until 1947. This was the second location of the W. F. Asimus Hardware and Grocery store. The original building went up in flames when the opera house burned down. In 1947, Guy Robison and Wayne Smith bought W. F. Asimus Hardware and Grocery and changed the name to Smith and Robison.

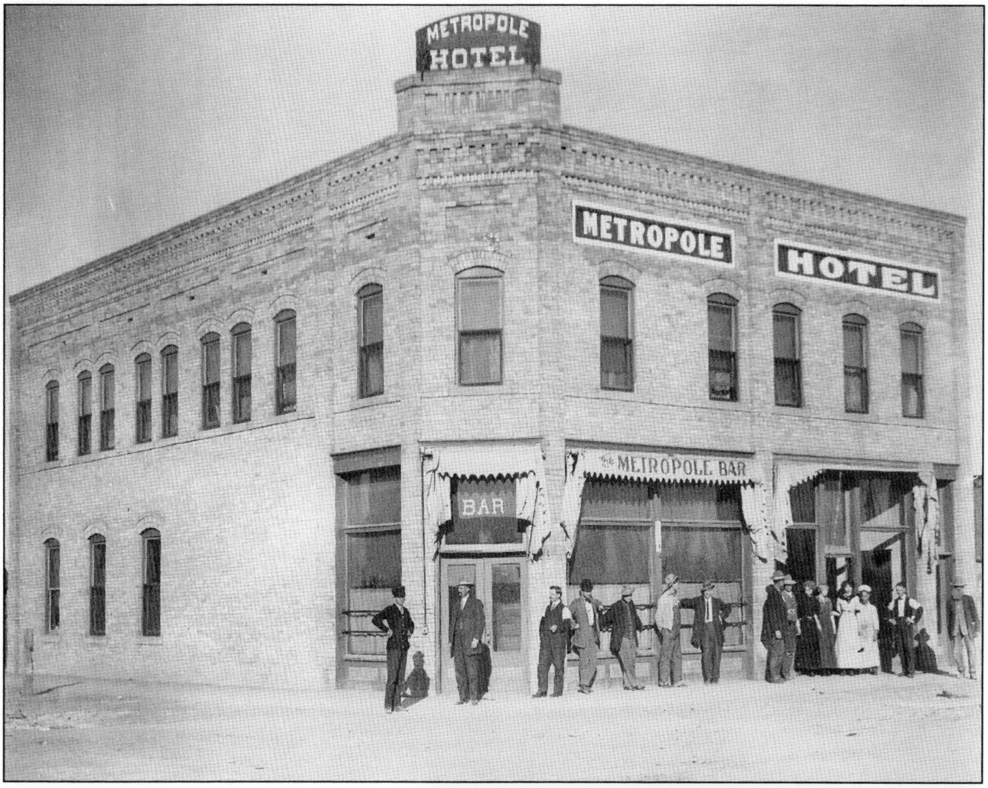

The Metropole Hotel and Bar was built by a partnership of two cousins: Charles Spadafora and Joe Politano. The Metropole was built on what was then called First Avenue. It burned to the ground in 1949. Later they purchased the cement block building on Broadway Street, the former Mariell-Bolinger Hardware; it was established as an amusement hall.

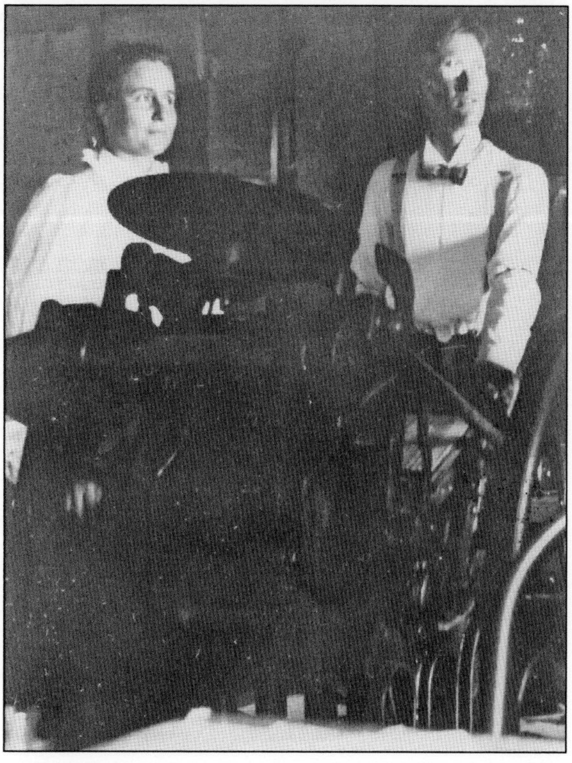

B. F. "Frank" Miller was the founder and publisher of the *Green River Dispatch*, Green River's second newspaper. The first newspaper was the *Green River Star*, which only had one issue. Another newspaper was the *Journal*, which ran for several years. The location of the newspaper shop was an old school, once the first Latter-day Saint chapel in Green River and now the old Senior Citizens Center.

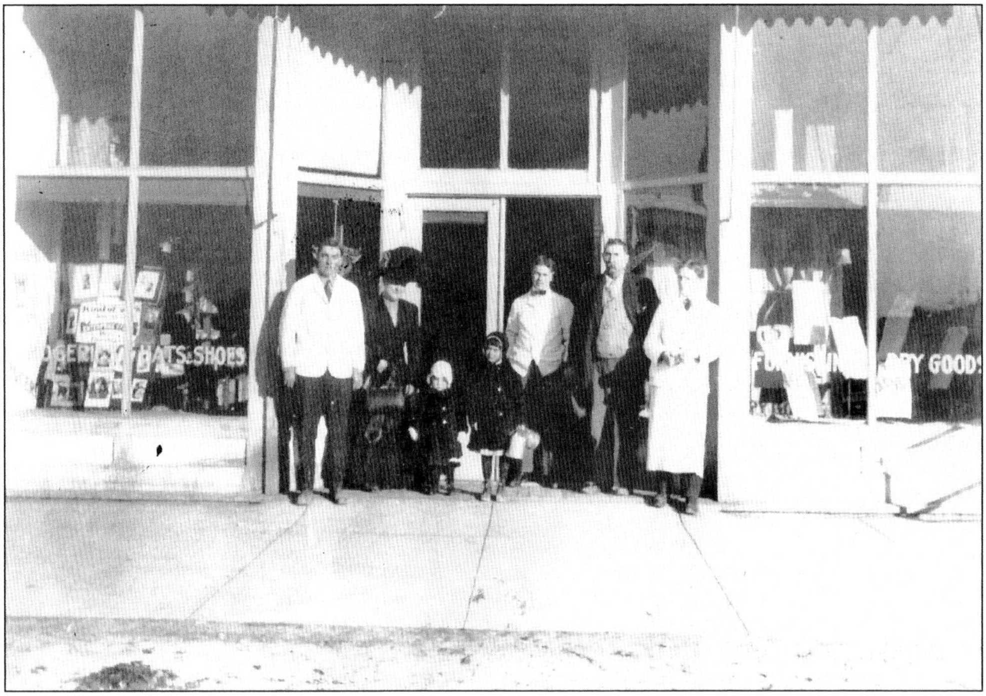

Price and Sons Store, a dry-goods business, operated from 1907 until 1911, when it burned down on June 11th. There are only two individuals identified in this photograph: Walter Price, the son referred to in the title of the store is on the far right. Ray Diehl, a nephew, is wearing the white coat and standing in the doorway.

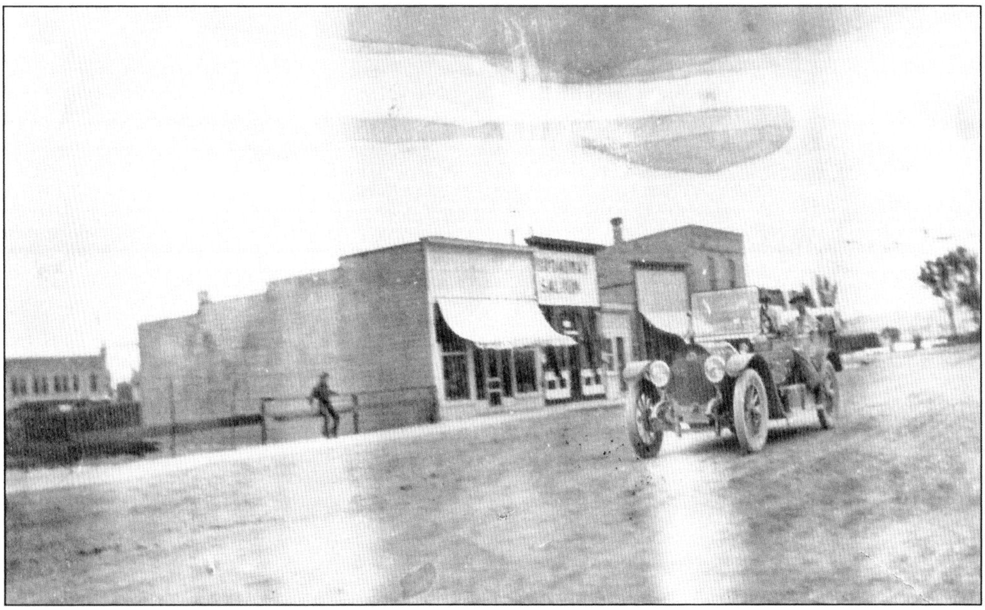

This photograph was taken in Green River of Hoosier Day in 1910. Hoosier Day was a caravan of Indiana-built cars. There were about 25 cars here that day. The manufacturers were on their way to San Francisco, California. The participants called the route to California "the Golden Trail."

Six

LEARNING, SPIRITUAL AND ACADEMIC

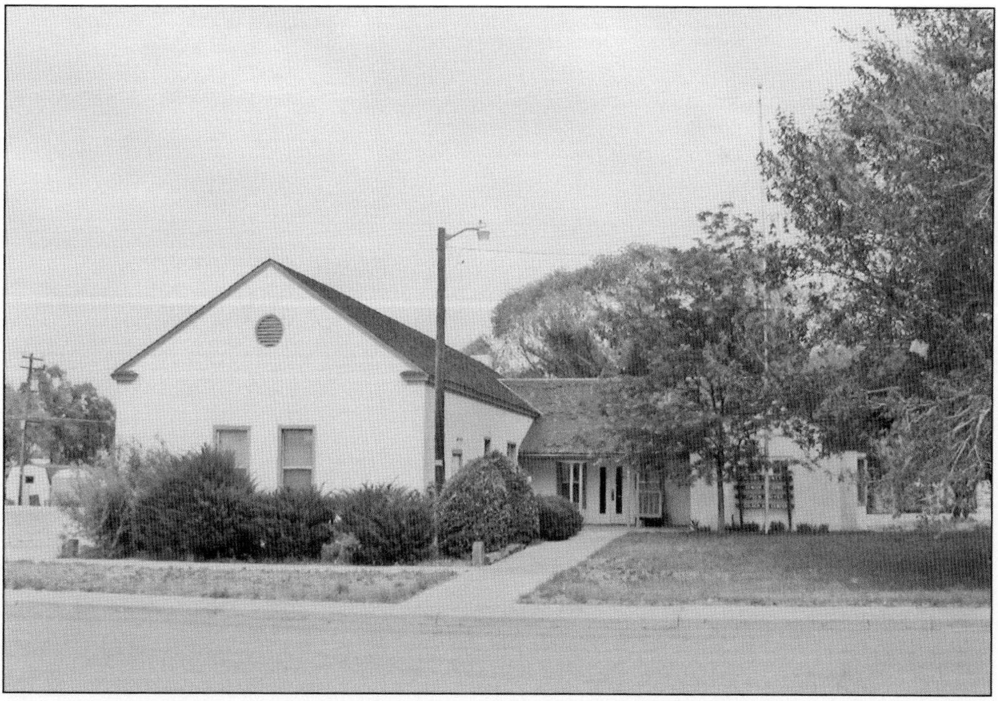

This is the current Senior Citizens Center as of the summer of 2008. There is another one being built in Green River today. This building housed many businesses and functions over the years. It was first a school, then a newspaper printing shop, the first chapel for the Latter-day Saints (LDS) church, and the meeting place of American Legion Post No. 103. Members of the Baptist faith later met here, and finally, it became the Senior Citizens Center.

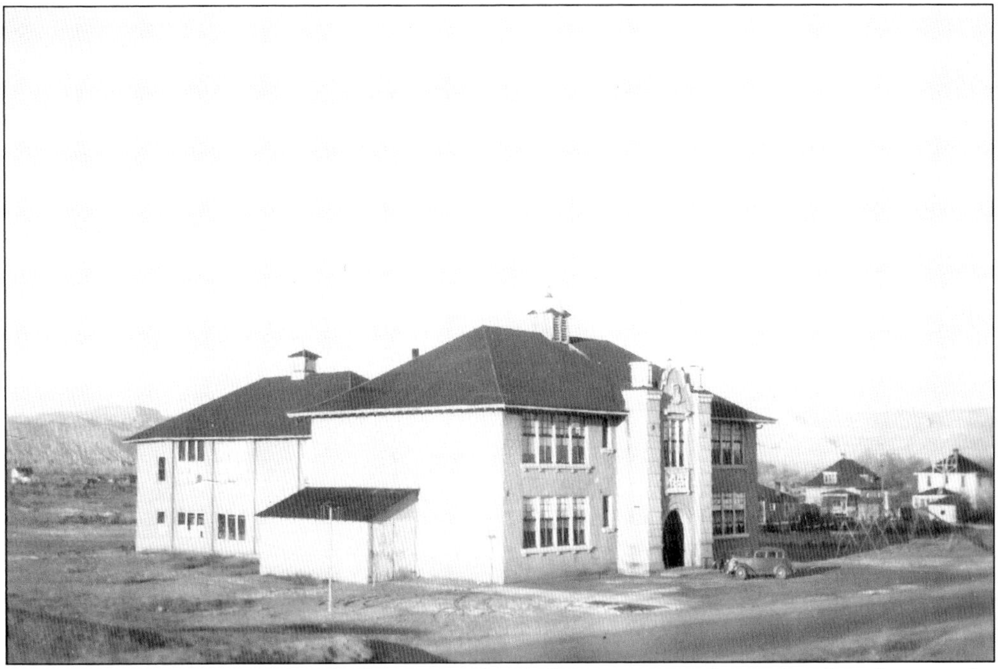

This school was demolished in the late 1960s, but before it was torn down, the class that was the last to use it gave it a wild send-off party. One of the graduating class members said, "There were more people there than had actually graduated that year."

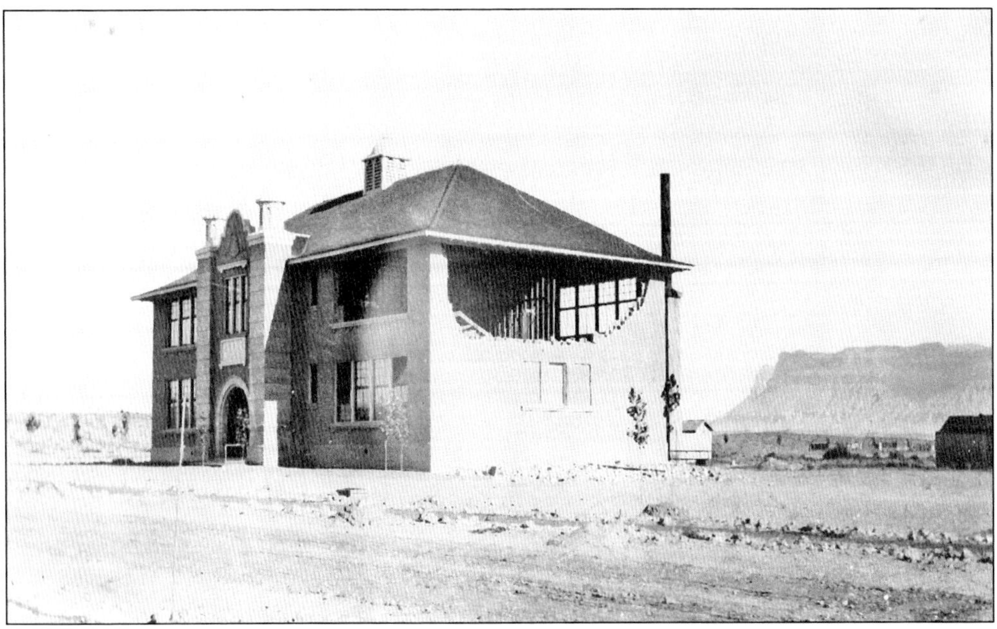

"A Little Desert Wind Dismissed School" reads the original caption of this photograph of the Green River School. Notice that part of the outside east wall is now missing several rows of bricks. In 1955, the new high school was built. This building was used for the Hometown Industries business before it collapsed on the Mancos shale it was built on.

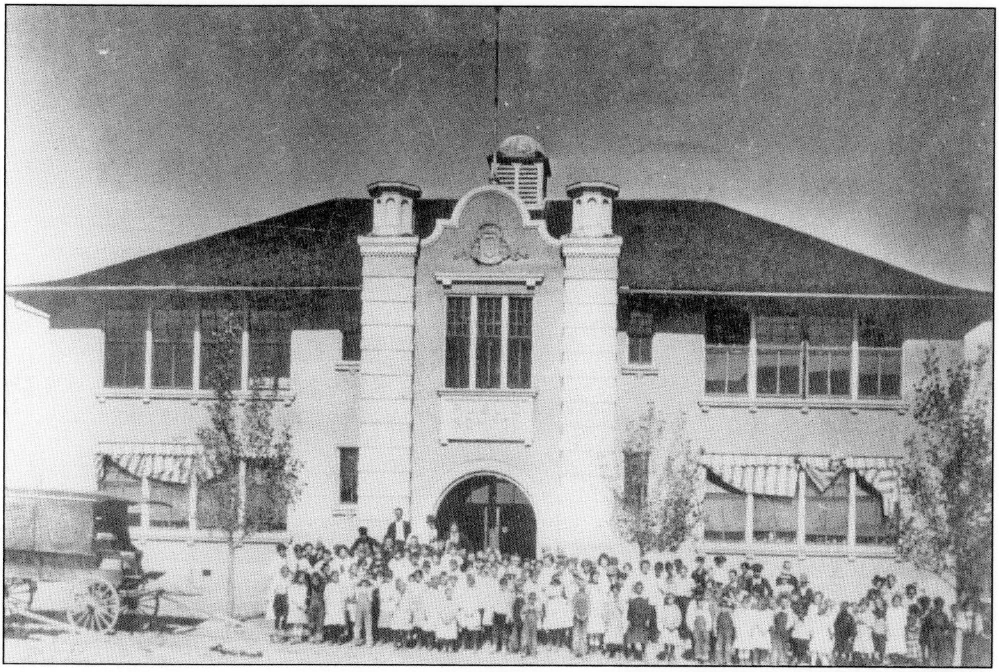

This is a photograph of the Green River High School in 1918. Notice the wagon out in front of the school. It is the school bus, which was used to pick up the students who lived farther away from town. It does not look like there was much room for the students in the bus. It appears to be full of boxes.

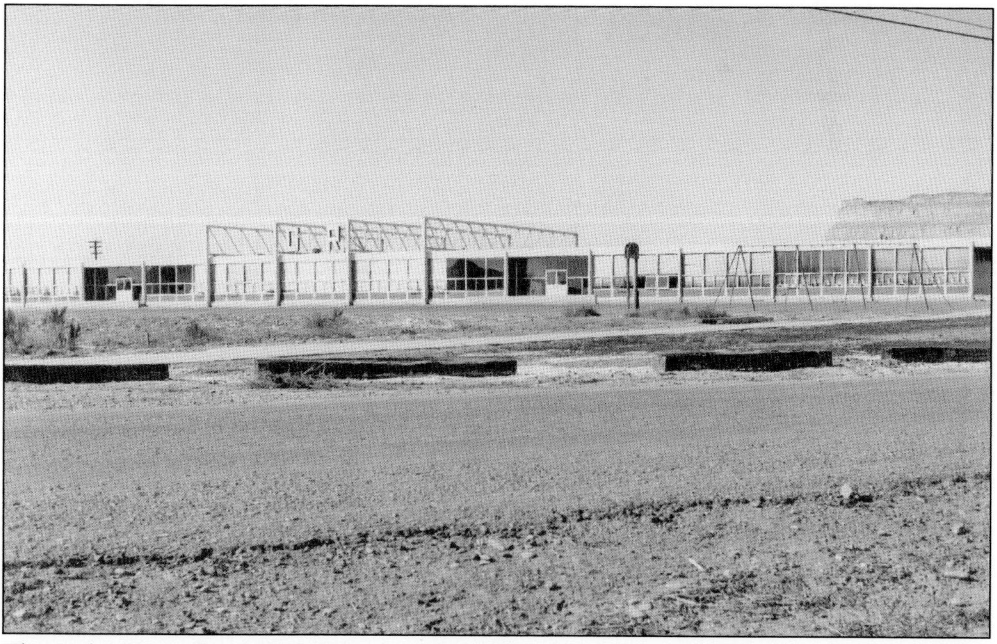

This is the Green River High School in 1955. This school was approximately where the county road shed is today. The gym of this school was underground and was built on Mancos shale. In later years, because of the Mancos shale, the floor became uneven. If a ball was set on the east end of the gymnasium floor, it would quickly roll itself to the west end of the floor.

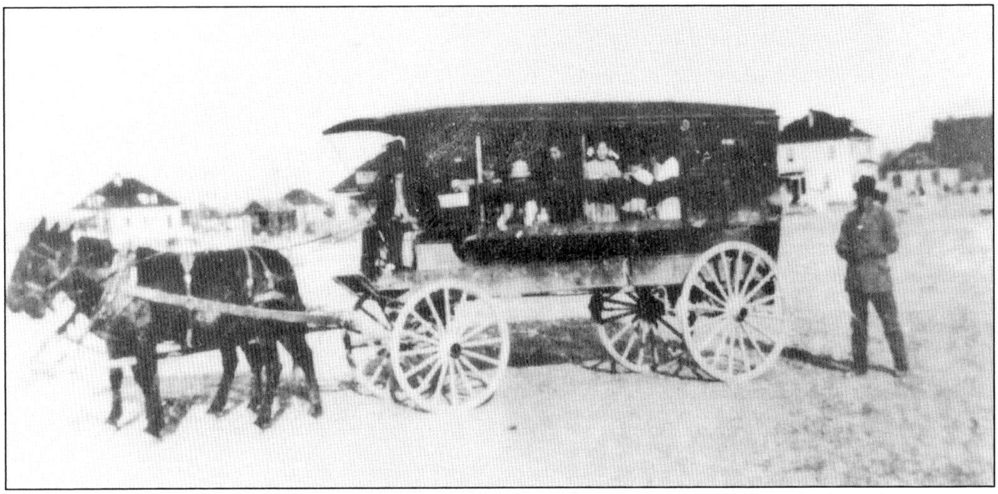

This is a 1911 photograph of one of the earliest school buses. Among the several students is one young girl in pigtails. The bus driver is standing outside of the school bus. This bus does not look like it could transport more than 20 students at a time.

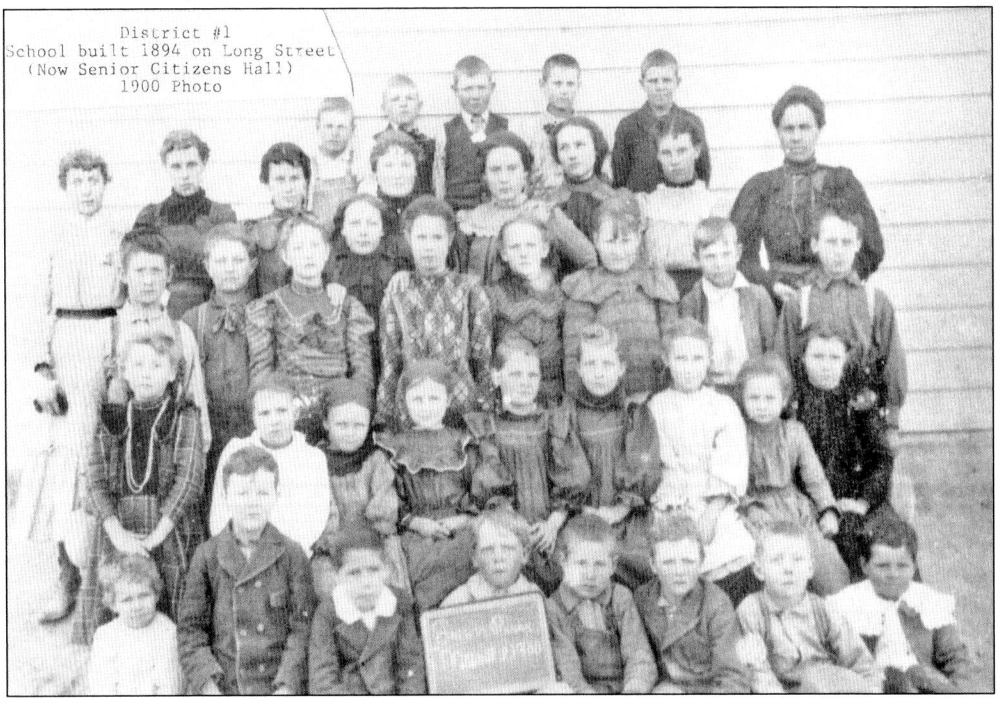

This photograph was taken in 1900 at the school located where the current Senior Citizens Center is. From left to right are (first row) Vern Henry, Melvin Henry, Malcolm Politano Sr., Huston Brown, Will Farrer, Clyde Farrer, Charley Farrer, and Clarence Farrer; (second row) Ruth Farrer, Lula Johnson, Jennie Fulmer, Mary Fulmer, Alline Brown, Zina Brown, Iva Stanton, Eva Farrer, and ? Hancock; (third row) Vern Hancock, Clyde Fulmer, Minnie Farrer, Vida Fulmer, Myra Hancock, Mary Simpson, Alberta Farrer, Earl Dahling, and Calud Thompson; (fourth row) Lillie Dahling, Ida Johnson, Agnes Thompson, Rosie Farrer, Sadie Hancock, Julia Fulmer, Mabel Henry, and Luella Curtis (teacher); (fifth row) Bill Dahling, Ernie Farrer, Albert Farrer, Bill Hancock, and Ollie Johnson.

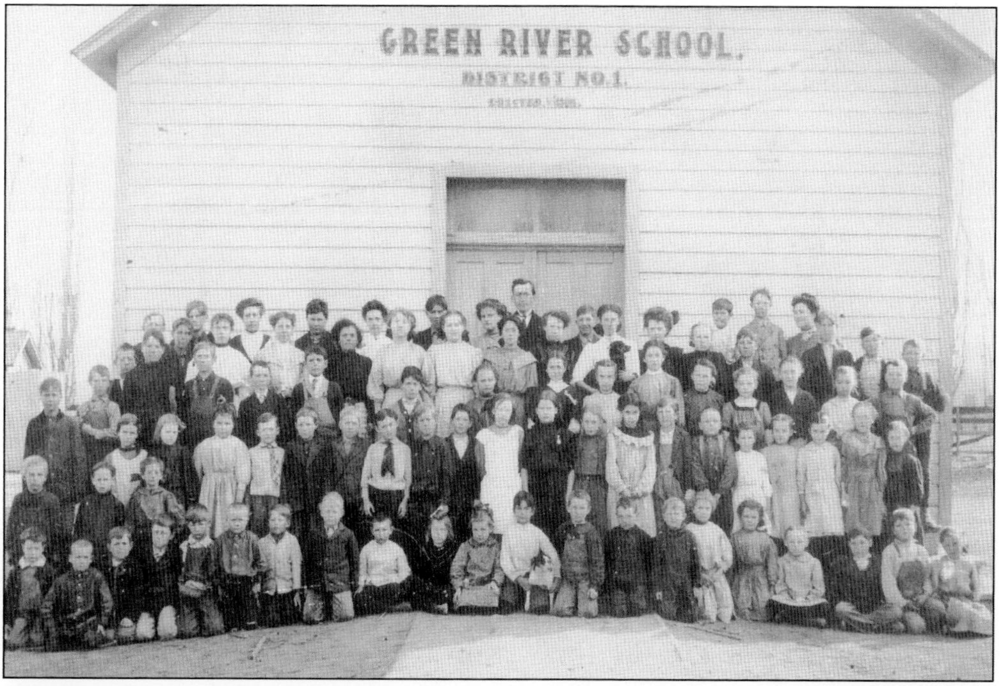

The Green River School is pictured in 1907. These students came to school in what today would be considered their best clothes. All of the girls are wearing dresses, and there are ties on many of the boys.

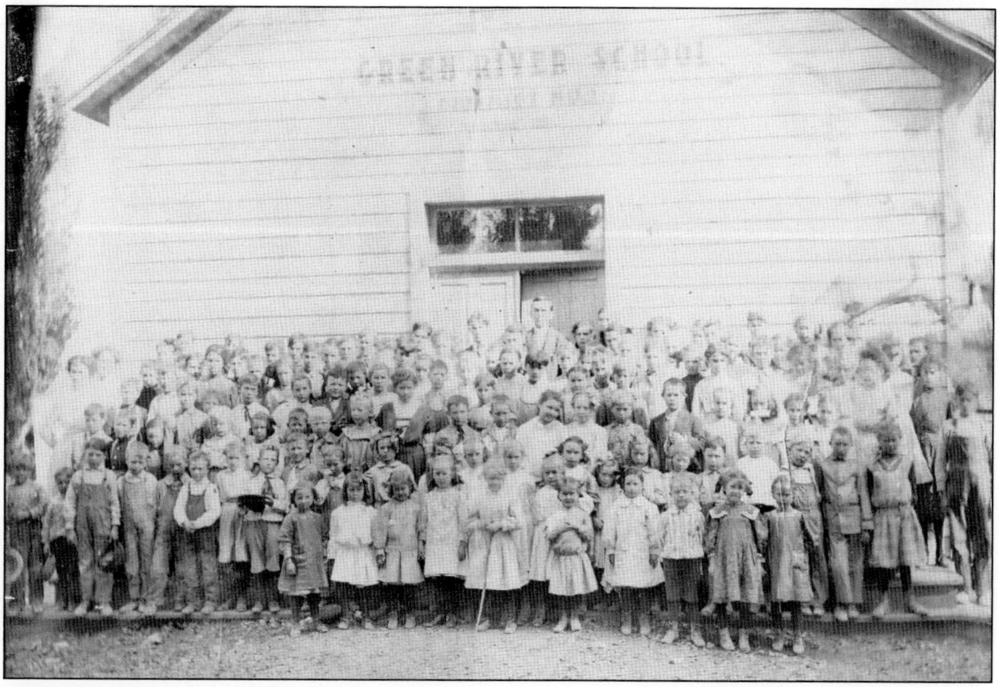

This is a photograph of the Green River School taken in 1900. Only two of the students are identified in the photograph: Melvin and Ed Cotrell. They are both in the first row on the left side of the photograph.

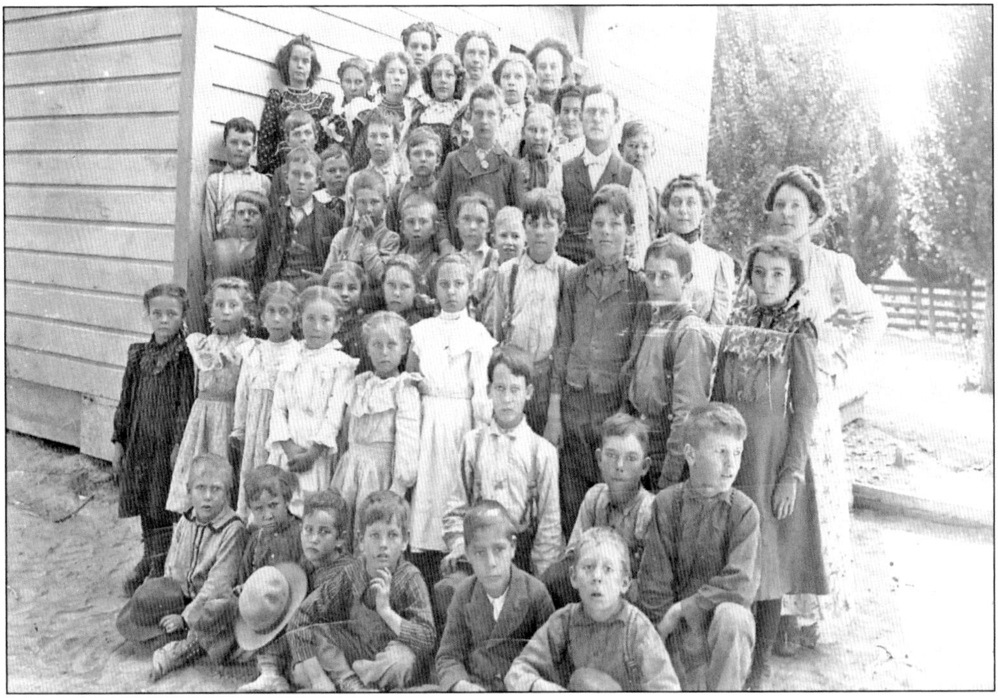

This is a school photograph from the original school on Long Street. There are two adults shown. One is probably the teacher; the school principal is likely the man featured here. Some of the older students look as if they are the same age as the teacher.

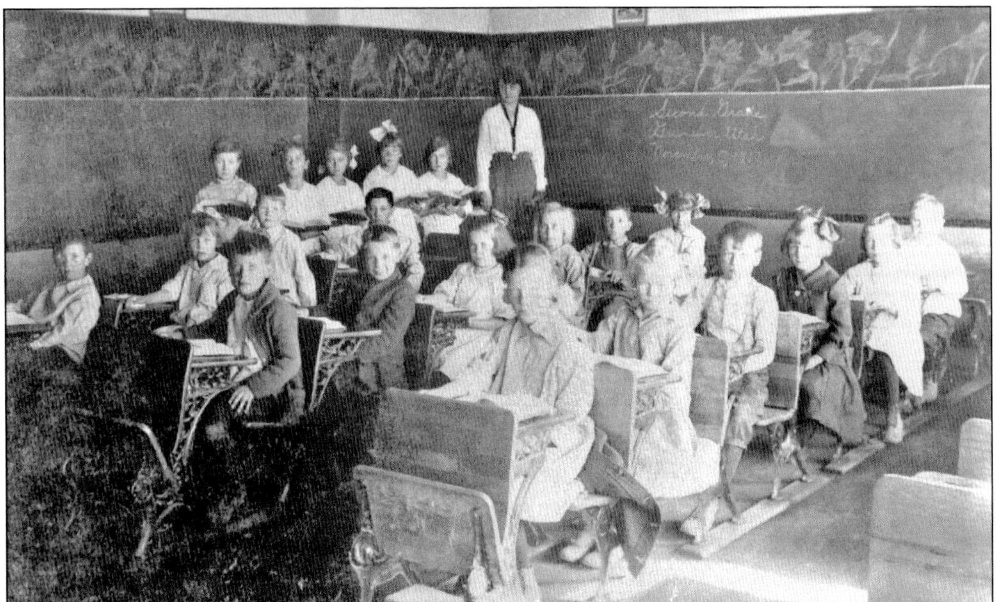

This photograph is of the second grade in 1917. This is one of the few photographs with an exact date. It was taken on November 5, 1917. Not many of the identities of the individuals are known. Those available are Raymond Thurman (first row, far left) and Zeta Louise Thurman (second row, second from left).

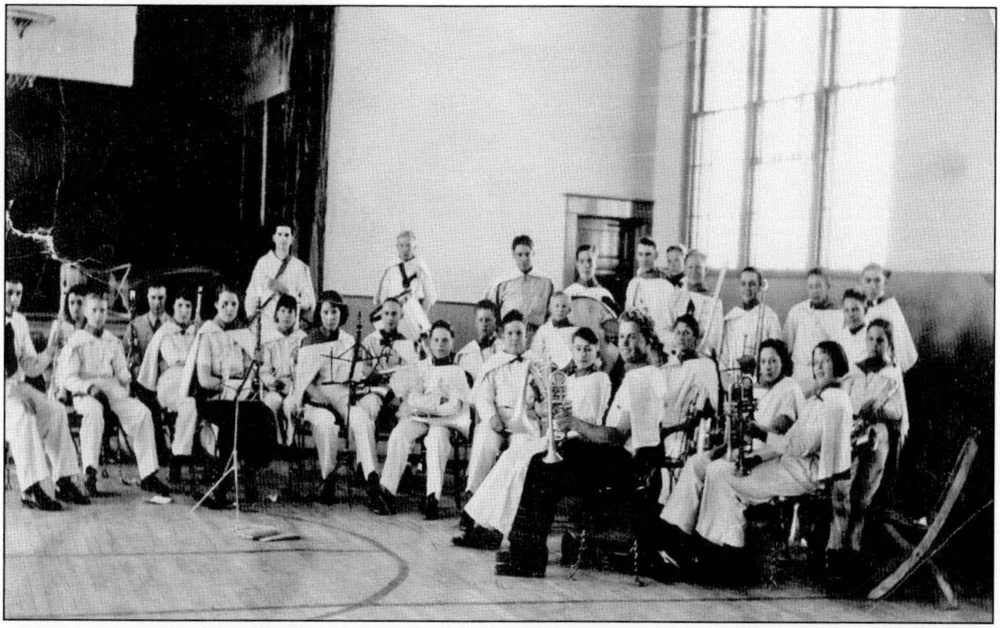

This is a photograph of the Green River School band taken around the 1920s. It is unknown why the children wore these particular uniforms, maybe to protect their clothes from getting dirty, or maybe this uniform is just simply to help the children feel unified. Another possibility is that this was the style at the time.

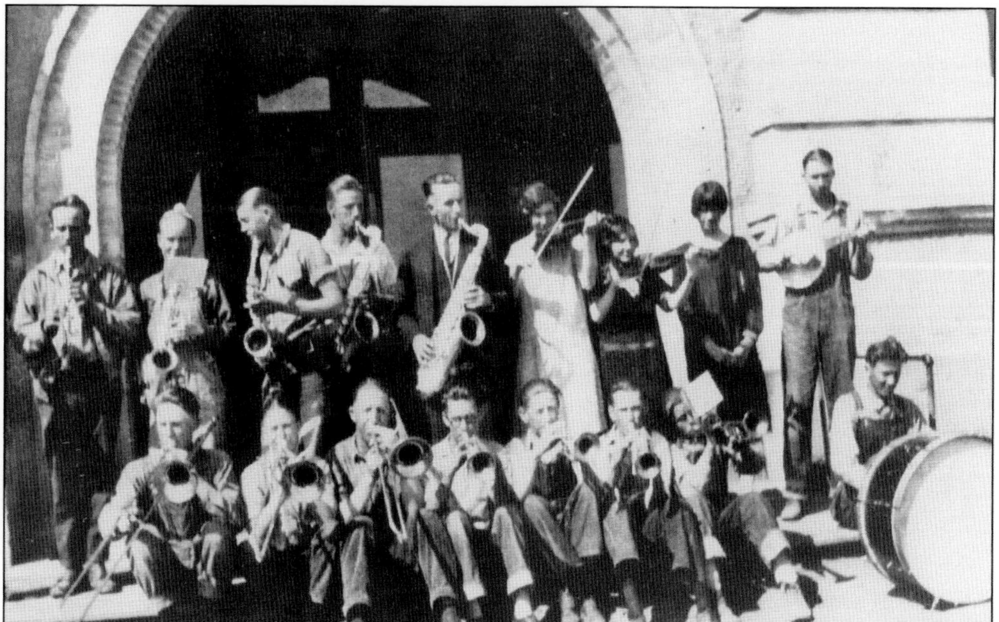

This is the Green River School band in 1926. Among those pictured are (first row) Claude Beebe, Phillip Dufford, Gordon Adams, Lewis Green, Harold Anderson, George Green, Francis Wilson, and Morris Tasker; (second row) Sinclair Gillies, Julius Thurman, Orville Swanson, Bill McClurg, Ray Thurman, Orville Christenson, Principal, Helen Beebe, Alwilda Adams, Zelpha McPherson, and Charles ("Babe") Tasker.

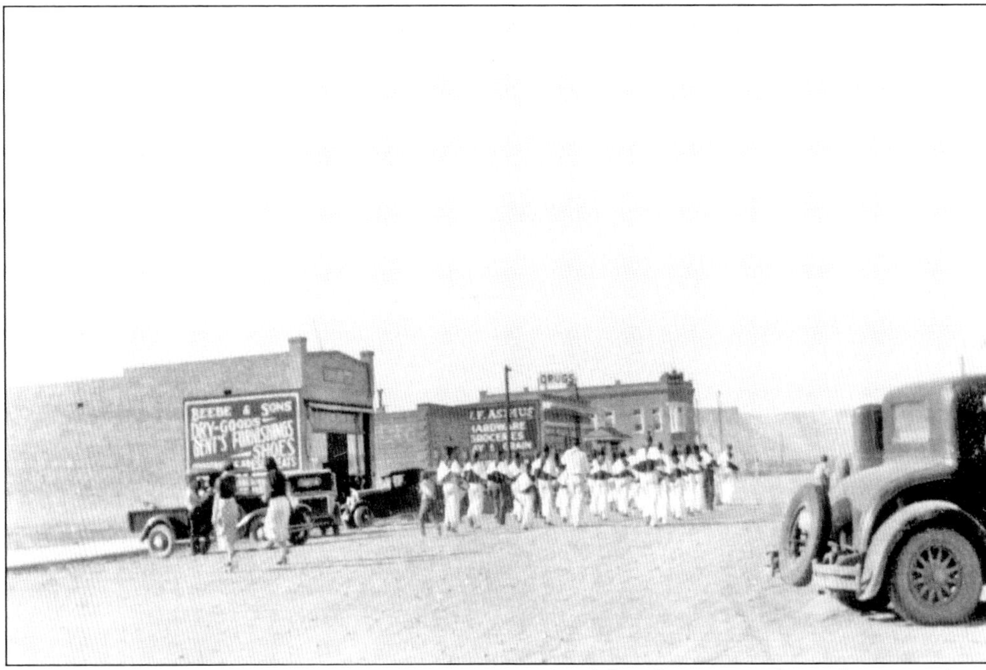

This is an early photograph of the Green River school band in a parade walking north up Broadway Street. At the center right of the photograph is the bank building. The bank building still stands to this day but is now empty. Before it closed, it had several different businesses operate inside it.

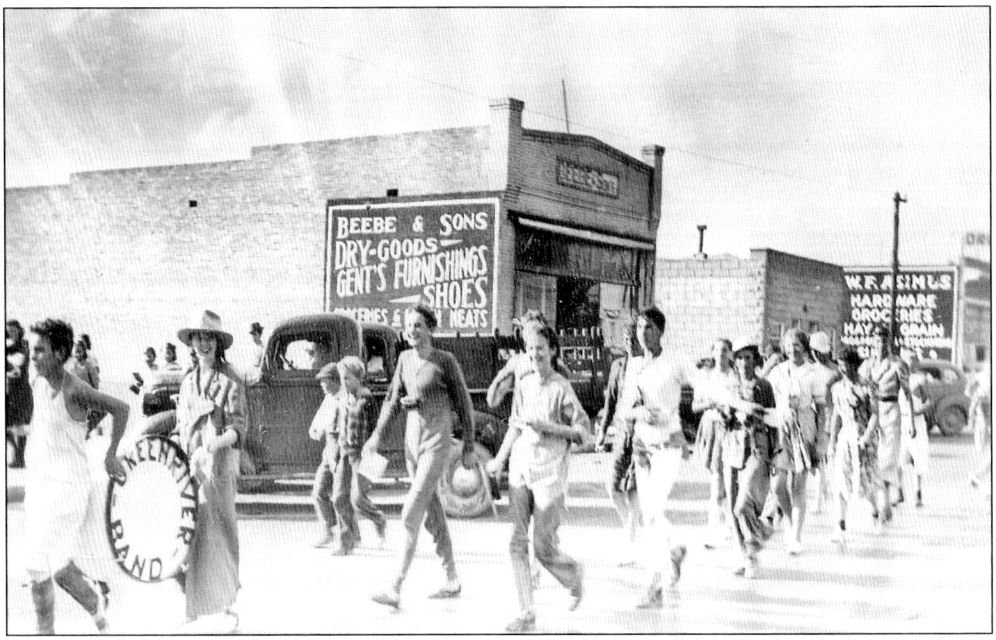

This is a photograph of a freshmen initiation. This parade gave the upperclassmen a chance to see who was available to be picked on during the upcoming school year. The freshmen are walking south down Broadway Street. The Beebe and Sons store and the W. F. Asimus store are visible in this photograph.

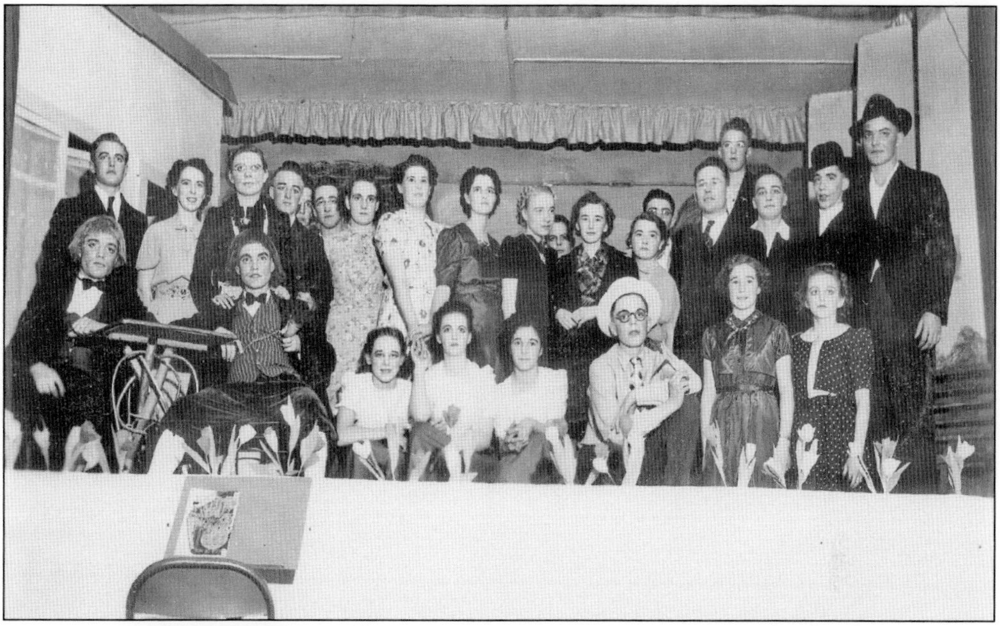

At one time in the Green River High School experience, operettas were held. This is a photograph of some of the participants in one year's performance. The performers are heavily made up to get ready for the glare of the lights on stage. This year, the operetta was held in March.

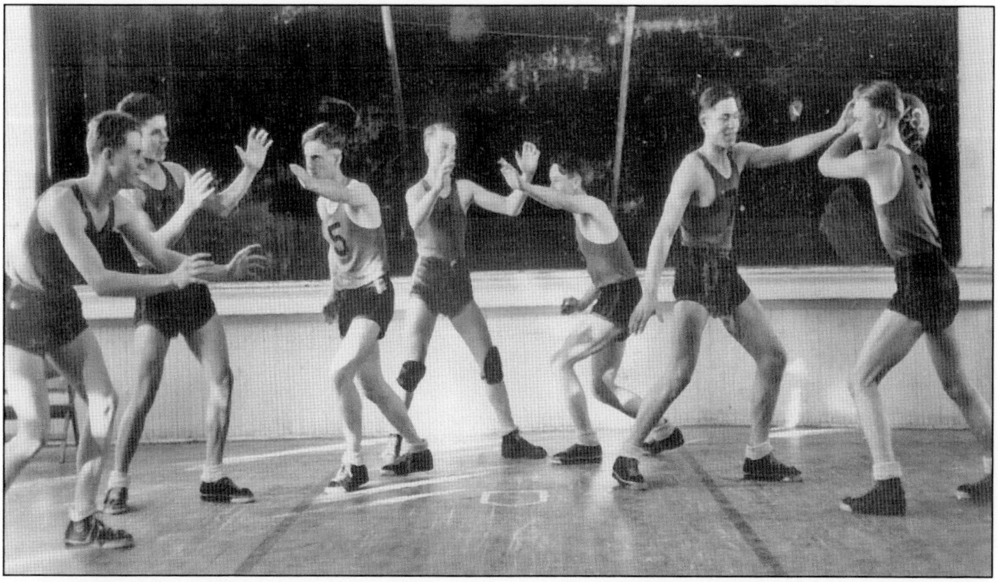

The caption for this photograph originally read "Basketball Practice," but it looks more like boxing or sparring practice. Only the uniforms being worn indicate that it is actually basketball practice.

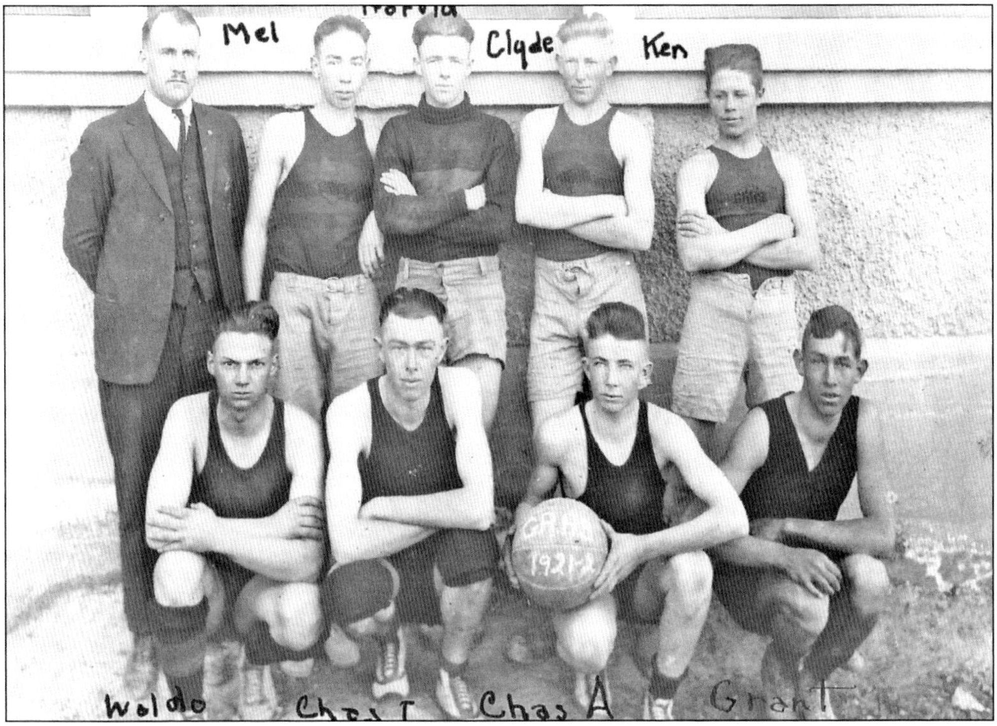

Here is Green River's basketball team in 1921. The coach is unidentified. The rest of the players are identified only by first name: from left to right are (first row) Waldo, Chas J., Chas A., and Grant; (second row) coach, Mel, Harold, Clyde, and Ken.

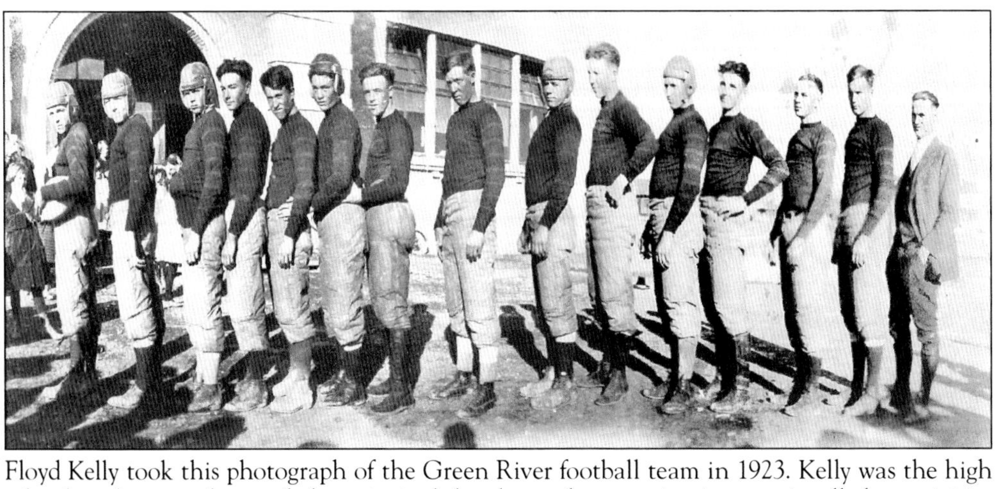

Floyd Kelly took this photograph of the Green River football team in 1923. Kelly was the high school geology teacher and the principal, but he took an active interest in all the activities happening at the Green River High School. Probably some if not all of these football players were in his geology classes.

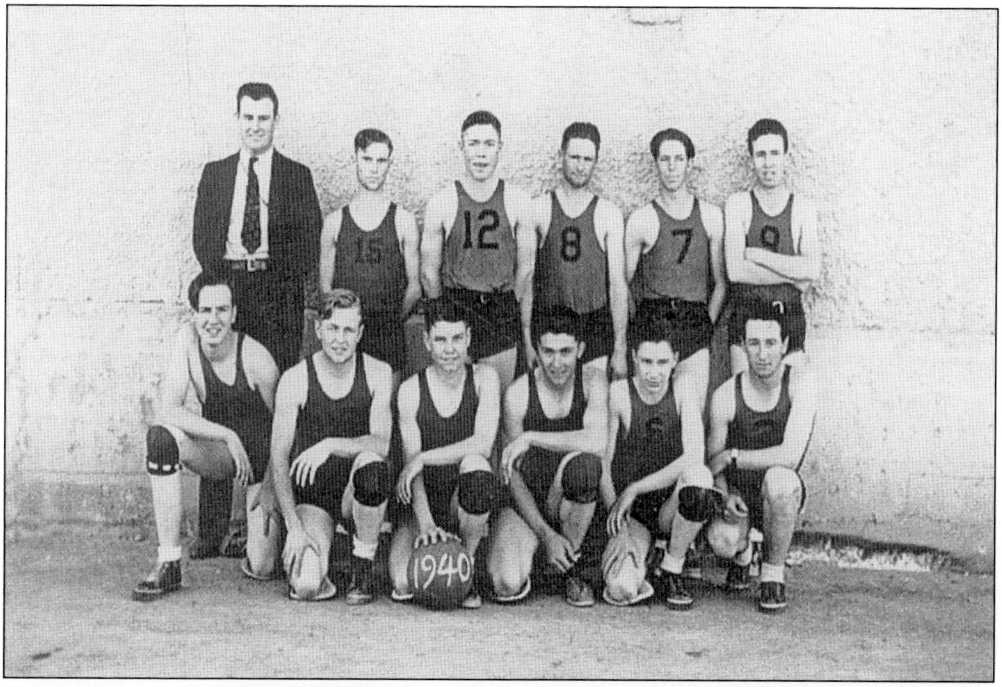

Pictured here is the 1940 basketball team. Vail Hatt is the team member holding the basketball. Louis Vetere is in the first row, fourth from left. Clell Duncan is also likely pictured here.

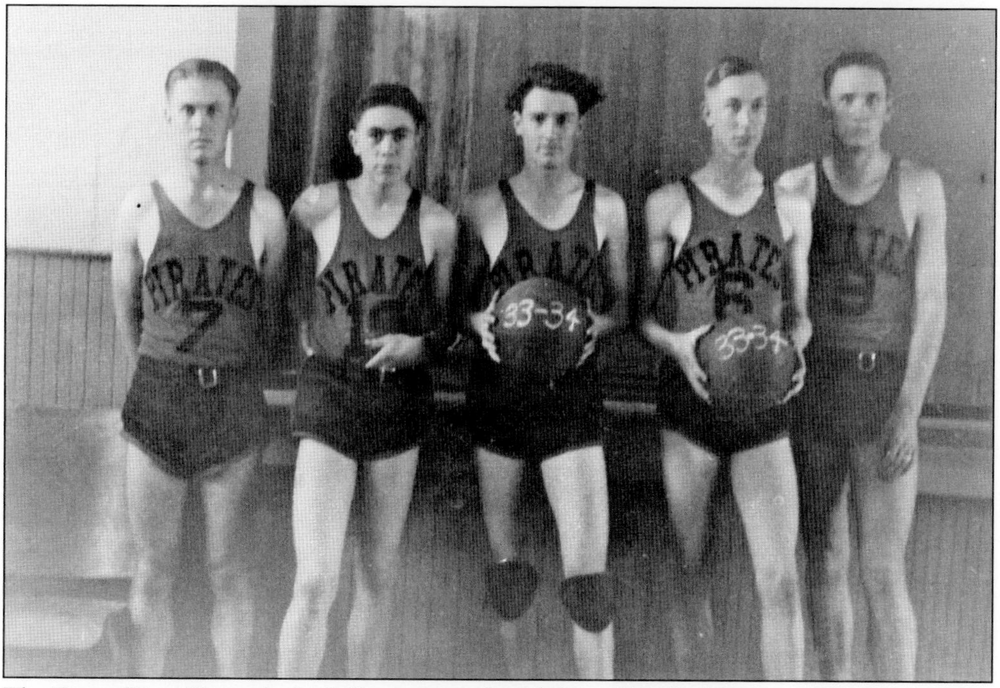

The Green River Pirates basketball team was, from left to right, Fred Hinson, John Bigelow, Lee Smith, Jordan Jorgenson, and Lauren Beebe. They played during the 1933–1934 school year. Some of the boys photographed have relatives who still live in Green River today. Other names are no longer in the Green River telephone book.

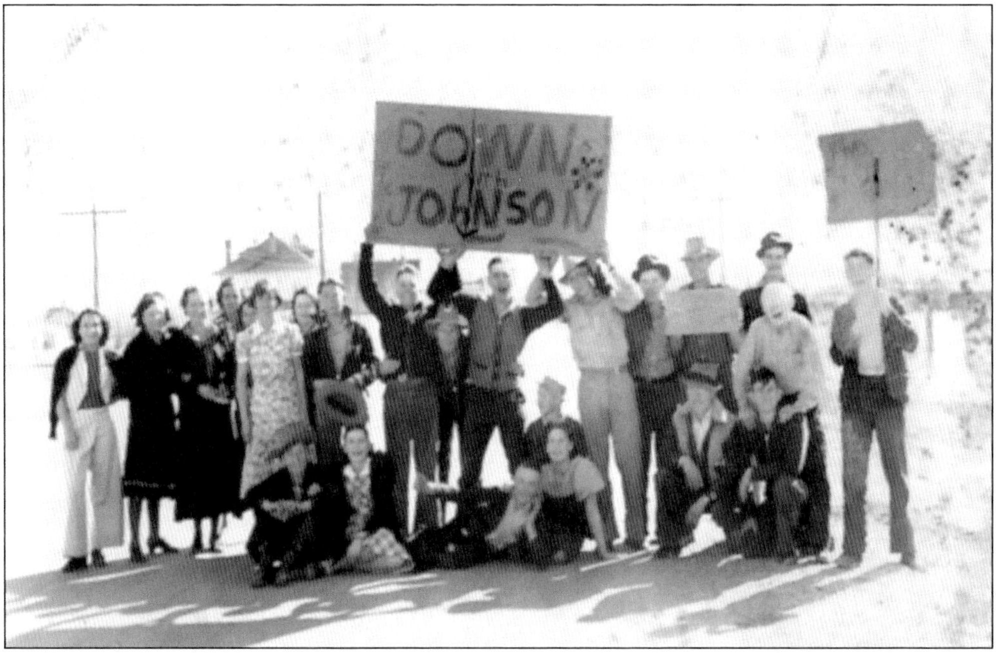

In 1938, several Green River students became angry with a teacher and held a protest. What caused the students' anger is unknown, but a "Down with Johnson" sign is visible. The teacher kept his job, and the students, after making their feelings known, returned to class for the rest of the year.

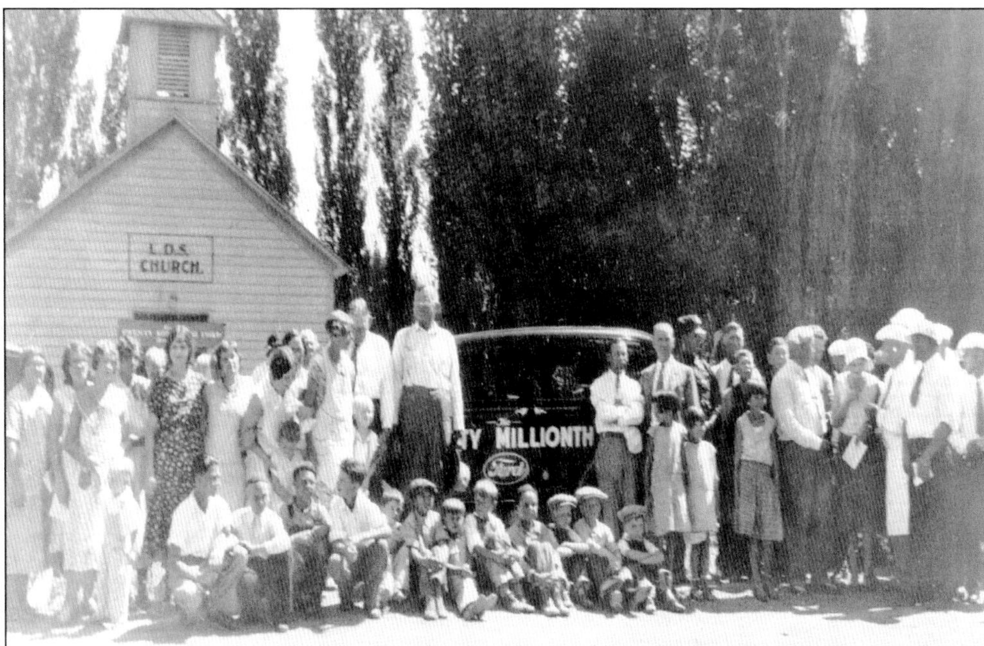

In an effort to boost sales and advertise Ford automobiles, a gathering of Green River residents met at the LDS Church when the 20-millionth car made by Ford passed through Green River, Utah. This photograph was taken on the grounds of the LDS Church in 1932.

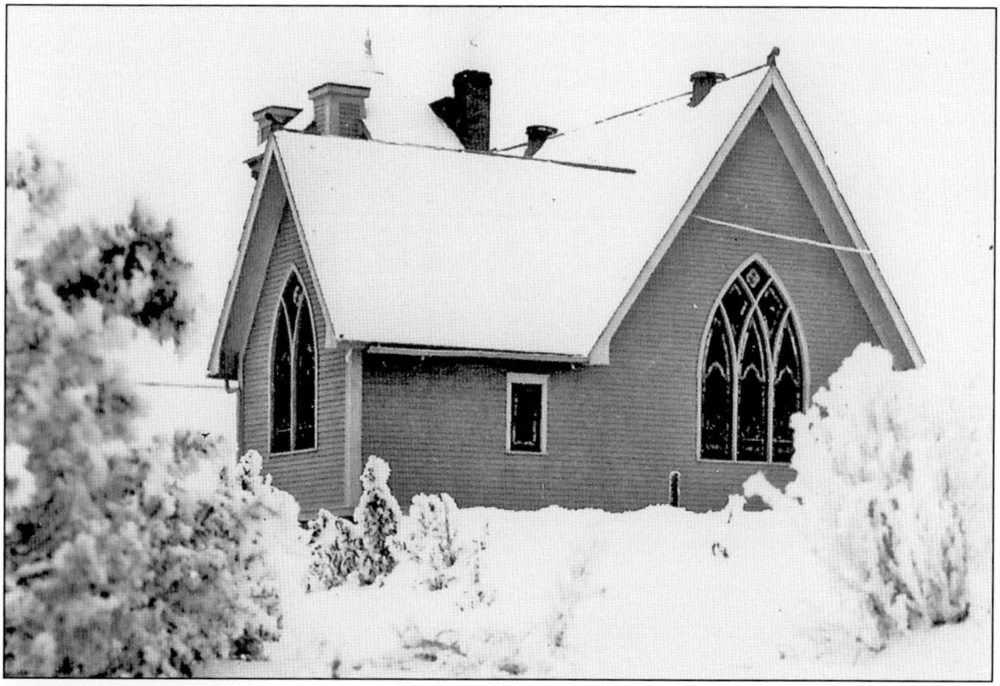

The photograph above is of the Green River Bible Church. The photograph below is of the First Presbyterian Church of Green River. The two photographs are the same church used by different denominations. The Presbyterian church was the first church built in Green River. It was dedicated on October 20, 1907. The building is still located on Main Street in Green River but is now used solely by the Green River Bible Church, an independent interdenominational church. The change of religious affiliation was made in 1959. It was decided that it would be easier to get ministers of different faiths to serve in Green River rather than just a minister of the Presbyterian faith.

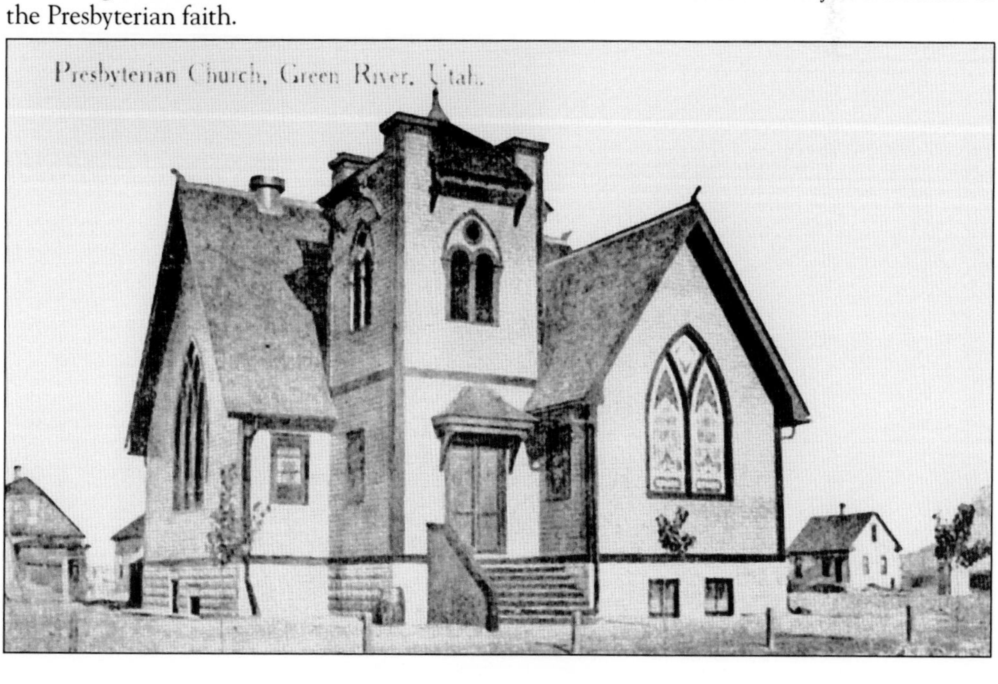

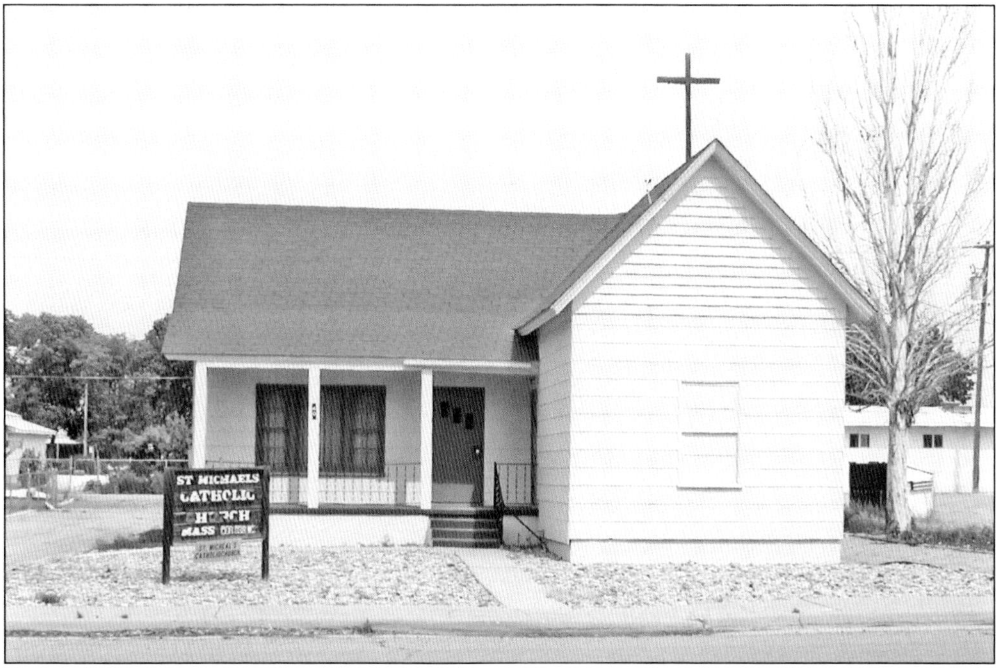

St. Michaels Catholic Church began as a mission in Green River in 1949. The congregation held services in the Midland Hotel until a house was converted to a church. Mary S. Vetere was the driving force in establishing a Catholic church in Green River. While services were being held in the Midland Hotel, Lillian F. Cline asked officials if the Episcopalian members could meet in the Catholic church at alternate times. Permission was given.

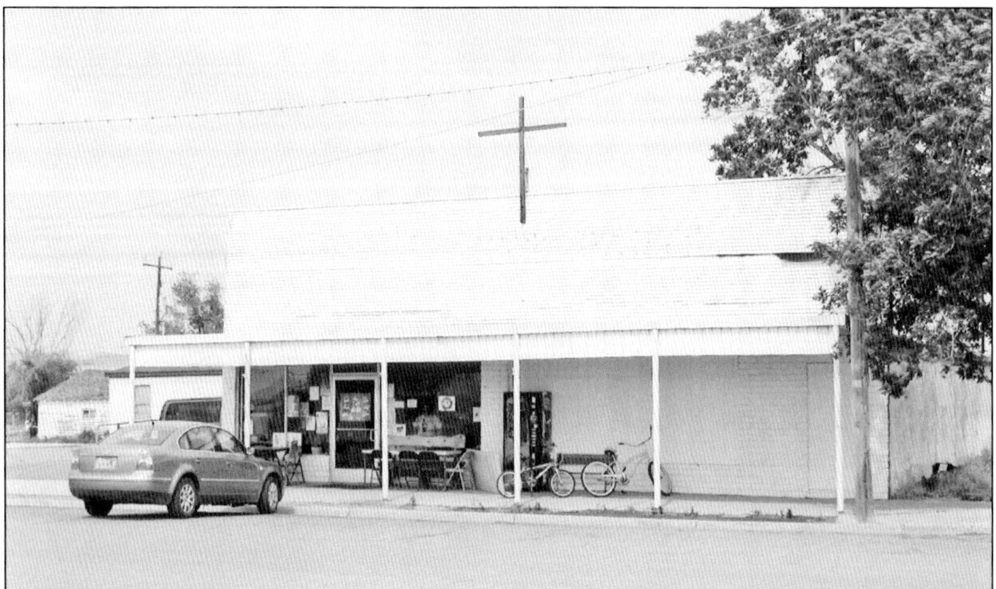

Members of the First Baptist Church first met at the American Legion Hall, which is now the Senior Citizens Center, during the 1960s. In 1984, they purchased the Malcolm Politano Sr. store. It was remodeled and carpeted throughout. The building still exists but has since been an auto parts store and is now the site of the Green River Community Center.

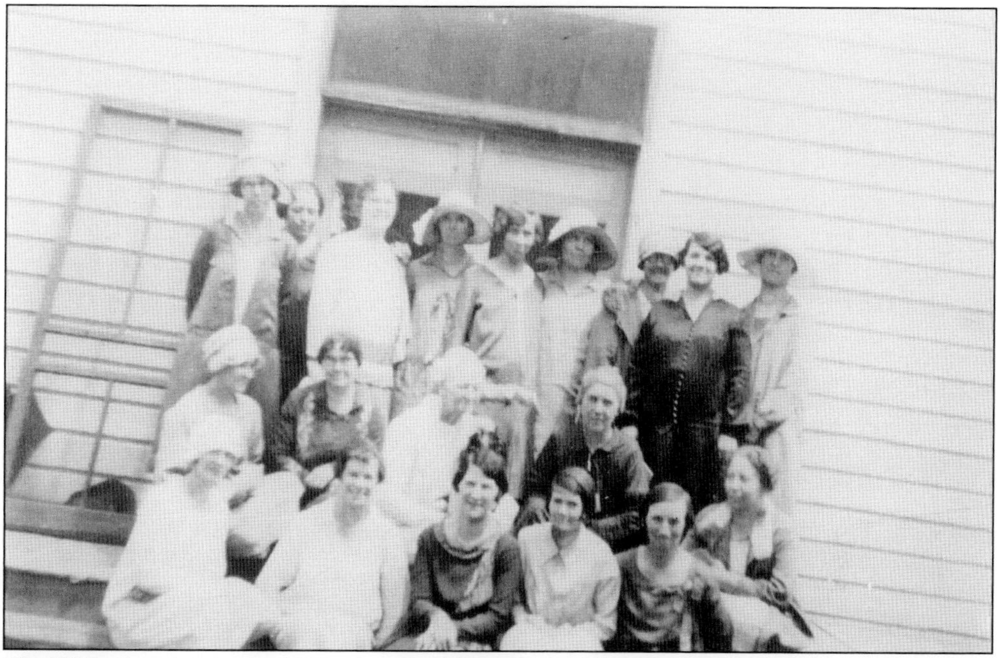

The LDS Church is in the 1894 school building on Long Street. From left to right are (first row) Chloe Moore, Rua Hunt, Ethelyn Stott, Mae Bigelow, Eva Hunt, and ? Howlett; (second row) Phoebe Holt, Alice Hanks, ? Porter, and Nellie Thompson; (third row) Elvira Stott, Carmelia Brown, Mabel Smith, Sarah Smith, Mae Hunt, Hazel Powell, Annie Allen, Amanda Curtis, and Lavina Hunt.

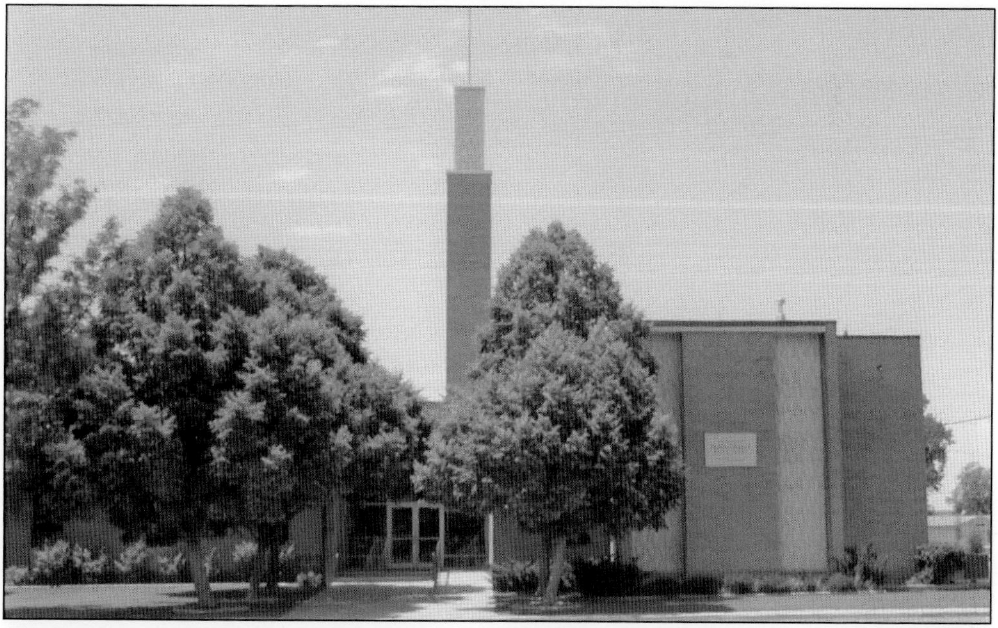

The building for the Church of Jesus Christ of Latter-day Saints (LDS) was completed in March 1962 and dedicated January 7, 1968. Those of the LDS faith did not found Green River, but there were a few members since the beginning of Green River's history. Before meeting in what is now the Senior Citizens Center, the members would meet in homes.

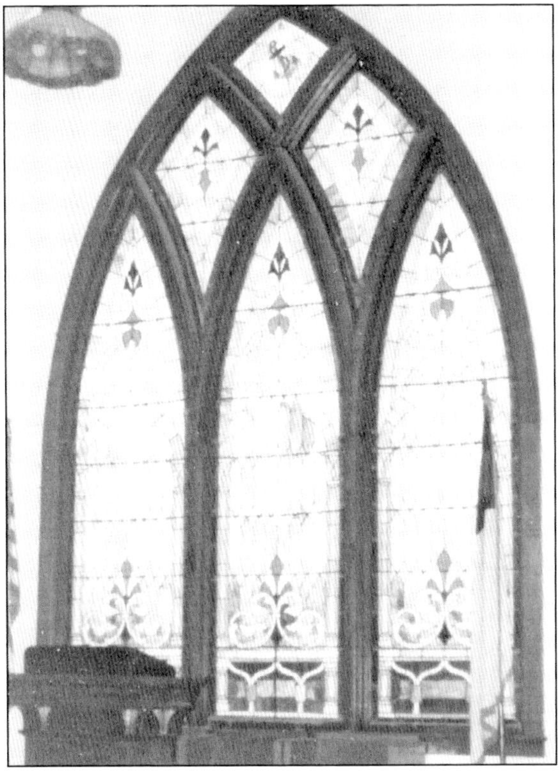

George Thurman insisted that the Presbyterian church have stained-glass windows, while the members thought cut-glass windows would be fine. These windows, which Thurman paid for, are on the north side of the building and were made in Germany. Thurman was a supervisor of the foundation and cement work of the building.

The Green River School 1910 girls' basketball team included, (first row) Helen Spaulding and Gladys French; (second row) Alta Cottrell, Hester Rutt, and Kathleen Nyland. Their "game day" uniforms are formal and almost look like a school uniform with their white blouses, black skirts, and black ties. Nyland must have wanted a more distinctive-looking tie.

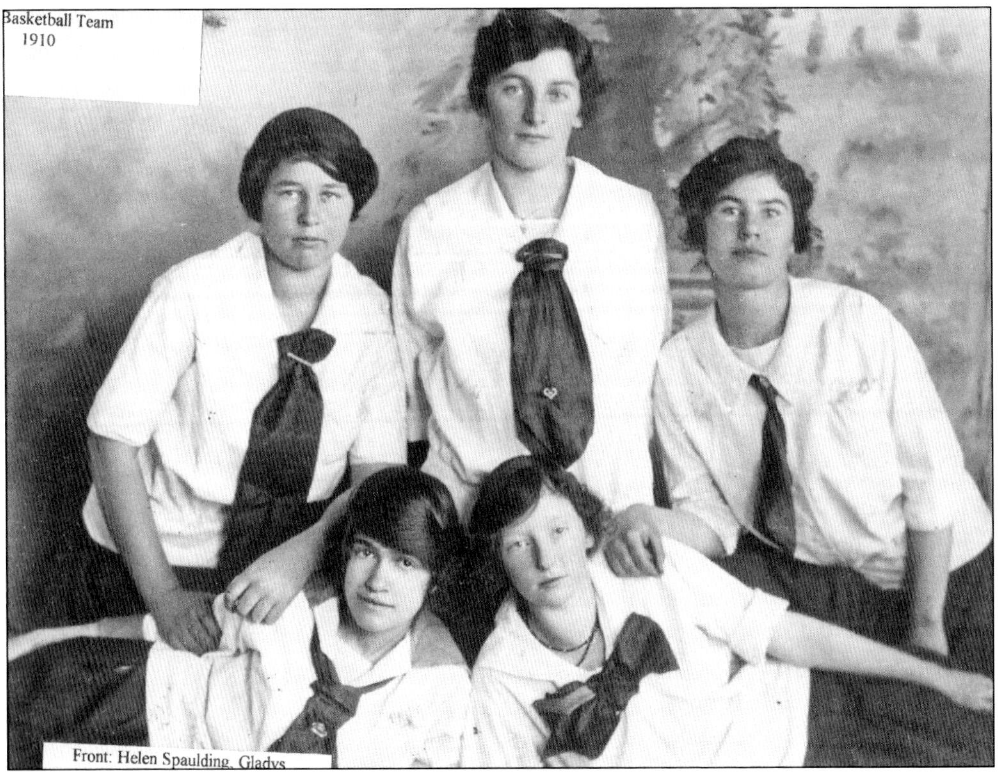

Seven

The John Wesley Powell River History Museum

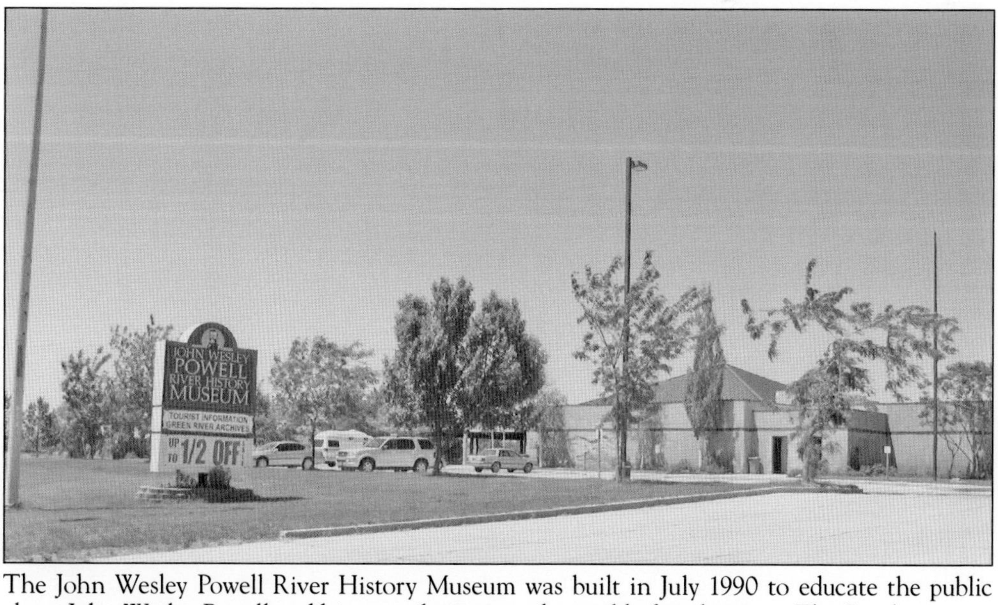

The John Wesley Powell River History Museum was built in July 1990 to educate the public about John Wesley Powell and his contributions to the world of exploration. The Southwest was one of the last places to be explored in the United States. Powell took two trips down the Green and Colorado Rivers in 1869 and 1871, during which he discovered the unknown.

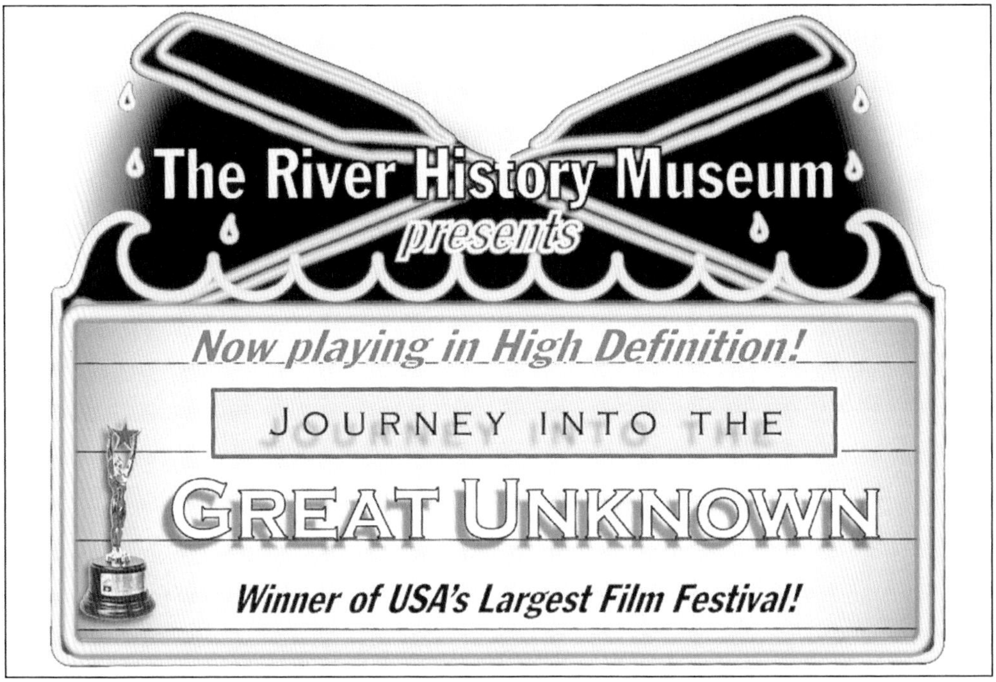

Journey into the Great Unknown is the award-winning movie featured at the John Wesley Powell River History Museum with HD Surround Sound. It re-creates the journey Powell took down the Green and Colorado Rivers. The narration of the film comes from Powell's journal and the journals of Powell's crewmembers. Visitors learn what Powell and his crew thought of the journey and of each other.

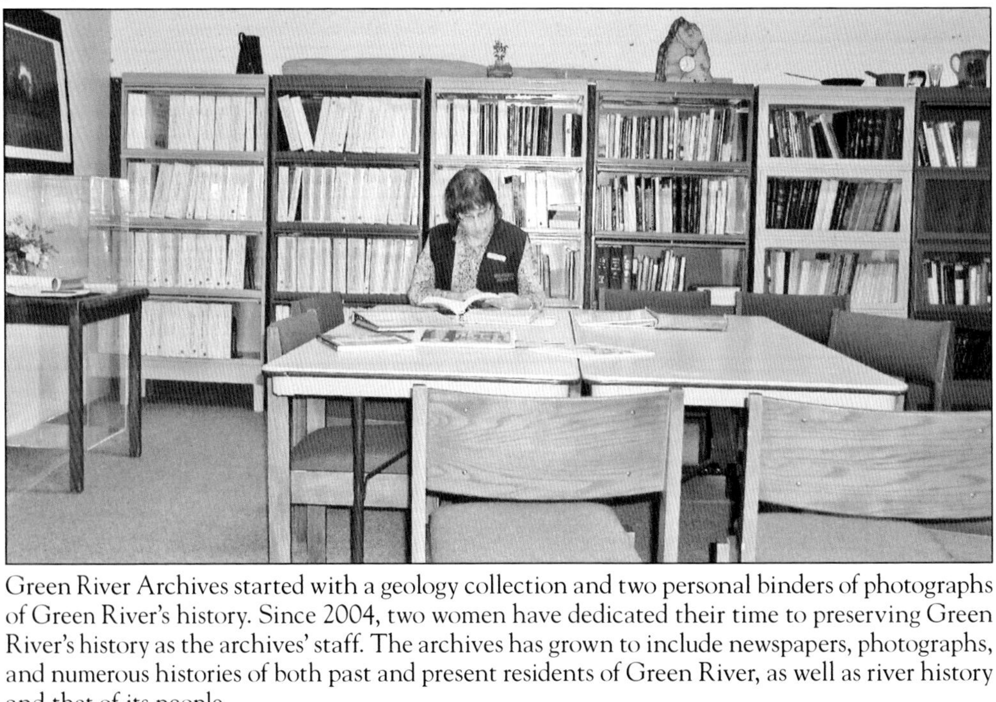

Green River Archives started with a geology collection and two personal binders of photographs of Green River's history. Since 2004, two women have dedicated their time to preserving Green River's history as the archives' staff. The archives has grown to include newspapers, photographs, and numerous histories of both past and present residents of Green River, as well as river history and that of its people.

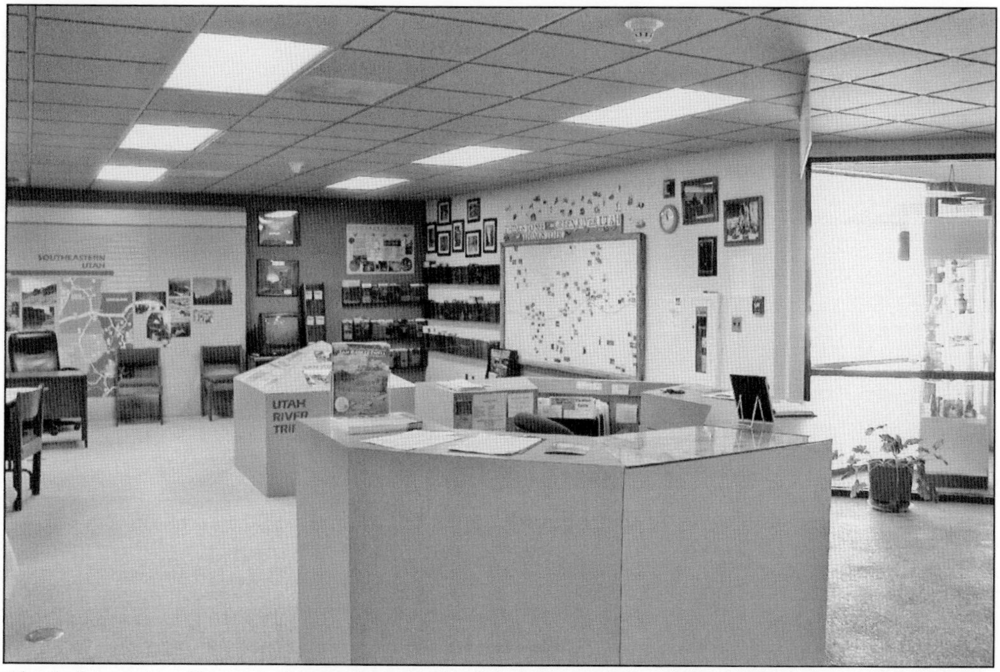

The Information Center is located inside the John Wesley Powell River History Museum. Inside are many free brochures to guide visitors to attractions in and around Green River. There is also a friendly and knowledgeable staff ready to help answer questions or help plan the next adventure while in Green River.

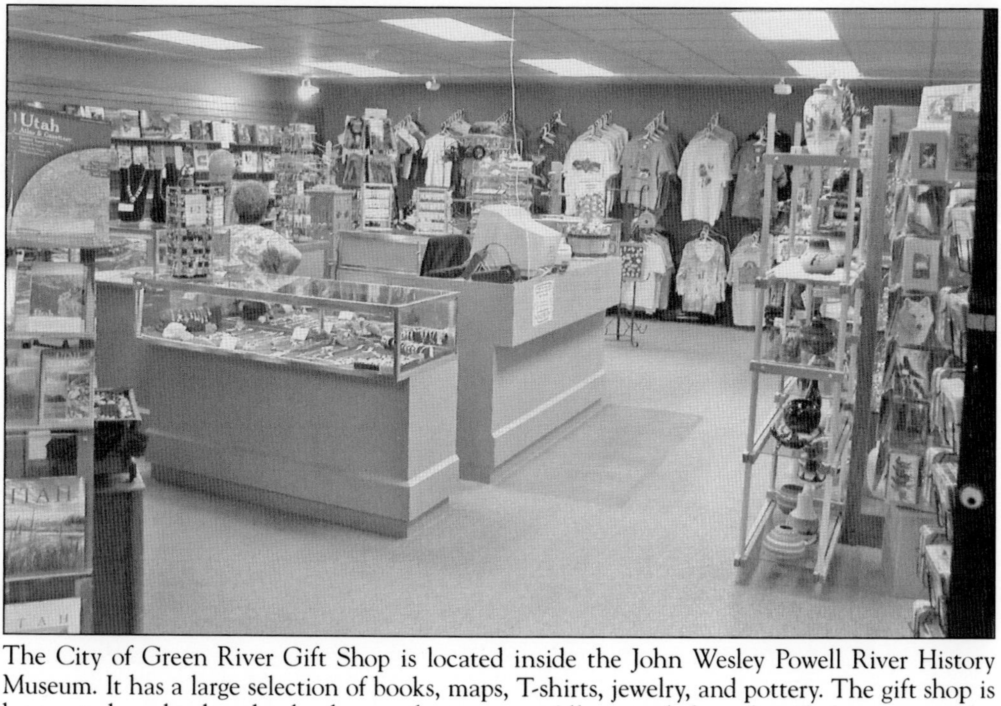

The City of Green River Gift Shop is located inside the John Wesley Powell River History Museum. It has a large selection of books, maps, T-shirts, jewelry, and pottery. The gift shop is known to have books other bookstores do not carry. All proceeds from the gift shop support the John Wesley Powell River History Museum.